GLADSTONE AND
DISRAELI

Gladstone and Disraeli surveys and compares the careers of these two influential Prime Ministers of nineteenth-century Britain. Stephen J. Lee examines how Gladstone and Disraeli emerged as leaders of the two leading parties and goes on to consider their time in power, analysing many different aspects of their careers. Using a wide variety of sources and historiography, Stephen J. Lee compares and contrasts the beliefs of Gladstone and Disraeli, and the effect of the two men on the economy, social reform, the Irish problem, parliamentary reform, and foreign policy.

Stephen J. Lee is Head of History at Bromsgrove School. His many publications include *The European Dictatorships, 1918–1945* (2nd edition, 2000) and, in this series, *Imperial Germany, 1871–1918* (1998), *Hitler and Nazi Germany* (1998) and *Lenin and Revolutionary Russia* (2003).

QUESTIONS AND ANALYSIS IN HISTORY

Edited by Stephen J. Lee, Sean Lang and Jocelyn Hunt

Other titles in this series:

Modern History

Imperial Germany, 1871–1918
Stephen J. Lee

The Weimar Republic
Stephen J. Lee

Hitler and Nazi Germany
Stephen J. Lee

The Spanish Civil War
Andrew Forrest

The Cold War
Bradley Lightbody

Stalin and the Soviet Union
Stephen J. Lee

Parliamentary Reform, 1785–1928
Sean Lang

British Foreign and Imperial Policy,
1865–1919
Graham D. Goodlad

The French Revolution
Jocelyn Hunt

The First World War
*Ian C. Cawood and
David McKinnon-Bell*

Anglo-Irish Relations, 1798–1922
Nick Pelling

Churchill
Samantha Heywood

Mussolini and Fascism
Patricia Knight

Lenin and Revolutionary Russia
Stephen J. Lee

Early Modern History

The English Wars and Republic,
1636–1660
Graham E. Seel

The Renaissance
Jocelyn Hunt

Tudor Government
T. A. Morris

Spain, 1474–1598
Jocelyn Hunt

The Early Stuart Kings,
1603–1642
*Graham E. Seel and
David L. Smith*

GLADSTONE AND DISRAELI

STEPHEN J. LEE

ROUTLEDGE

London and New York

For Charlotte

First published 2005
by Routledge
2 Park Square, Milton Park, Abingdon, Oxon OX14 4RN

Simultaneously published in the USA and Canada
by Routledge
270 Madison Ave, New York, NY 10016

Transferred to Digital Printing 2008

Routledge is an imprint of the Taylor & Francis Group, an informa business

© 2005 Stephen J. Lee

Typeset in Akzidenz Grotesk and Perpetua by Keystroke, Jacaranda Lodge,
Wolverhampton
Printed and bound in Great Britain by TJI Digital, Padstow,
Cornwall

British Library Cataloguing in Publication Data
A catalogue record for this book is available from the British Library

Library of Congress Cataloging in Publication Data
A catalog record has been requested

ISBN 10: 0-415-32356-8 (hbk)
ISBN 10: 0-415-32357-6 (pbk)

ISBN 13: 978-0-415-32356-7 (hbk)
ISBN 13: 978-0-415-32357-4 (pbk)

CONTENTS

ILLUSTRATIONS

INTRODUCTION

The *Questions and Analysis* series is based on the belief that the student actively benefits from explicit interpretation of key issues and help with source-based technique. Each volume therefore separates narrative from analysis and sources; it follows an overall structure of Background Narrative, Analyses, and Sources with questions and worked answers.

This volume, *Gladstone and Disraeli*, adds another dimension. Sixth-form and university courses have given more and more importance to historical debates, requiring proficiency in historiography as well as in history. The revised format takes this development into account.

Each of the eight chapters follows a common pattern. The Background is confined to essential introductory perspectives or narrative. Analysis 1 focuses on a key historical issue (as in previous volumes), while Analysis 2 now examines the historiographical dimensions of the same issue, considering the extent of and reasons for changes of emphasis. There is now a similar distinction between two types of sources in most chapters (although this is not always appropriate). Sources 1 reflect revised approaches to sources at intermediate levels like AS, and relate to an event covered in Analysis 1. Sources 2 are mainly secondary, giving specific examples of differing lines of interpretation already introduced in Analysis 2; these are intended more for A2 or university students. In Chapter 1 there are complete worked answers for all the source-based questions, along with advice on the techniques needed. These answers and advice are also relevant to the questions set in Chapters 2 to 8.

The subject of this volume is well suited to this approach. The reputations of Gladstone and Disraeli have experienced a wide range of views from historians, which are reflected in Analysis 2 and Sources 2 within each chapter. These are categorised and compared. In some cases explanations are provided for the differences between them, and it is intended that the more general observations and comments made in some chapters will be relevant to the subject matter in all the others.

It is hoped that the student or general reader will want to contribute to the debate on all the topics dealt with in this book. Provided that they can be substantiated, all views are valid – and they all count. This is what makes history so creative.

ACKNOWLEDGEMENTS

The author and publisher are grateful to the following for permission to reproduce copyright material:

Chapter 3 source 8, Chapter 7 source 7 and Chapter 8 source 8: Eugenio F. Biagini, *Gladstone* © 2000 Macmillan, reproduced with permission of Palgrave Macmillan.

Chapter 1 source 9, Chapter 2 source 7, Chapter 7 source 8 and Chapter 8 source 9: J. Parry, *The Rise and Fall of Liberal Government in Victorian Britain* © 1993 Yale University Press.

Every care has been taken to trace copyright holders and obtain permission to reproduce the material. If any proper acknowledgement has not been made, we would be grateful if copyright holders would inform us of the oversight.

OUTLINE CHRONOLOGY OF MINISTERIAL POSTS

GLADSTONE (1809–98)		DISRAELI (1804–81)
	1841	
	1842	
1843–5 President of the Board of Trade	1843	
	1844	
1845–6 Colonial Secretary	1845	
	1846	
	1847	
	1848	
	1849	
	1850	
	1851	
1852–5 Chancellor of the Exchequer	1852	Chancellor of the Exchequer* 1852
	1853	
	1854	

1855

1856

1857

1858 Chancellor of the Exchequer*
                1858–9
1859

1859–66 Chancellor of the
        Exchequer   1860

1861

1862

1863

1864

1865

1866 Chancellor of the Exchequer*
                1866–8
1867

      Prime Minister (1) 1868
1868

1868–74 Prime Minister (1)
        and   1869
1873–4 Chancellor of the
        Exchequer   1870

1871

1872

1873

1874 Prime Minister (2) 1874–80

1875

	1876	(created Earl of Beaconsfield 1876)
	1877	
	1878	
	1879	
1880–5 Prime Minister (2) and 1880–2 Chancellor of the Exchequer	1880	
	1881	Death of Disraeli 1881
	1882	
	1883	
	1884	
	1885	
1886 Prime Minister (3)	1886	
	1887	
	1888	
	1889	
	1890	
	1891	
1892–4 Prime Minister (4)	1892	Tory/Conservative governments
	1893	
	1894	**Peelite, Whig–Liberal or Liberal governments**
	1895	
	1896	* Disraeli was also Leader of the Commons in 1852, 1858–9, 1866–8, and Lord Privy Seal 1876–8
	1897	
Death of Gladstone 1898	1898	

1

GLADSTONE AND DISRAELI BEFORE 1868

BACKGROUND

Phase 1: 1812–41

British politics were controlled, from the later stages of the Napoleonic Wars until 1830, by the Tories under the premiership of Lord Liverpool (1812–27), George Canning (1827), the Earl of Goderich (1827–8) and the Duke of Wellington (1828–30). Following their victory in the 1830 general election, however, the Whigs dominated the next decade under Earl Grey (1830–4) and Lord Melbourne (1835–41). Despite a brief minority government under Robert Peel between 1834 and 1835, the Tories experienced a period of disarray as Peel tried to modernise the party's approach and extend the basis of its appeal following the publication of his Tamworth Manifesto in 1835.

It was in this period of reconstruction that both Gladstone and Disraeli entered Parliament as Tory MPs. Their family backgrounds and their first experience of politics have both parallels and differences.

Gladstone's father was a successful businessman, a convert from Presbyterianism to the Church of England and, from 1818, a Tory MP. The son started with evangelical beliefs but swung increasingly towards the high church and, for a while, considered a possible career in the ministry. Instead, he took a double first at Oxford in classics and mathematics, before entering the House of Commons as MP for Newark in 1832. Although initially seen as a 'stern' and 'unbending' Tory, Gladstone's administrative ability was recognised by Peel, who gave him a junior post in the brief 1834–5 Tory government. By the end of the 1830s it was already clear that a close political partnership was being forged between Peel and Gladstone – which might transform the party once it again managed to win a general election.

Disraeli came from a Jewish business background, his grandfathers having migrated from Italy in the mid-eighteenth century. After the family's conversion to Christianity in 1817, he seemed set for a career in law. During the 1820s, however, he became involved in financial speculation which left him badly in debt. He was also renowned as a sharp dresser with an extravagant lifestyle. He made five attempts to enter the House of Commons after 1832, finally succeeding in being elected Tory member for Maidstone in 1837. At this stage in his career he took his stand on resisting what he saw as radical and Whig attempts to undermine Britain's key institutions – the monarchy and the Church. He failed, however, to impress and his maiden speech in the Commons was badly heckled. He tried – but failed – to gain the attention and patronage of his party leader and, by end of the 1830s, the mutual antagonism of Disraeli and Peel was already apparent. Disraeli's prospects for future office were therefore much more limited than Gladstone's.

Phase 2: 1841–6

In 1841 Peel's reforms within the Tory party paid off as the newly renamed Conservatives won a forty-one-seat majority over the Whigs. In his second ministry (1841–6) Peel now focused on economic and financial reform, introducing a series of budgets which reduced duties on a variety of imports and exports. His main target, however, was the repeal of the Corn Laws of 1815 and 1828, which provided British farmers with protection against imports of cheaper foreign grain. In forcing the repeal through in 1846 Peel split the Conservative party. The protectionists defied their party leader, which meant that Peel had to rely on Whig votes to supplement those Conservatives supporting the repeal of the Corn Laws. During the crisis Gladstone and Disraeli lined up on different sides: Gladstone gave unequivocal support to Peel's actions, while Disraeli was part of the Conservative majority opposing them.

Gladstone's support for Peel was the logical result of a close political cooperation which was further strengthened during the 1841–6 Conservative government. As vice-president, and then president, of the Board of Trade, Gladstone was directly involved in drawing up and implementing Peel's free-trade budgets which were designed to stimulate Britain's manufacturing industries. But he also agreed with Peel about the need to extend the reforming measures to cover agriculture as well, even though these were opposed by the protectionist and farming interests within the party. It was Gladstone who emphasised the urgency of repeal of the Corn Laws in 1846 to try to offset the economic and human disaster facing Ireland as a result of the potato famine. Economic *laissez-faire* therefore converged with moral principle as Gladstone and Peel risked bringing down the most productive government seen in Britain since 1800.

Disraeli's perspective was entirely different. He had no reason to back the leader who had denied him access to government office – or, for that matter, to pursue free trade into the potentially dangerous field of agriculture. Instead, he emerged as one of the focal points of opposition to Peel. He was one of the leaders of the 'Young England' movement which criticised the social record of Peel's government and, when the opportunity arose in 1846 to remove Peel, he aligned himself with the protectionists. While Gladstone had supported his leader against the party, Disraeli held with the party against its leader. The result was a parting of the ways.

Phase 3: 1846–68

Peel's government fell in 1846. Although the support of the Whigs was sufficient to help him force through the repeal of the Corn Laws against the opposition of most of the Conservatives, he was forced to resign when the Whigs subsequently introduced a vote of no confidence on Peel's Coercion Bill to deal with Irish disorders. For the next two decades the Whigs dominated the British political scene, as a comparison of the records of the two parties shows. The Whigs were in power under Russell (1846–52 and 1865–6) and Palmerston (1855–8 and 1859–65); they also provided most of the ministers for Aberdeen's coalition government (1852–5). Russell was, without doubt, the most experienced politician of the period, with a pedigree that went back to the 1832 Reform Act, while Palmerston became arguably the most powerful and popular prime minister of the whole of the nineteenth century. Meanwhile, the Conservatives managed only three minority ministries (1852, 1858–9 and 1866–8), all under the Earl of Derby. The Conservatives were, of course, depleted by the permanent loss of Peel's supporters in 1846; these proceeded to form a new political grouping known as the Peelites. This sub-party continued even after the death of Peel in 1851, and one of its members, Aberdeen, collaborated with the Whigs in his coalition government of 1852–5.

Between 1846 and 1868 there were therefore three main trends in British politics. First, the Whigs dominated under two particularly influential statesmen – Russell and Palmerston. Second, the Conservatives, under the overall leadership of Derby, did what they could to keep themselves from disintegrating, gradually establishing the base for a permanent recovery. And third, the Peelites existed for a while as a separate group of ex-Conservatives who had more in common with the Whigs and who contributed individual ministers to Whig governments. Then, in 1861 an event of particular significance took place. At the Willis's Rooms meeting a formal alliance was drawn up between the Whigs and Peelites which became the basis of a new Whig–Liberal party. For four years this secured Palmerston's position as the 'great unmoveable' in British politics. The Conservatives who had, by the 1860s, done much to put their house in order, despaired of ever being able to break his political monopoly. But shortly after Palmerston's death in 1865 the political situation was transformed and Britain experienced two decades of more evenly balanced two-party politics. For part of this period the two great protagonists were Gladstone and Disraeli.

Each of these had played a crucial role in the political developments between 1846 and 1865. As Conservative leader in the House of Commons Disraeli had skilfully prevented further splits within the party and also persuaded it to come to terms with free trade, even if this had been a *fait accompli*. In doing this, he was moving away from his ultra-Conservative and protectionist roots, developing an awareness of the need to reform the party and broaden its appeal. He also gained experience as Chancellor of the Exchequer in Derby's government of 1852. After the latter's death in 1868, Disraeli became overall leader of the Conservative party and, for a few months in 1868, Prime Minister. His rival by this time was Gladstone, who had taken over the leadership of the Whig–Liberals in 1867. Between 1846 and 1852 he had been in the political wilderness, before joining Aberdeen's coalition government as Chancellor of the Exchequer in 1862. In 1859 he played an important part in fusing the Whigs and Peelites into the Liberals, also serving with distinction as Chancellor of the Exchequer between 1859 and 1865.

The new dominance of Gladstone and Disraeli was established by the next three general elections. In 1868 Gladstone's Liberals won a majority of 116 seats; Disraeli reversed this in 1874 through a 39-seat victory for the Conservatives, before Gladstone regained the initiative in 1880 with a Liberal majority of 64. For a while, at least, two-party politics had returned to Britain.

ANALYSIS 1: COMPARE THE CONTRIBUTIONS MADE TO BRITISH POLITICS BETWEEN 1832 AND 1868 BY GLADSTONE AND DISRAELI.

Gladstone and Disraeli made a variety of contributions, the extent and value of which may be compared under three main criteria. The first two are their service in public office and the contribution they made to the party of their origin, especially their subsequent role in redefining party politics. Third, a comparison should also be drawn between their ideas and the way in which they tried to enhance the political image of the parties they led by 1868.

Before 1867 both men had experience of public office, although Gladstone had served longer and in more roles than Disraeli. Gladstone was, for example, an important member of the ministries of Peel, Aberdeen, Palmerston and Russell – as President of the Board of Trade (1843–5), Colonial Secretary (1845–6) and Chancellor of the Exchequer (1852–5 and 1859–66). Disraeli's experience was confined to three spells as Chancellor of the Exchequer under Derby (1852, 1858–9 and 1866–8). Disraeli's opportunity was, admittedly, reduced by the comparative weakness of the Conservative political performance between 1846 and 1866, while Gladstone's experience was greatly enhanced by the ascendancy of the Whigs during the same period. Disraeli's experience as Chancellor of the Exchequer was also combined with the office of Leader of the Commons, a significant role which evaded Gladstone.

The contributions of Gladstone and Disraeli to party politics differed fundamentally. The first contrast is in their role within the party of their origin – the Conservatives. The defining influence appears to have been the leadership and ideas of Robert Peel, Prime Minister in 1834 and 1841–6. Although initially 'the rising hope of the stern, unbending Tories', Gladstone was won over by Peel's more progressive approach – especially over economic policy. There was a strong affinity between the two politicians which meant that Gladstone was a natural inclusion in Peel's second cabinet and provided consistent support for the repeal of the Corn Laws in 1846. Disraeli, by contrast, found himself excluded by Peel from government office. By the early 1840s he was firmly established as a volatile critic of Peel's economic ideas and played a major part in the revolt of Conservative backbenchers against the government policy on the Corn Laws. Gladstone followed Peel's brand of Conservatism – but to the point of the destruction of party unity in 1846. Disraeli had the reverse effect, dividing the party during Peel's ascendancy but staying with the majority who opposed the repeal of the Corn Laws in 1846. Gladstone departed with his leader from the party; Disraeli, in defying his leader, forced the latter's departure but kept together what was left of the party between 1846 and 1866. Both, therefore, had unifying and divisive influences, although chronologically in the opposite order.

The year 1846 represents a watershed in redefining party politics in the nineteenth century, with Gladstone and Disraeli heading the flow in opposite directions. Gladstone spent the next decade outside political parties, belonging rather to a Peelite splinter group which gradually shrank in size. Disraeli remained within the Conservative party and, as its leader in the Commons, played an important role in holding it together during the period 1846–66. Gladstone, meanwhile, helped to bring about a fundamental party realignment. In 1859 he brought the Peelites into a permanent alliance with the Whigs and Radicals to form what was soon to become known as the Liberal party. Both Gladstone and Disraeli were, for a while, overshadowed by more traditional aristocrats. The Conservatives were led by the Earl of Derby, who formed three minority governments (1852, 1858–9 and 1866–8), the Whigs by Lord Palmerston, who dominated British politics as Prime Minister (1855–8 and 1859–65). Disraeli and Gladstone were very much their subor-dinates and, although they provided many of the progressive ideas of their respective parties, were in no position to implement them fully until Derby's retirement in 1868 and Palmerston's death in 1865. The relationship between Disraeli and Derby was generally harmonious: both had been strong opponents of the repeal of the Corn Laws in 1846, only to accept free trade in the 1850s as a *fait accompli*. There was also close cooperation between them over the 1867 Reform Act. By contrast, Gladstone and Palmerston were frequent antagonists, whether over foreign policy or over the extension of the franchise.

This brings us to the next key contribution which can be attributed to both Gladstone and Disraeli – the broadening of the base of support for their respective parties. Gladstone contributed to a new consensus among the more progressive elements in politics: this involved a coalition of Peelites and Whigs under Aberdeen (1852–5), with the inclusion of the Radicals as well in Palmerston's second ministry (1859–65). Gladstone's influence was pivotal in transforming *ad hoc* coalition governments into a permanent coalition party and he was well placed as a new moderate amongst old Whigs and old Radicals. He also pressed for the expansion of the electorate to support the Liberal claim to be the natural force for progress. Meanwhile, Disraeli was providing a similar boost to Conservative appeal. He prevented his party from retreating into the reactionary and entrenched rump of a once larger body. Instead, he aimed to give the Conservatives a vision which involved competing with the Whigs. The latter he considered corrupt oligarchs who had 'no object but their own aggrandisement'. Conservatism, by contrast, was more in the interest of the nation as a whole, since it would appeal 'with a keener sympathy to the passions of the millions'. But the implementation of 'Tory democracy' would involve a layer of voters from the upper working class – which Disraeli achieved through the Second Reform Act (1867). The overall trend, especially during the 1860s, was for Gladstone and Disraeli to extend their parties' bases, each hoping to undermine the other in the process.

Both statesmen added substantially to the ideas which underlay political action in the mid-nineteenth century. Both were conscious of widespread exploitation and presented a case for measured reform. Disraeli's contrast between rich and deprived in the *Two Nations* provided a case for measured social reform, eventually attempted between 1874 and 1880. Gladstone's focus was more on the corruption within institutions, his chance to deal with these coming in his first ministry (1868–74). Neither envisaged a radical break with the past – but rather a process of regeneration. All this would be accomplished within the political framework either of 'Tory Democracy' or 'Gladstonian Liberalism'. In the sector of economics, Gladstone made the earlier impression, embedding *laissez-faire* principles within the Peelite–Whig–Radical coalition and making free trade a fundamental Liberal policy. Disraeli's approach was more pragmatic – but he came to accept free trade in the 1850s and managed to persuade the Conservatives of its inevitability. This meant that the policies pursued as Chancellor of the

Exchequer by Gladstone (1852–5 and 1859–65) and Disraeli (1852, 1848–9 and 1866–8) were often complementary.

The middle third of the nineteenth century therefore saw major political trends, with which Gladstone and Disraeli were closely associated – often in direct opposition to each other. Depending on the perspective used, the roles of the two men can be seen as either positive or negative – or both. It would, however, be hard to argue that they were unimportant.

Questions

1. Disraeli's contribution to the Conservative party before 1868 was constructive, while Gladstone's was destructive. Do you agree?
2. Who contributed more to extending the popular base of party politics before 1868 – Gladstone or Disraeli?

ANALYSIS 2: HOW AND WHY HAVE INTERPRETATIONS DIFFERED ABOUT THE ACHIEVEMENTS OF GLADSTONE AND DISRAELI BEFORE 1868?

The year 1868 is a crucial date in the history of Gladstone and Disraeli, of Liberalism and Conservatism. It was the year in which Disraeli succeeded Derby as Prime Minister, only to give way to Gladstone following the Liberal party's victory over the Conservatives in a general election. It also initiated a period of two-party politics. But the very notion of a post-1868 rivalry between two parties equipoised under two combative leaders automatically raises the question as to what role these leaders had been playing within their parties *before* 1868.

How have they been interpreted?

There are two main perspectives on what Gladstone and Disraeli contributed before 1868 towards the development of their parties as they existed *by* 1868. The first is based on an assumption that they were directly responsible for the strengthening of their parties and that they provided much of the ideology and inspiration behind them. The second view is the exact opposite: that the Liberal and Conservative parties developed largely *irrespective* of the input of Gladstone or Disraeli, a view which seems to apply particularly to the Conservatives under Disraeli.

Many historians have put the case for Gladstone making a crucial contribution to the evolution of Liberalism and the Liberal party: these range from Gladstone's first biographer, Morley, to mid-twentieth-century historians such as Hammond and Foot and, more recently, Hamer. The usual case made is that Gladstone made possible a new combination in British politics. This followed his conversion to the free-trade policies pursued by Peel, especially in the Conservative government of 1841–6, and his willingness to follow Peel into political exile after the repeal of the Corn Laws in 1846. In government Gladstone had 'a principal share in the fiscal revolution that was necessary to the prosperity of British trade'. In exile he became a 'political freelance' between 1846 and 1852 but his liberal principles became increasingly apparent both in domestic issues (such as his opposition to Russell's 1851 Ecclesiastical Titles Bill) and in foreign policy (especially in his attack on Palmerston's policy over Don Pacifico in 1850). He contributed extensively to the further development of free trade as Chancellor of the Exchequer in 1852–5 and 1859–66 and played a major part in helping establish a permanent bond between the Whigs, Radicals and Peelites in the form of a new Liberal party. Although the initiative for this was taken in 1859 under Palmerston's premiership, it was Gladstone who provided the reforming impetus which made possible all the later changes to the British electoral system and institutions. The pace accelerated once the restraining hand of Palmerston had been lifted by the latter's death in 1865. By the time that he had been installed in power after his victory in the 1868 general election, Gladstone was ready to initiate an unprecedented wave of reform. Indeed, 'When Gladstone died in 1898 it was universally recognised that he had been the leading figure of the nineteenth century in the history of Liberalism.'[1]

Another emphasis on Gladstone's importance was provided by Hamer – although with an interesting twist. This time, the argument is based on the premise that there was no coherent development of any 'liberal' philosophy. But the importance of Gladstone is undiminished because his personality and drive enabled him to establish an artificial dimension and unity for Liberalism through his personal focus on 'crusading politics', as in the case of Home Rule for Ireland in the 1880s.[2] This preference for conviction – and single-issue politics – had already been strongly established by Gladstone before 1868. With it were implanted the seeds of dissension which threatened to split the Liberal party from the moment of its formation.

Disraeli, too, has been considered the key influence behind the emergence of a more modern party. The case for this was first put by Monypenny and Buckle, Disraeli's earliest biographers.[3] More recently,

Smith[4] pointed to a twofold contribution. In the first place, Disraeli held the Conservatives together after the traumatic split over the 1846 repeal of the Corn Laws. Secondly, he provided a new and more appealing ideological structure which emphasised the need to broaden the base of electoral support and adopt a policy of social reform. These ideas modernised the Conservatives and put them back into contention for office. Disraeli was therefore preparing to tap into the working-class vote in a similar way to Peel's attraction of the middle classes in the 1830s and 1840s.

The contributions of Gladstone and Disraeli before 1868 have been strongly argued. They have, however, been equally firmly downgraded. Disraeli's record was affected first. Blake, for example, maintained that his achievements before 1866 were strictly limited and that his career was salvaged only by 'brilliant parliamentary conjuring tricks' in turning to his advantage the Reform Bill crisis of 1867.[5] There was no longer-term basis to Disraeli's contribution; indeed, his influence was shallow and divisive. He adopted a different approach from Peel, who 'wished to cement an alliance of moderate men against a Whig party that seemed to be perpetual prey to the intrigue and agitation of extremists'.[6] Disraeli's approach was never as coherent as Peel's and seemed to rely on exploiting 'the differences between capital and labour' and proposing 'a sort of benevolent aristocratic paternalism'.[7] Peel's search for reconciliation with the middle classes had made more practical sense within the context of a still very limited electorate. This was, however, destroyed by the Conservative split over the repeal of the Corn Laws – in which Disraeli played a crucial part. Indeed, 'In wrecking Peel's career, Bentinck and Disraeli came very near to wrecking his and their party too.'[8] There was nothing particularly idealistic about this – but rather a return to an earlier ultra-Conservative position based on the very antithesis of reform. The impact of such negative behaviour was so serious that there was not much that Disraeli could do to pull the Conservatives back together after 1846. This meant that 'Disraeli was to spend a longer time in opposition than almost any statesman of comparable stature in our history.' The logical outcome of this view is that 'During those years Disraeli did very little. If he had died or retired in 1865 or 1866 his influence on his country and his party would have seemed to the historian to be as negative as that of Charles James Fox.'[9]

Some historians have gone even further: Vincent, for example, considered Disraeli's whole career – before and after 1868 – a 'failure'.[10] Smith, often equally critical about Disraeli's impact on the Conservative party, nevertheless felt that his career was less a 'failure' than a 'sideshow', albeit 'a sparkling and dramatic sideshow'. He 'made little immediate difference to the Conservative party' and his political importance in mid-century is 'greatly exaggerated'. Smith even denied Disraeli any credit for being the unwitting founder of the Liberal party. 'Peel rode for a fall, and was unhorsed by his wilful incomprehension of the conditions of party politics.' The Conservative split was therefore brought about by Peel, not by Disraeli.[11] Nor should Disraeli's role after Peel be exaggerated. 'No Conservative leader in the middle of the nineteenth century could have overcome the disadvantage imposed by Peel's failure . . . to graft urban appeal on to an agricultural base.' All he could do was 'to maintain a brave face and a ready wit'.[12] The remnant of the Conservative party after 1846 therefore held together irrespective of Disraeli rather than because of him.

The positive picture of Gladstone before 1868 has been similarly undermined, especially the claim that he blended the three ingredients of Whiggery, Radicalism and Peelism into the new compound of Liberalism. In a particularly interesting departure from the conventional view, Parry maintained that Gladstone was never the main influence in the formation of the Liberal party. In fact, he remained Conservative at heart and never really changed from his earlier influences (this is examined further in Chapter 2). Instead, the key input into Victorian Liberalism was 'whig' rather than Gladstonian. This was evident politically in the 1832 Reform Act, which 'inaugurated the era of parliamentary government'[13] and, in turn, increased government potential to 'take positive action on behalf of the people' and to 'initiate bold and moralising legislation'.[14] Another root of Liberalism was the 'liberal Toryism', of which Canning and Palmerston had been important representatives in the late 1820s. It was Palmerston, rather than Gladstone, who was the key to the emergence of the Liberal party. As Prime Minister Palmerston was much more progressive than he is usually portrayed, especially during his second ministry (1859–65). He was a 'tireless administrator' who, with the assistance of 'members of the old Grey connection' introduced a considerable amount of 'worthy and necessary' legislation.[15] Palmerston it was who focused on the use of parliamentary commissions and who directed attention to the need for institutional reform, especially of the civil service. Gladstone, who normally gets the credit for this after 1868, simply carried through a policy which had already been started. It was also Palmerston who brought together the reforming parties in 1859, under the dominant influence of the Whigs. If, indeed, Gladstone did play a role, it was a divisive one. Pursuing 'the politics of conviction not consensus' he later undid the Liberal coalition which had actually been set up by Palmerston and Russell – not by Gladstone.

At the academic poles of debate, therefore, Disraeli has been seen either as a moulder of a new form of Conservatism or as a shifting opportunist; Gladstone as the creator of a new progressive synthesis in the form of Liberalism or as a divisive force which threatened rather than created this synthesis. By now, any genuine student of history will have raised questions or perhaps developed some alternative ideas. The potential for further analysis is considerable and a wide range of perspectives needs to be addressed. Two groups of questions about Gladstone and Disraeli might be used as a starting point. First, does a positive – or negative – view of one of them necessarily involve a similar view of the other; and, if not, why not? And second, should an assessment of each be sought somewhere on the scale between the positive and the negative; if so, where – both between the poles and in relation to each other? This assessment should, however, bear in mind some of the *reasons* for differential analysis suggested next.

Why have historians differed?

History is by nature controversial, driven by the search for alternatives. Individuals as diverse as Gladstone and Disraeli add a special edge.

Historians nearly always aim to maintain a balanced approach to their study; providing their conclusion or verdict only after considering alternatives. Those who do not, invite the criticism that they are creating stereotypes. Yet the way in which this balance is set may well differ. It is the difference in the blending of the ingredients rather than the ingredients themselves which defines academic historiography. In the case of the early careers of Gladstone and Disraeli, this could work in several ways to produce the type of arguments we have already seen.

In the first place, some historians will be more obviously drawn than others to the drama of the events and the strength of the personalities involved. Here the focus may well be on the contribution – whether positive or negative – of these personalities. Consider Disraeli. He has been seen as the main force behind the revival of Conservatism after the near-fatal split in 1846 – provoked, incidentally, by the determination of another individual, Peel, to achieve *his* objectives. Alternatively, he is seen as a negative influence, the main agency behind the Conservative split and the subsequent growth of the politics of the 'greasy pole'. Either way, the events are related to the personality. Similarly, we have a choice of Gladstones. Either he was the man who, on a point of principle, unwittingly helped Peel wreck one party before going on to apply his principles in putting together another. Or he was a more consistent 'wrecker' who implanted in the new party the same seeds of destruction he had helped sow in the old. Just as the threads of Conservatism pass through Disraeli's hands, so those of Liberalism are held by Gladstone. In each case the individual plays a vital role in the way in which the threads of Conservatism and Liberalism extend into the future.

The historian's attraction to the importance of the individual may be enhanced by the notion of 'paradox'. In each case, an early career interacted with the political scene through a search to reconcile apparently conflicting character traits. British politics between 1832 and 1868 therefore were defined substantially by the paradox of Gladstone as the 'stern unbending Tory' who went on to create the new Liberal amalgam. Disraeli was the descendant of Jewish immigrants, who rose to the leadership of Britain's most orthodox party and became the ardent leader of the Church establishment. The complexities involved in these transitions can easily be related to the political developments of the time and a personalised interpretation advanced.

Not all historians wish to go down this route. Some prefer to allow individual personalities to recede into their habitat. The focus changes and sharpens the details of the political background. We see the development of dynamics of a different kind, less concerned with individuals and more with trends such as the emergence of class consciousness and interest groups, the growth of the constituency organisation of political parties, and changes in population patterns. This is not to deny the importance of individuals: they do, after all, pursue policies which accelerate change. It is more to reduce the influence of *specific* individuals like Peel, Gladstone and Disraeli and to place them in the broader context of others like Russell, Derby and Palmerston. It is more a case of denying Gladstone and Disraeli a pre-eminent influence by rearranging the perspective. Or, to use another metaphor, the threads pass through too many hands for any individual pull on them to have been decisive.

These considerations may well have helped shape the type of book written. Some authors will adopt an openly statesman-centred approach; indeed a whole series might be based on this premise. The purpose of the *Teach Yourself History* series, published by the English University Press from the 1950s, was to put key historical changes in the context of great lives and, of course, the other way round. This is explicitly stated by A.L. Rowse in the general introduction to the series: it 'is the intention by way of a biography of a great man to open up a significant historical theme'; eventually, 'as the series fills out and completes itself, by a sufficient number of biographies to cover whole periods and subjects in that way'.[16] This is bound to boost the role of Gladstone, although, one has to say, at the expense of Disraeli, Peel and Palmerston, none of whom feature in the series.

The alternative to personality-based history is the more impersonal approach found in an increasing number of monographs. These often make use of evidence and methods which overlap into other academic disciplines, connecting history with economics, demography, politics, and sociology. The motive is undoubtedly to expand the range of research into new areas and reflects the multi-disciplined approach of some modern historians. Research has itself become increasingly important in academic circles and is now a basic requirement in higher education. Research, in turn, opens up new possibilities for development, the scope for which is exponential. The monographs which result from this will, in turn, inform new waves of more general works, many of which will try to integrate perspectives which go beyond the personal influence of individuals.

We should, however, always allow for a 'reaction' against any 'trend'. Some research continues to be subject-based, showing the influence of an individual in ways which had not previously been considered. Gladstone and Disraeli can therefore move back into the foreground, although in an unexpected profile. It is even possible to base a neo-biographical approach on new impersonal criteria showing, perhaps, that different threads passed through individual hands.

Questions

1. Taking the situation before 1868, what should the predominant view of Gladstone and Disraeli be in line with the chart below? Justify your choice by considering alternative points of view.

Gladstone: Positive Mainly positive Neither Mainly negative Negative
Disraeli: Positive Mainly positive Neither Mainly negative Negative

2. 'Historians have taken a more positive approach to Gladstone's political contributions before 1868 than they have to Disraeli's.' Do you agree with this view?

SOURCES

1. DISRAELI AND THE CONSERVATIVE PARTY BEFORE 1866

(Time allowed: 60 minutes)

Source 1: A cartoon from *Punch*, 1847.

THE RISING GENERATION – IN PARLIAMENT
Peel: 'Well, my little man, what are you going to do this session, eh?'
D—li (the Juvenile): 'Why – aw – aw – I've made arrangements – aw – to smash – aw – everybody.'

Source 2: From Disraeli's *Sybil; or the Two Nations*, published in 1845.

'Well, society may be in its infancy,' said Egremont, slightly smiling, 'but, say what you like, our Queen reigns over the greatest nation that ever existed.'

'Which nation?' asked the stranger, 'for she reigns over two.'

The stranger paused; Egremont was silent, but looked inquiringly.

'Yes,' resumed the younger stranger after a moment's interval. 'Two nations; between whom there is no intercourse and no sympathy; who are as ignorant of each other's habits, thoughts and feelings, as if they were dwellers in different zones, or inhabitants of different planets; who are formed by a different breeding, and are fed by a different food, are ordered by different manners and are not governed by the same laws.'

'You speak of – ' said Egremont, hesitatingly.

'THE RICH AND THE POOR'.

Source 3: From *The Times* in 1860.

Let the Conservative Party never forget the hopeless state in which they were when fortune sent them Mr Disraeli for a leader. They had grown weary of a chief who was too liberal for their views of national policy, and avenged themselves upon him by an act of renunciation which left them without leaders. They were irretrievably committed to an unpopular cause. Gradually, Mr Disraeli has weaned his party from their most flagrant errors. He has taught them to profess a sympathy for the great body of their countrymen and to recognise the necessity of looking to public opinion for support. When he found the Tory Party, they were armed in impenetrable prejudice; under him, they have become competitors with the Liberals in the career of progress.

Source 4: From P. Adelman, *Gladstone, Disraeli and Later Victorian Politics* published in 1970.

The policy of Sir Robert Peel in trying to provide a more progressive ethos for his party in the early nineteenth century ground to a halt in 1846. By 1865, after twenty years in the wilderness under the leadership of the Earl of Derby in the Lords and, more precariously, Disraeli in the Commons, little had been done to provide the Conservative Party with new supporters, new policies or any new enthusiasm.

Questions

1. Using Source 1 and your own knowledge, explain why Disraeli is represented in this way. (20)

2. Compare Sources 3 and 4 as evidence on Disraeli's contribution to the Conservative party between 1846 and 1865. (40)

3. Using Sources 1 to 4, and your own knowledge, discuss the view that, before 1865, Disraeli had few ideas and little political ability. (60)

Total (120)

Worked answers

1. *[About 10 minutes should be spent on this question. References should be made directly to the cartoon and caption in the light of your 'own knowledge'.]*

The cartoon depicts Disraeli as an iconoclastic politician, making arrangements 'to smash everybody' and with little respect for the unity of the Conservative party or for its leader, Peel (shown as a traditional and imposing figure). This is an allusion to the role played by Disraeli in opposing the policy pursued by Peel the year before in repealing the Corn Laws. Disraeli and Bentinck had mobilised a large section of the party to resist this, the result being a major split. The cartoon also comments on Disraeli's well-known reputation for being an extravagant dresser: this is seen as part of his rebellious nature. The caption gives the impression that he is an awkward speaker. This is rather harsh on Disraeli – but could be a reference to his disastrous maiden speech in the Commons in 1837 or to Disraeli's perceived lack of a coherent policy at this stage. 'The rising generation' could be seen as a forecast of extensive political change for the rest of the 1840s and 1850s.

2. *[The answer to this question should take about 20 minutes and should be about twice the length of the answer to 1. 'Compare' means providing an integrated comparison based on selected extracts from the two sources, not an end-on description of both sources; it also involves considering similarities and differences. 'Compare as evidence' involves two processes. The first is 'evidence' as content: the similarities and differences in what the sources actually say and imply, in general terms and through any details. The second is 'evidence' in terms of the type of source, insofar as it influences the scope of the content. This should not, however, become a generalised discussion on provenance or reliability. There may well be a clue within the source's attribution, which can be used in the answer. A useful stylistic device is to put comments from both sources into one sentence and separate them by a semicolon.]*

A comparison of the evidence of Sources 3 and 4 in terms of their content reveals several broad similarities. One is a general comment on the point reached by Disraeli's leadership of the Conservative party in the early 1860s. Another is a reference to Disraeli's predecessor, Robert Peel, who had left the Conservative party in 1846; according to Source 3 this was because he had been 'too liberal for their views', while Source 4 refers to his 'more progressive ethos'. In both cases this is the starting point for an analysis of Disraeli's succession. Beyond that, however, there are major differences. The overall impression from Source 3 is that Disraeli had achieved major success, whereas the verdict of Source 4 is largely negative. Source 3 points to real progress as Disraeli 'weaned his party from their most flagrant errors' and their commitment to an 'unpopular cause'; according to Source 4, on the other hand, 'little had been done' in terms of developing 'new policies'. There is also a difference in the perception of the appeal of the Conservative party; Source 3 considers that they had now become 'competitors with the Liberals', whereas Source 4 maintains that there were no 'new supporters'. Leadership is clearly the key issue for all of this. Source 4 seems to be more favourable to Derby, referring to Disraeli's leadership in the Commons as 'more precarious'; this is a striking contrast with the man who, according to Source 3, was 'sent' by 'fortune'.

The content is influenced by the purpose and approach of the sources, which also affect their usefulness as evidence. Both sources consider their subject briefly – *The Times* within the context of an editorial, and Adelman as the starting point for the real scope of his book – *later* Victorian politics. But there is also a difference in purpose, which might well explain the difference in approach. *The Times* was seeking to generate support for a new Conservatism by focusing on a personality, a common device used by newspapers. Adelman's intention was to preview Disraeli's early career before going on to cover his subsequent achievements. Both, therefore, are likely to be highly selective. Beyond that, *The Times* offers an insight into media interpretations of popular feeling at the time, whereas Adelman's writing has the advantage of hindsight and wider research.

3. *[About 30 minutes should be spent on this question. Its length should therefore be equivalent to that of 1 and 2 together. One possible technique for tackling 3 would be as follows.*

- *In the first paragraph, briefly summarise where the four sources stand in relation to the statement in the question.*
- *Then move on to a consideration of each source in more detail. Avoid*

a sequential and descriptive approach. Use your own knowledge to comment on the sources' handling of 'ideas' and 'political ability' with, perhaps, a paragraph on each. A few comments should be included on issues of reliability – but relate these directly to whether they strengthen or weaken the weight you would give to the argument in the source.

- *Next, there will be some material excluded from the sources which is still relevant to the quotation. This is a second use of your own knowledge.*
- *Remember to come to an overall conclusion which resolves the arguments you have used throughout. This should be brief but decisive.*

Some of the material in 3 may overlap with 1 and 2. This is likely, since the questions are intended to move from specific comments towards an overall assessment. Remember, however, that each question has a different purpose within this, which means that simple repetition will be inappropriate.]

None of the sources provide a direct response to the quotation but all can be used directly in parts or indirectly throughout. Bearing this in mind, Sources 1 and 4 have a largely negative approach and seem to approach the quotation more closely than do Sources 2 and 3, which are more positive.

Any reputation which Disraeli did have as an original thinker is based on works such as *Sybil* (Source 2). Although he was not the first to use the idea of the 'two nations' as 'rich and poor', this particular extract was to achieve prominence in later social reform. Whether or not this reputation for progressive ideas is deserved has produced major controversy, of which the differences between Sources 3 and 4 are representative. Source 3 clearly took seriously Disraeli's emerging reputation for 'progress'. In a direct reference to the ideas contained in *Sybil*, Source 3 emphasises that Disraeli taught 'sympathy for the great body of their countrymen'. An alternative view is that too much can be read into what was, by literary standards, an ordinary novel. Source 4, for example, omits any reference – direct or indirect – to Disraeli's writing. This leaves Source 1, which stands out as an attack on someone who not only lacks ideas, but who is not even articulate ('aw', 'aw'). This has to be taken with a pinch of salt, since the purpose of any cartoon is to satirise through one-sided and eye-catching generalisation.

None of the sources deal with 'organisation' as such, but much can be inferred from them. The focus of Source 3 is actually the 'hopeless state' of the party after its members had 'avenged themselves' on Peel and left themselves 'without leaders'. Disraeli effected a transformation which involved the broadening of Conservative support through, it has to be deduced, greater organisation. Similarly, there is nothing explicit in Source 2. But if *Sybil* is seen in any way as diagnostic, then it would require organisation to provide solutions, and perhaps to deal with the situation in which 'rich and poor' were 'not governed by the same laws'. Source 4, by contrast, considers Disraeli's leadership 'precarious' and the lack of effective organisation is implicit in the comments about the party's absence of any kind of development. Source 1 is even more negative. Disraeli is given the credit of having 'arrangements' but these are entirely destructive, the intention being 'to smash everybody'.

Careful consideration of the hidden meaning of the sources can, therefore, reveal two clear sides. There are, however, additional points which the sources do not consider, which tend to favour the more positive approach. Disraeli's ideas were based on rather more than a reference to 'two nations' in *Sybil*. He was a prolific writer not only of novels but also of political commentaries. He also played an active part in developing a Conservative variant of free trade, the origins of which were apparent in his 1852 budget and developed further after 1866. Some historians have said that all the ingredients for Conservative policy (based on main-taining institutions, preserving the Empire and improving the condition of the people) were present well in advance of their public utterance in the 1872 Crystal Palace speech. Even if this is not proven, it is still unlikely that Disraeli's later 'ideas' and 'organisation' emerged from a vacuum. The period between 1846 and 1865 therefore played a significant part in the development of both.

2. INTERPRETATIONS OF THE INFLUENCE OF PEEL ON GLADSTONE

(Time allowed: 45 minutes)

Source 5: From Gladstone's book *Protectionism*, published in 1860.

I learned the cause of the different trades out of the mouths of the deputations which were sent up to remit our proposals. So that by the close of the session I began really to know something about the matter and my faith in Protection except as a system of transition crumbled rapidly away.

From this time [1842] down to 1860 or thereabouts the question of Protection mainly determined the parliamentary history of the country and it became my fate to bear a very active part in it especially after the death of Sir Robert Peel. For my part I am a Free Trader on moral no less than on economic grounds: for I think human greed and selfishness are interwoven with every thread of the Protective system. In this great controversy Peel as I think displayed perfect honesty and inflexible courage. From the language he held to me in December 1845 I think he expected to carry the repeal of the Corn Law without breaking up his party. But meant at all hazards to carry it.

Source 6: From Norman Gash, 'The Peelites after Peel'. This is an extract from an article originally published in *Modern History Review*.

Many [of the Peelites] bore lasting resentment at the unscrupulous personal attacks on Peel by the Protectionists during the Corn Law debates of 1846 and despised Disraeli as an unprincipled adventurer. This was particularly true of Gladstone. Although of all the leading Peelites he felt perhaps least loyalty to Peel's memory and remained on cordial terms with Lord Derby, he had an unconquerable aversion to his lieutenant in the Commons. The hard inner truth was that if Gladstone rejoined the main body of Conservatives, he would either have to displace Disraeli or reconcile himself to serving under him.

Gladstone is an illustration in one man of the perplexities of the Peelites as a whole. He was by common consent the ablest of the Peelites and their natural leader in the lower house. As a Conservative and a High Churchman he hankered intellectually for a reunion with the rump of the old Conservative Party, while year by year his personal emotions, his liberal sympathies and his political ambitions were carrying him in an opposite direction. It is not surprising, therefore, that none of the prominent Peelites felt able to give a forceful lead in guiding his colleagues towards one or other of the two main parties. If Gladstone was not in a position to do so, it was unlikely that any of the other younger men would take the task on himself; and the older Peelites, Aberdeen and Graham, had few political ambitions left.

Source 7: From Michael Winstanley, *Gladstone and the Liberal Party*, published in 1990.

International peace and domestic prosperity could best be achieved, he maintained, by removing barriers to reciprocal trade between nations, thus encouraging economic interdependence and mutual self-interest. Although he was to become the most prominent proponent of this view, he was not its originator. The period of so-called 'Liberal-Toryism' of the 1820s witnessed the first tentative reductions in trade barriers, and Peel's administration of 1841–6 hastened the process, pushing through wide-ranging reductions in duties, particularly in the budget of 1842, and repealing the detested Corn Laws in 1846. It was only during this period that Gladstone became convinced of the virtues of economic liberalism and abandoned his protectionist views. Even then, his conversion arose from his administrative experience at the Board of Trade where he had discovered the illogical complexities of the tariff structure. Only later did he come to espouse the internationalist ideology of the free-trade movement which had been so eloquently expressed at the time by Richard Cobden and the Anti-Corn Law League. By the time Peel's government fell apart over the issue of the repeal of the Corn Laws in 1846, however, Gladstone was firmly wedded to free-trade principles and found himself increasingly at odds with the rump of his old party.

Source 8: From J. Morley, *The Life of William Ewart Gladstone*, first published in 1903.

It was during these years of labour under Peel that he first acquired principles of administrative and parliamentary practice that afterward stood him in good stead: on no account to try to deal with a question before it is ripe: never to go the length of submitting a difference between two departments to the prime minister before the case is exhausted and complete: never to press a proposal forward beyond the particular stage at which it has arrived. . . . We cannot forget that Peel and Mr Gladstone were in the strict line of political succession. They were alike in social origin and academic antecedents. They started from the same point of view as to the great organs of national life, the monarchy, the territorial peerage and the commons, the church, the universities. They showed the same clear knowledge that it was not by its decorative parts, or what Burke styled 'solemn plausibilities', that the community derived its strength: but that it rested for its real foundations on its manufactures, its commerce, and its credit. Even in the lesser things, in reading Sir Robert Peel's letters, those who in later years served under Mr Gladstone can recognise the school to which he went for his methods, the habits of mind, the practices of business, and even the phrases which he employed when his own time came to assume the direction of public affairs.

Source 9: From Jonathan Parry, *The Rise and Fall of Liberal Government in Victorian Britain*, published in 1993.

Gladstone came not from the Liberal tradition but from the Conservative one which had had difficulty adjusting to Reformed politics after 1832. He was a disciple of the Conservative leader Peel, and had ambivalent feelings about whig-Liberalism – like all Peelites, though they were forced to ally with the Liberal party from the 1850s. As Gladstone grew older, he built on Peel's legacy by developing a number of personal enthusiasms and traits which led him into controversial initiatives after he became Liberal leader. The result was a series of tensions within the party.

Questions

1. Compare the explanations given in Sources 6, 7 and 8 for Gladstone's relations with the Conservative party in the development of his career between 1841 and 1866. (15)
2. 'The first part of Gladstone's career (1832–68) was shaped by the benevolent influence of Peel.' How far do Sources 5 to 9, and your own knowledge of the historiographical debate on Gladstone, confirm this view? (30)

Total (45)

Worked answers

1. [Spend about 15 minutes on this question. Unless instructed otherwise, confine the answer to a comparison of the ideas; any historiographical comment should arise only from this comparison. Comparisons should be integrated and quotations should be brief. A possible technique for integrated comparison is to look for the theme of each source and then some of the details. The sources do not have to be dealt with in the order given; it might actually make more sense not to.]

The three sources provide different overall perspectives on how Gladstone's career developed in relation to the Conservative party, both in and out of office. Morley (Source 8) points to an evolutionary process, in which Gladstone developed his ideas within the party in parallel with Peel. The extract does not deal explicitly with the period after 1846 but the assumption is that the process continued outside the party which, in a sense, became irrelevant. Winstanley (Source 7) also outlines a gradual change in Gladstone, although over a longer period. His formative influences were from the ideas of the 1820s, hastened by his 'administrative experience' in Peel's administration; the logical continuation of this was that he became 'increasingly at odds with the rump of his old party'. The emphasis of Morley and Winstanley on continuity is not, however, reflected in Source 6. Gash opts rather for an explanation of Gladstone's relations with the party based on 'perplexities', on the opposing influences of attraction and repulsion; the latter eventually prevailed and prevented any reconciliation.

The main reason for this variety of views is the different perceptions of the influence of Peel on Gladstone. Morley establishes the strongest connection. Gladstone gained from Peel 'principles of administrative and parliamentary practice'; hence Peel and Gladstone were 'in the strict line of political succession' (Source 8). Winstanley also attributes much to

Peel's example, although the line of influence extends back also to 'Liberal-Toryism' (Source 7). Gash reduces the importance of Peel and emphasises Gladstone's continued links with the Conservatives because he 'remained on cordial terms with Lord Derby' (the Conservative leader). What prevented him from rejoining the party was not so much the continuing influence of Peel as the 'unconquerable aversion' he felt for Disraeli (Source 6).

2. *[Spend about 30 minutes on this question. It requires careful handling of:*

(1) *The wording of the question.*
(2) *The extracts provided.*
(3) *Your own knowledge of the historiographical debate.*
(4) *Your own historical knowledge of the period.*

You should frame the overall answer in accordance with (1), *using material from* (3) *to illustrate the broad debate, into which* (2) *can be inserted as specific examples. The appropriateness of viewpoints within the historiography can be commented on by reference to* (4). *Material for this answer can also be used from other chapters, particularly Chapter 2.]*

There are two propositions in this quotation. One is that Peel exerted a strong influence on Gladstone's early career. The second is that this influence was for the good. The four sources reflect the range of historiographical debate, although the extracts do not necessarily summarise the overall approach of the books from which they are taken. Bearing that in mind, it seems that Sources 5 and 8 agree with both parts of the statement, while Source 6 tends to disagree. Source 7 seems partially to agree – to the extent that Peel was an influence – but makes no assessment of whether it was beneficial. Source 9 stands out as confirmation of the first part of the proposition – but also makes it clear that Peel's influence was the start of a damaging process.

One of the more widely argued interpretations is that Peel influenced the development of Gladstone's ideas and the subsequent redefining of British party politics. Morley certainly felt that this was the case; after all, it was under Peel that Gladstone 'first acquired principles of administrative and parliamentary practice' and that they came to share ideas about 'the great organs of national life' (Source 8). This view is hardly surprising since Gladstone, in turn, was Morley's political mentor and Morley would have been fully conversant with Gladstone's own tributes to Peel, as expressed, for example, in Source 5. The connection has also been acknowledged by a range of historians in the twentieth century, including Hammond and Foot and, above all, by Ghosh. The campaign for free trade, started by Peel and continued by Gladstone, was seen as central to their departure from Conservatism and to Gladstone's movement towards Liberalism. There were, of course, strong connections with religion and an underlying moral sense. But this is connected with free trade; Gladstone was convinced of the correctness of free trade 'on moral no less than on economic grounds' (Source 5). It is also significant that all of Gladstone's years in office outside the Conservative party were spent either as Chancellor of the Exchequer or as Prime Minister – or as both.

Not everyone has been convinced by this approach. Gash reflects in Source 6 the line of argument that relations between Peel and Gladstone could be inconsistent, at times even stormy. According to Gash, Gladstone felt 'perhaps least loyalty to Peel's memory'. There were certainly instances of open conflict: in 1835, for example, Gladstone resigned his post of President of the Board of Trade in protest against Peel's policy on the Maynooth Grant. Historians like Butler have also stressed the importance of Gladstone's early attachment to high-church Anglicanism. This is also alluded to by Gash, who maintains that as a 'High Churchman' Gladstone 'hankered intellectually' for reunion with the Conservatives' (Source 6). Another way of reducing the importance of Peel's influence has been to connect Gladstone's ideas with those of Huskisson and Robinson – the 'liberal' Tories of the 1820s, of whom Peel was not one. This point is made by Winstanley in Source 7, although he gives greater credit to Gladstone's 'administrative experience at the Board of Trade'.

The most radical approach is also the most recent. According to this, Peelite influences were strong, but not beneficial. Some historians have emphasised that it was not Disraeli who split the Conservative party – but Peel, who ignored its sensibilities and preferred to impose a new policy rather than persuade the majority of Tories to come to terms with it. Gladstone, Peel's pupil, then went on to do exactly the same thing to the Liberals. Parry's view is that Gladstone came from the 'Conservative tradition' and, because he was Peel's 'disciple', had difficulty in forming a genuine alliance with the Liberals (Source 9). Elsewhere Parry has also argued that Liberalism was better served by the Whigs, including Palmerston, who had originally been one of the 'liberal Tories' of the 1820s. Gladstone damaged the Whig legacy to the Liberals by undermining the consensus of early Liberalism. In this he 'built on Peel's legacy', since this involved the 'pursuit of personal enthusiasms and traits', leading to 'controversial initiatives'. (Source 9)

Overall, the balance is more even than it once was. Gladstone's continuation of Peel's work is not considered quite so smooth, and his 'Peelite' contributions to Liberalism not quite so obvious or positive. But, for all that, they are still there. They are also within the broader tradition of British party politics, which has seen numerous splits and departures: Palmerston, as an ex-Tory, probably ruffled as many Whig feathers as Gladstone, an ex-Conservative and Peelite.

2

THE IDEAS OF GLADSTONE AND DISRAELI

BACKGROUND

This chapter provides an overview of the ideas of Gladstone and Disraeli; these are developed further in the specific areas covered by Chapters 3 to 8.

Gladstone and Disraeli were both prolific writers. There is therefore no shortage of evidence for their ideas and policies. Gladstone's repository comprises the *Diaries* (14 volumes), the *Gladstone Papers* (750 volumes), a huge quantity of correspondence and speeches, and over twenty published books: these included commentaries on religion (for example, *The State in its Relations with the Church*), works on classical themes (*Studies in Homer and the Homeric Age*) and his own life (*A Chapter of Autobiography*). Disraeli generated a similar mountain of speeches and correspondence, as well as political commentaries (*Vindication of the English Constitution* and *The Spirit of Whiggism*) and satirical novels (*Coningsby* and *Sybil*). None of these works provide an explicit and coherent summary of their overall ideas, but they do give insights into particular characteristics at particular times.

ANALYSIS 1: COMPARE AND CONTRAST THE MAIN IDEAS OF GLADSTONE AND DISRAELI.

Both Gladstone and Disraeli had much to say about institutions and structures within the United Kingdom. Disraeli took it for granted that the natural guarantors of British cohesion were the aristocracy, the gentry, the Church and the monarchy, and directed his attack more at what he saw as corrupting influences coming from the parties – specifically the Whig 'oligarchy'. This was 'a small knot of great families who have no object but their own aggrandisement, and who seek to gratify it by all possible means'.[1] The best antidote to Whig exclusiveness was the broader and more inclusive approach of the reformed Conservatives, which 'in this country is the national party'. For this reason Disraeli is sometimes accredited with giving Conservatism an emphasis on a nationwide appeal rather than on sectional alliances. Gladstone's criticism was directed more at problems *within* the institutions rather than at threats from outside them. He warned particularly of administrative corruption and inefficiency, as well as privilege and patronage. His remedy was greater equality of opportunity, which would allow the emergence of a meritocracy. To Gladstone the enemy was not an external 'Whig oligarchy' seeking to pervert institutions but rather oligarchic tendencies within the institutions themselves. The priority in his first ministry (1868–74) was therefore to clean up the civil service, the army, the structure of state education, admissions to Oxford and Cambridge, and the Irish Church. Disraeli's institutional reform between 1874 and 1880 was, by comparison, limited.

Attitudes to institutions were directly related to perceptions of the broad mass of the population. Both Gladstone and Disraeli extended the base of support for their respective parties. Disraeli saw this as a means of strengthening the Tories and combating the negative influence of the Whigs. The latter had widened the gap between the ruling and working classes, reducing Britain to 'two nations'. Conservatism provided the political antidote since 'It appeals with a keener sympathy to the passions of the millions; it studies their interests with a more comprehensive solicitude.'[2] This would lead to a series of social reforms to 'secure the social welfare of the people'.[3] The theme of his second ministry (1874–80) was a series of measures concerned with issues like public health; this might be seen as evidence of a different approach from Gladstone's focus on institutional reform. Neither leader saw the necessity to enlarge substantially the scope of state intervention to ensure improved living standards. It was, however, Gladstonian Liberalism which made a positive virtue of constraints on such intervention.

He was firmly in favour of 'self help' and opposed any move towards using taxation as a means of redistributing wealth; indeed, he pressed harder than Disraeli for the ending of income tax altogether – an objective he never achieved.

Disraeli might, therefore, be allowed the edge in social legislation. Certainly 'one-nation Toryism' had a greater influence than 'self-help Liberalism' on subsequent party development in the twentieth century. Both, however, saw the virtue of electoral reform, thus extending the franchise well into the working class. Disraeli saw a natural Tory reservoir there, which led him to conclude that the Tories were 'the naturally democratic party of England'.[4] This is why he doubled the suffrage in the 1867 Reform Act. There is, however, always the suspicion that this was done to secure future electoral success. Gladstone had a stronger belief in the inherent 'goodness' of the masses, although he never aspired to be a 'democrat'. His contribution to the broadening of the electorate was the 1884 Reform Act which enfranchised about half the remaining men in the working class.

Ideas related to the economy also overlapped – but for different motives. Gladstone came much closer than Disraeli to an ideological approach. He had a strong commitment to *laissez-faire*, allied to careful financial management. He saw wealth as a 'trust' which should be increased so that it would 'fructify in the pockets of the people'. He maintained Peel's free-trade policies, his budgets of 1853 and 1860 being a logical continuation of the financial reforms of Peel's second ministry (1841–6). This is hardly surprising since he took the first of two major decisions of his political career: in 1846 he supported the repeal of the protectionist Corn Laws and followed Peel out of the Conservative party. Disraeli was initially as dogmatic, throwing his weight behind the opposition to repeal and supporting all the protectionist arguments. He was, however, prepared to adjust to the new economic order after 1846 and managed to persuade most of the rest of the party to accept free trade. But this was, however, a pragmatic approach. He merely accepted the inevitable, discovering in the process the cut-off point of his earlier views. Not surprisingly, he never expressed the same enthusiasm as Gladstone for *laissez-faire* as an economic principle. This did not prevent him from contributing to the process in his own budgets. But his was a conversion of necessity, not of commitment. Gladstone abandoned his party for his belief, whereas Disraeli abandoned his belief for his party.

Attitudes to party were also polarised. To Disraeli, party was the fount of principle and ideology, whereas to Gladstone it was the means whereby principle and ideology could be achieved in practice. In a more candid moment, Disraeli said: 'Damn your principles! Stick to your party.'

In doing the latter he sometimes changed his ideas, especially on economic issues. He saw reform and progress as a means of enhancing Conservatism while, at the same time, justifying Conservatism as an agent of progress. The two are, of course, interconnected – but it is not hard to see which is the more important. In Gladstone's case, principle transcended party. We have seen that the first crisis of his career took him out of the Conservatives in 1846. The second, the decision to press for Home Rule for Ireland after 1885, brought about a split in the Liberal party. So convinced was he of the justice of the cause that he took a major risk. The Home Rule campaign involved more than just the possibility of defeat in Parliament or in a general election; like the Corn Laws issue in 1846, it involved the future integrity of the party itself. Disraeli never took that risk.

Foreign policy involved a distinctive contrast in the heritage as well as the preferences of the two leaders. Gladstone preferred the multilateral approach which went back through the line of Aberdeen (Prime Minister in 1855 and Conservative Foreign Secretary 1841–6). He hoped to revive the traditional Concert of Europe and to keep the pursuit of British interests within the recognition of international law. Disraeli, by contrast, was a firm unilateralist, preferring to protect British interests in the most direct way possible. In this he shared the approach of Palmerston (Whig Prime Minister 1855–8 and 1859–65) and Canning (Tory Foreign Secretary 1822–7 and Prime Minister 1827). Gladstone accused him of undermining 'all the most fundamental interests of Christian society'.[5] The contrast was most marked over the Eastern Question during the late 1870s. Gladstone castigated the Ottoman Empire for repressing its Christian provinces, whereas Disraeli sought to maintain it as a strategic barrier to the threat of Russian expansion. Gladstone's strongest criticisms were expressed in his Midlothian campaign. There were occasions when Gladstone felt impelled to take direct action – but this was always a last resort. For Disraeli the priorities were the reverse: conferences were usually the result of the failure of preferred unilateralism.

The Empire featured prominently during the administrations of both men. Again, their ideas differed substantially but practice proved not always to be in line with theory. For Disraeli, Empire was one of Britain's key attributes. He said in 1871 that 'England is no longer a mere European Power; she is the metropolis of a great maritime empire, extending to the boundaries of the farthest ocean'.[6] Maintaining this was a key commitment for any government. Gladstone reversed the priority. He considered that the Empire was 'satiated' and that the government's obligation was the 'care of her own children within her own shores'.[7] In practice, however, Gladstone presided over more substantial additions to the Empire than did Disraeli, the result of being drawn into east and north Africa by unpredictable crises. He also came to accept that imperialism was popular and that 'the sentiment of empire may be called innate in every Briton'.[8] Thus, while Disraeli was an ardent exponent of the theory of imperialism, Gladstone became its reluctant practitioner.

The Irish issue similarly divided the two leaders and their parties, although this time there was no convergence of practice – willing or unwilling. Disraeli considered that the 1800 Act of Union should be permanently upheld: Ireland was an integral part of the United Kingdom and therefore within the core of the Empire. Any surrender of sovereignty would have the most drastic consequences for both. He therefore opposed virtually all the policies put forward by Gladstone and defined the longer-term Conservative approach down to 1914. Gladstone saw the pacification of Ireland as his 'mission' and gave it considerable attention in all four of his ministries. He disliked the embedded privilege of Anglicanism in Ireland and had some sympathy with the argument for Irish self-determination. The former he dealt with at the beginning of his first government (1868–74), while the latter became the key issue of his third and fourth ministries (1886 and 1892–4) when the 'mission' took on more the appearance of a crusade. Eventually his Home Rule policy dwarfed every other political issue and split the Liberal party. Disraeli had been careful to use Ireland as a unifying factor for the Conservatives.

Was there an overall driving force behind the attitudes of the two men? In the case of Gladstone, religion could be seen as a constant and defining influence. Initially a right-wing Tory who upheld the full authority and status of the Church of England, he became more tolerant of other forms of Christian faith, believing instead that religion should express itself politically through the equation of private morality with public action. This is apparent in the way in which he justified virtually all his policies in moral terms – and also in the energy with which he pursued them. Disraeli seemed to have no such driving force. His energy was given to adjusting and adapting – sometimes reactively, sometimes proactively. His ideas were readily adaptable to public policy and often showed little of the person behind them. This could have been the consequence of his personal background, which had involved the anglicisation of the D'Israeli family.

ANALYSIS 2: HOW HAVE HISTORIANS ASSESSED THE IDEAS AND ATTITUDES OF GLADSTONE AND DISRAELI? WHY HAVE THEIR EXPLANATIONS DIFFERED?

The debate on Gladstone seems to rest on how his ideas developed in relation to his career and policies. The controversy over Disraeli is probably more basic: did he have ideas which were sufficiently distinctive to influence his policies at all?

Gladstone's ideas and attitudes were an integral part of his own development as a politician, statesman – and person. They therefore changed. From being a high-church Anglican keen to defend the status of the Church of England he became broadly tolerant towards all forms of Christianity and disestablished the Church in Ireland. From being a protectionist he became an ardent free-trader. From being a defender of the establishment he came to target specific forms of corruption and patronage within the establishment. From defending the narrowness of the franchise before 1832 he came to accept the need to extend the franchise in 1867 and 1884. And from holding to the integrity of the United Kingdom he came to propose the granting of Home Rule to Ireland in 1885.

But how quickly and how consistently did these changes actually occur? There has been some disagreement over the momentum as well as over the intensity. Gladstone certainly acknowledged the latter; looking back from 1894 over a long career, he emphasised the limitations of his early ideas as a right-wing Tory. But the subsequent change was difficult. 'There was', he concluded, 'a singular slowness in the development of my mind, so far as regarded its opening into the ordinary aptitudes of the man of the world.'[1] Gradually, however, he came to accept new positions and change his ideas in line with new influences and necessities. In modern terminology, although he did not experience a sharp learning curve, the curve was nevertheless substantial because of the time-span involved. His earliest biographer, Morley, argued that Gladstone had exaggerated the slowness of his development through excessive modesty or 'embarrassed judgement'. Instead, there were periods when 'the way was clear' and in these circumstances 'nobody could run more straight, at higher speed, or with more powerful stride'.[2] A particular example of this was Gladstone's pursuit of the principle of free trade during the 1840s and 1850s. Yet there were constraints as well, which meant that rapid progress was intermittent. 'Hard as he strove for a broad basis in general theory and high abstract principle, yet always aiming at practical ends he kept in sight the opportune.'[3]

An alternative approach was put forward in the early 1950s by

Hammond and Foot.[4] They emphasised a more consistent development of Gladstone's ideas and policies than Morley admitted, while accelerating the pace. Gladstone, they argued, had 'a principal share in the fiscal revolution that was necessary to the prosperity of British trade'. He was converted by Peel to free trade and supported the repeal of the Corn Laws. In political exile he became a 'political freelance' between 1846 and 1852. But his liberal principles became increasingly apparent in his support for Russell's bill for the removal of Jewish disabilities (1847) and his opposition to Russell's Ecclesiastical Titles Bill in 1851. He supported the New Zealand Bill in 1852 and opposed Palmerston's policy over Don Pacifico. He also attacked the Neapolitan regime as 'the negation of God erected into a system of government'. He turned down an offer to join a Conservative government in 1851, instead entering Aberdeen's coalition, and supported the Balkan peoples in the Crimean War. These, and many other examples, were used to show the intensity and sustained momentum of his political activity.[5] This is very much in line with the argument of Wemyss Reid half a century earlier: 'Inconsistency . . . is not a phrase which really applies to Mr Gladstone's apparent changes of opinion and undoubted changes of policy. Rightly or wrongly, in all those changes he believed that he was advancing nearer to the light, and that his conscience compelled him to make that advance, no matter what the cost might be to himself or to his friends.'[6]

Reid saw the 1850s and 1860s as part of an accelerated pace of change. Three other historians have attached different approaches to that decade. F.W. Hirst, contributing to the same volume as Reid, stressed that different strands of Gladstone's policies developed at different speeds. 'The relation in which Mr Gladstone stood to English parties – if the personal cliques of a wretched era deserve so dignified an appellation – is puzzling in the extreme.' The same did not, however, apply to the economic side. 'Indeed, on the economic side, Mr Gladstone's opinions had continued to advance with an almost alarming rapidity.'[7] Agatha Ramm connected the two strands within a more uniform pace. Gladstone made a 'fresh start' in 1851, partly because of the realignment of party political forces and partly as the year in which 'he began to feel a particular liking for audiences of working men'. The year 1851 also represents the first stage in his interest in institutional reform, his commitment against Neapolitan tyranny and the beginning of his interest in the common man. The machinations of party were a secondary factor since 'It was to be the essence of Gladstonian Liberalism that it claimed to appeal to men's convictions and not to their party loyalty.'[8] Magnus saw the 1850s as a contrast in a different way – political frustration leading to the discovery of the working class. Since Gladstone was in conflict with Palmerston he 'found an opportunity to overcome that frustration by summoning the masses to his aid'.[9] There are, of course, bound to be dissenting voices against the notion of progressive change – however rapid or disjointed. The main example is Parry, whose analysis of the development of the Liberal party has already been considered in Chapter 1. He argued that Gladstone was not the main influence in the formation of the Liberal party. In fact, Gladstone remained Conservative at heart and never really changed from his earlier influences. This is why he damaged the Liberal party after 1867. It was the Palmerston Whigs, not Gladstone, who gave the Liberals their progressive tendency. Any changes which Gladstone underwent personally therefore carried no political impact.[10]

Whereas the debate about Gladstone focuses mainly on when and how his ideas changed, that about Disraeli is more concerned with whether he had any meaningful ideas at all. There have been two main schools of thought here. One is that he was a first-rate politician – but you can forget about the ideas. The alternative is that he had ideas – but made a poor politician. There are, of course, variations somewhere between the two.

Historians who have argued that Disraeli was more adept at practical politics than at generating ideas include Hirst (1903), Blake (1966) and Feuchtwanger (2000). The time lapses between these indicate that it is a recurrent theme. According to Hirst, 'Only a man whose political conscience was a blank could have tried; only a man whose political courage was an unlimited quantity could have succeeded. Divested of the one and invested with the other, Disraeli usurped Radicalism, dished Whiggism, and educated Toryism. From that time the Conservative party, having, in Lord Cranborne's words, "borrowed the ethics of the political adventurer," and having learned at the appropriate moment to sink its prejudices, ceased to be "stupid".'[11] According to Blake, Disraeli produced little constructive theory. 'His mind was like a catherine wheel shooting out sparks. Most of them fell on damp earth.' On the other hand, 'Where Disraeli excelled was in the art of presentation. He was an impresario and an actor manager. He was a superb parliamentarian, one of the half dozen greatest in our history.'[12] Feuchtwanger even deprived Disraeli of any credit for the term 'Tory Democracy', pointing out that Disraeli never used it. Instead, it was 'picked up in a burst of opportunism' by the Conservative party after Disraeli. 'Churchill was making a mark as a popular orator, filling the void which Disraeli and his colleagues had been unable to fill. He and his comrades were soon in full cry, using the Beaconsfield legacy and Tory Democracy as principal themes. Gorst was telling Churchill that the time was ripe for a "Democratic Tory party, which was always Dizzy's dream, at the head of which you might easily place yourself".[13] Disraeli's political greatness was therefore partly retrospective, as was any theoretical input.

Almost the exact opposite has been argued by Vincent, who put a strong case for the re-examination of Disraeli's ideas as a genuine contribution to the political and social thinking of the nineteenth century. In his *Vindication of the English Constitution* (1835), Disraeli developed 'his own theory, based on inferences from English history, as to the nature of political society' and stood 'in his historical materialism, at that point at which Burke met Marx in a common scepticism about historical abstractions'.[14] He was also 'unusual in challenging the narrowness of contemporary English psychology and sociology'.[15] His *Vindication* 'foreshadowed his Young England novels of the 1830s, his party leadership and his premiership'.[16] This involved a deliberate scheme to outflank the Whigs through a new and broader appeal to the working class, but one based on historic roots. In this way, Disraeli could be seen as the theorist behind a national party, in contrast with which the Whigs were mere social oligarchs. 'As a social thinker, Disraeli was before his time. Without using modern vocabulary, he often referred to the standard contrast between "crowd" and "community".' He also 'trusted the people at least as much as he trusted anyone'. Disraeli did, therefore, influence the future, but not through any practical abilities. 'His job was one in which it was impossible to succeed, except in the very long term and in a way which was more literary than governmental.'[17] Indeed, his practical politics were most unimpressive. 'Disraeli's record in losing six general elections and winning only one (1874) was uniquely bad.'[18]

Most historians would find their arguments somewhere between these two poles. Here are two examples, both involving the notion of a paradox. The first is the view of Lewis that the initial strength of Disraeli's theory was eventually subdued by his later discovery of expediency.[19] Disraeli may once have believed in the earlier prescriptions of Young England for healing the rifts in English society. But the revolutions of 1848 on the continent, together with the threats of disturbance in England, changed his attitude from one of positive hope to a more negative and opportunistic prevention of radicalism through measured and precautionary concessions. Another contradiction in Disraeli has been put forward by Ghosh, who attributed to Disraeli a doctrinaire approach, particularly to the economy, without his actually having a doctrine. According to Ghosh, Disraeli lacked Gladstone's doctrinal emphasis on controlling government expenditure at all times. Disraeli curbed it when it exceeded economic growth. This allowed him a degree of flexibility to finance imperial expansion and social reform.

Was there an underlying impetus for the ideas and attitudes of the two men? Here, as elsewhere, interpretations have varied.

The defining influence most commonly associated with Gladstone is his religious belief. Any debate over this influence is less concerned with its *existence* (since this would be hard to deny) than with the way in which it *operated*. Gladstone's biographer, Morley, acknowledged its presence: 'This, we can hardly repeat too often, is the fundamental fact of Mr Gladstone's history. Political life was only part of his religious life.'[20] Yet Morley gave remarkably little space, in his otherwise monumental work, to any detailed analysis or interpretation. This has been provided, instead, by Gladstone's later biographers, who seem to fall into three main categories. Some, like Magnus, saw religion as being far more important than anything else to Gladstone. Indeed, 'no statesman in modern times . . . has been in a position to dedicate such an extraordinary combination of qualities so unreservedly and effectively, on so grand a scale and for so long a period, to the task of giving effect in politics to the Christian religion. In that respect Gladstone's record is unique.'[21] Hence Gladstone brought to politics a high-mindedness combined with naivety which contrasted with the worldliness of his contemporaries. A second approach, favoured by many other historians, is to see Gladstone as a more practical politician, who brought his religious views into his schemes for reform. In fact, the connection between the two changed during the course of his career: as his religious ideas became more tolerant, they opened up areas for change, both to institutions and to the role of people within them. In other words, his changing religious emphasis made him less exclusive and more inclusive. A typical example of this approach was Butler: Gladstone moved 'from a belief in a Christian commonwealth towards the liberal ideal of a free Church in a free State'.[22] In contrast to this, a third possibility is that Gladstone's religious influences did *not* change, remaining instead a powerful force for tradition. This line was taken by Parry, who believed that Gladstone's background as a 'tory high churchman' never quite rubbed off and at times conflicted with the 'more self-consciously Protestant' ethos of the Whig–Liberals.[23] It was not Gladstone who provided Liberalism with its reforming impetus but the Whigs. If anything, Gladstone undermined these reforms by remaining inflexible and dogmatic.

The equivalent influence in Disraeli's case is not the inner religious self but, rather, the ethnic background. His 'Jewishness' has been a long-standing issue, attracting quite a variety of views. Some writers have dismissed the importance of Jewish influences altogether. Blake, for example, argued that, if there were any ethnic influences on Disraeli, they were Italian. This has echoes of a view widely held during the first half of the twentieth century, when issues of Disraeli's Jewishness were either ignored or evaded.

Others have shown that Disraeli's Jewishness actually helped shape his career. This might be categorised in three ways. First, it gave Disraeli a sense of *detachment* from British political life, enabling him to preside over it. The last part of the biography by Monypenny and Buckle (*Life of Benjamin Disraeli*) maintained that 'the fundamental fact' was that 'he was a Jew'; this meant that he was always 'a little detached when in the act of leading; always the spectator, almost the critic, as well as the principal performer'.[24] Paul Smith made a similar point about his theories. 'In a philosophical sense, he ended up securely tethered in no recognised body of belief or community of sentiment, not so much the wandering as the free-floating Jew.'[25] A second approach emphasises, by contrast, the *involvement* brought by his Jewishness. Vincent maintained that 'Disraeli was far more of a racial than a social or a religious thinker'.[26] Disraeli believed in racial superiority – but in a form which enabled Jewish influences to enhance the English strain; this was the opposite to the antisemitic assumption that Jewishness was a racial pollutant. A third interpretation, quite distinct from the other two, is that his Jewish antecedents provided Disraeli with a *broadening* influence, especially in foreign policy. Traditionally it has been assumed that Gladstone was Britain's most Eurocentric statesman, always aware of Europe's Christian and classical heritage. Endelman and Weintraub also claimed for Disraeli a European consciousness and identity, different from Gladstone's but providing an alternative perspective to the Eastern Question which was not entirely pragmatic. It could certainly be argued, for example, that Disraeli had a better understanding than Gladstone of eastern Mediterranean cultures, especially Turkish.

There is, finally, an interpretation which sees the defining influence on Gladstone and Disraeli as something quite outside religious conviction or ethnic origins, although the importance of these is not denied. Ghosh considered the economic ideas of Robert Peel as the key force behind the mid-careers of both. The connection with Gladstone is broadly recognised and his major impact on the 1850s and 1860s was carrying through to maturity the free-trade principles of Peel's 1841–6 ministry. But Ghosh applied the same connection to Disraeli, even though the latter had fiercely opposed the repeal of the Corn Laws in 1846. Disraeli came to realise that this was the only way he could go and that there was no alternative to competing with Gladstone to continue Peel's economic finance and moderation. Hence 'It is possible to trace a continuous development in ideas from the late 1840s through to the end of his career.'[27] There were ideas – but they were reactive rather than creative.

WHY HAVE INTERPRETATIONS DIFFERED?

Politicians apply political theory in practice. But they rarely produce the ideas on which political thought is based. Unless, that is, the politician was Edmund Burke – or perhaps Benjamin Disraeli? Normally there is a gap between the politician, who refines ideas, through simplification, into a workable system, and the political theorist who distils the complexities of the same ideas to show why that system needs to be changed. Historians study both – and probably have their own scale of values to judge their relative worth.

While political philosophers can be dismissed as being impractical, politicians are often accused of being superficial. This is because neither is much good at taking a leaf out of the other's book. Disraeli therefore had an inherent disadvantage. By being associated, even indirectly, with political theorists, he invites ridicule at worst and worthy inferiority at best. Gladstone comes out rather well by comparison. Despite his considerable academic strengths and a profound knowledge of theology and classics, no one has ever made direct comparisons between him and experts in those fields. The basic difference between Gladstone and Disraeli is probably one of psychology rather than of philosophy. Gladstone's ideas were internalised – focused on his own reactions and crises – and therefore considered to embody conviction and commitment. Disraeli was more effective at externalising his views, sometimes as a novelist and sometimes as a political theorist. In so doing, however, he invited comparisons with his betters in a way which Gladstone did not – since he was his *own* better.

Applying these observations may provide some perspective to the views of historians outlined. The better the politician, it seems, the worse the theorist. The judgement of A.J.P. Taylor (Source 2 below) was the harshest – but also the least informed. More serious were those of Hirst, Blake and Feuchtwanger. Hirst's assumption, it has to be said widely accepted, was that opportunists, by definition, make bad theorists. That is certainly one angle on Disraeli – an apparently timeless one which was taken even further by Blake: because he was a brilliant opportunist he can have had no theory of any merit.

Gladstone had a major advantage over Disraeli, which means that historians have generally taken him more seriously. He had an inner core of belief, which influenced everything else. He is therefore given credit for strength of conviction, whether this was for positive or negative ends. Disraeli may have had background influences helping him to shape his attitudes. But his ideas were more impersonal than Gladstone's and dwelt more impersonally on the nature of society. This made him more liable to comparison with contemporaries who were better philosophers or novelists or political theorists. Such criticisms range from the outright dismissive (Taylor) to the more considered (Blake, Smith). Vincent has gone against the trend by considering – seriously – the ideas of Disraeli in their own right.

An attempt has been made to deal with those fundamental influences which helped define the essence, possibly uniqueness, of Gladstone and Disraeli. This is particularly difficult since it involves different processes and different starting points. Perhaps the second of these – the starting point – is the crucial one.

Morley accepted the importance of religious belief to Gladstone – but chose not to dwell on it. The main reason for this was external to his subject. As an avowed agnostic, Morley was concerned that he could not do full justice to this aspect of Gladstone's make-up. There was, indeed, some opposition to Morley doing the biography at all. Harcourt, for example, told Morley: 'You cannot write about his religion because you don't believe it.'[28] Gladstone's family had a direct influence on the outcome: they were prepared for Morley to do the work, provided that he treated the religious side as something essentially private. Since the publication of the *Life of Gladstone* in 1903, there have been other approaches to the religious influence on Gladstone, with two different ways of seeing the connection between the personality and the political career. Should the career be seen as the outcome of the personality, as influenced by religion (the approach of Magnus)? Or should the personality be deduced from the career, with religion either adjusting with the change (possibly the most common approach) or preventing any change at all (Vincent)? None of these perspectives is in any way 'superior' to the others since each is based on extensive academic research and each interpretation is based on a different reading of the same evidence.

There is, however, a further issue involved in analysing the 'Jewishness' of Disraeli. This is the influence of the prevailing attitude towards ethnicity – especially *Jewish* ethnicity. During the Victorian era there was some openness in its treatment, whether positively or negatively. The former was facilitated by the more libertarian environment following the admission of Jewish members to Parliament, but the latter emerged in parallel under the influence of antisemitism and social darwinism. The frank discussion of Disraeli's Jewishness was most evident in the final volume of Monypenny and Buckle's biography, after which there was a substantial decrease in such studies. During the 1930s, 1940s and 1950s, especially, this may well have been an attempt to steer away from a sensitive issue to avoid any possible misunderstanding or suggestion of antisemitism. Blake's biography emerged, perhaps, in the climax of this trend.

Blake might also be seen as the *end* of the trend. For while most British historians were wary of analysing Jewishness, a number of Jewish studies were doing just that – before, during and after the Holocaust. From the 1970s onwards these began to enter the mainstream and, by the end of the 1980s, were part of the flow of interpretations on Disraeli. Since 1990 it has been, for example, unusual to read a book or article on Disraeli which does *not* refer to his Jewish background. Hence Endelman, Vincent, Smith and others have all built it into their interpretations, although in different ways. Perhaps it is even becoming the equivalent of Gladstone's religious beliefs: few question that it is the inner core, but there is disagreement as to how it affects the rest.

Questions

1. 'Gladstone based his political career on ideas and principles, whereas Disraeli adjusted his ideas and principles to his political career.'
   a. How far have historians argued this?
   b. How far do you agree with it as a proposition?
2. How 'constant' an influence were
   a. Gladstone's religious commitment, and
   b. Disraeli's Jewishness?
3. 'Historians disagree over the actual importance of the ideas of Gladstone and Disraeli merely for the sake of disagreement.' How far do you agree with this?

SOURCES

1. 'DISRAELIAN CONSERVATISM' AND 'TORY DEMOCRACY'

Source 1: A cartoon from *Punch*, 1868. The caption reads: 'At last'. The cartoon shows Disraeli having reached the top of the greasy pole.

See Figure 2.

Source 2: From A.J.P. Taylor, 'Dizzy' in *Essays in English History*, published in 1976. This is one of a series of essays on a wide variety of historical topics. The author had a reputation for originality and for courting controversy.

Figure 2.

Disraeli had a flighty mind which drifted from smart triviality to adolescent day-dreaming and back again. He was first and last a great actor, watching his own performance and that of others with ironic detachment. He cared for causes only as a means of combat. His novel *Sybil* is supposed to contain a profound social analysis. In fact it says no more than that the rich are very rich and the poor very poor – by no means a new discovery. His own policy, when he came to power, turned out to be nothing more startling than municipal wash-houses. His only genuine emotion in politics sprang from personal dislike – of Peel in his early career, of Gladstone even more strongly towards the end.

Source 3: From a speech made by Disraeli at the Crystal Palace, 24 June 1872.

Gentlemen, I have referred to what I look upon as the first object of the Tory party – namely, to maintain the institutions of the country, and reviewing what has occurred, and referring to the present temper of the times upon these subjects, I think that the Tory party, or, as I will venture to call it, the National party, has everything to encourage it. I think that the nation, tested by many and severe trials, has arrived at the conclusion which we have always maintained, that it is the first duty of England to maintain its institutions, because to them we principally ascribe the power and prosperity of the country.

Gentlemen, there is another and second great object of the Tory party. If the first is to maintain the institutions of the country, the second is, in my opinion, to uphold the Empire of England. If you look to the history of this country since the advent of Liberalism – forty years ago – you will find that there has been no effort so continuous, so subtle, supported by so much energy, and carried on with so much ability and acumen, as the attempts of Liberalism to effect the disintegration of the Empire of England. Gentlemen, another great object of the Tory party, and one not inferior to the maintenance of the Empire, or the upholding of our institutions, is the elevation of the condition of the people.

Source 4: From T.L. Jarman, *Democracy and World Conflict 1868–1970*, published in 1963. The book is an outline history of Britain aimed at the general reader and as an introduction to students of British history.

Monarchy and Empire were cardinal points in his political creed. Nor had Disraeli forgotten social reform which, according to the ideal he had expressed in his novels, should bridge the gap between rich and poor. His was a bold, new attitude in face of the prevailing ideas of *laissez-faire*, and an early pointer towards the welfare state.

Questions

1. What does Source 1 contribute to a discussion about Disraeli's 'ideas'? (20)
2. Compare Sources 2 and 4 as evidence for the importance of Disraeli's ideas on social reform. (40)
3. 'Disraeli was a practical politician – without any real ideas.' Discuss this view, using Sources 1 to 4 and your own knowledge. (60)

Total (120)

2. INTERPRETATIONS OF THE ROLE OF RELIGION IN GLADSTONE'S IDEAS

(Time allowed: 45 minutes)

Source 5: From Philip Magnus, *Gladstone: A Biography*, first published in 1954.

Gladstone's heart was not in politics, which he had chosen early as his field of action from motives with which he was never wholly satisfied. He had resolved, as far as possible, to make politics conform with the highest Christian ethic. He was conscious of the possession of great gifts, and he loved power for the opportunities which it gives; but all his affections were centred upon the universal Christian society, and not upon any local temporal kingdom. After he had abandoned his exalted theory of a union between Church and State, he was content to see the Church become a voluntary body. But the problem of the right relationship between two societies – the one, eternal and divine, the other, mortal and mundane – which has troubled the conscience of Europe for two thousand years, continued to torment Gladstone and to plunge his mind into a seething ferment of restlessness. Throughout the ages, the parties to that ancient dispute have constantly shifted their positions, and Gladstone also shifted his own position. The increasing secularization of nineteenth-century thought made him desist from the intellectual search for a unifying principle. He continued, however, to thirst for it emotionally, pending the full conversion of the leading nations of mankind to the Christian way of life.

Many, perhaps at first a majority, of Gladstone's contemporaries saw as clearly as he did the hand of God at work, behind all the transient phenomena of history, to propel mankind towards some transcendent and, as yet, imperfectly apprehended goal. No statesman in modern times, however, has made so little concession to human weakness; and none has been in a position to dedicate such an extraordinary combination of qualities so unreservedly and effectively, on so grand a scale and for so long a period, to the task of giving effect in politics to the Christian religion. In that respect Gladstone's record is unique.

Source 6: From Richard Shannon, *Gladstone: Heroic Minister 1865–1898*, published in 1999.

Gladstone's political life had been shaped by three profoundly formative influences. Most obvious, and well understood in the public domain, was his devotion to the principles and policies of Sir Robert Peel, prime minister in 1834–5 and 1841–6. . . . Secondly, there was Gladstone's discovery of 'the people' as a great resource of beneficent public energy to be mobilized and manipulated to good political ends. . . . Not at all well understood in the public domain, but more profoundly formative than either, was Gladstone's Anglican Christianity: his unswerving conviction, whether as young Evangelical or mature High Churchman, of the manifest providential government of the world, and his growing sense of his own assigned role as an instrument, however unworthy, of God Almighty.

It was this Christian providentialism which was, primarily and ultimately, most significant in explaining the contours and courses of Gladstone's life. It was necessarily, in the nature of the case, occult: revealed in the privacy of his diaries, rarely alluded to in public. It would not be in fact until 1878 that Gladstone finally satisfied himself that the intimations he had received throughout his career hitherto of his accredited servitude to the 'deep and hidden agencies' of God's providential plan had accrued into an evident reality. But his awareness of those deep and hidden agencies had been of long existence. In the years before 1865 he was feeling his way as a Christian statesman determined to fulfil the will of God in Christ through political struggle, anxious all the while to discern correctly what that will was and to find the appropriate mode of action to realize it.

Gladstone asserted throughout his life that his true vocation was for the Church; he entered politics at his father's behest, not unwillingly, yet ever with an awareness that for him politics uninformed and undirected by religion would be a vain and futile exercise.

Source 7: From Jonathan Parry, *The Rise and Fall of Liberal Government in Victorian Britain*, published in 1993.

The conservatism of Gladstone's *ends* gives an inadequate impression of the destabilising effect on the party of his *means of* achieving them. His particular political concerns were with finance, religion and the immorality of coercive or careless government; everything else in politics was to him just mundane administration. His economising zeal, his foreign policy, his instincts about Ireland, his hostility to clumsy parliamentary interference with the doctrine and discipline of his beloved Church of England, all took the form they did because of his drive to eradicate incompetent, boastful over-government. The problem for the Liberal party was that these attitudes could be very controversial, because of Gladstone's own forcefulness in promoting them, and because they meshed, or seemed to mesh, so well with the intemperate agitations by provincial Liberal groups for severe retrenchment, religious radicalism, 'sentimental' foreign policy, or Irish self-government. It was in these areas that the Gladstonian party came to look so different from Palmerston's.

Source 8: from T.A. Jenkins, *Gladstone, Whiggery and the Liberal Party 1874–1886*, published in 1988.

Experience as a minister in Peel's government [compelled Gladstone] to recognize that adaptability was a necessary part of the politician's craft. This liberation from the intellectual strait-jacket of his early years marked the beginning of that process of 'growth', which John Morley identified many years ago as the principal feature of Gladstone's political career.

The fact that Gladstone never found an alternative guiding creed to his discredited theory of Church–State relations poses a serious problem, however, for it is by no means clear that his subsequent political career was sustained by anything more than personal ambition and opportunism.

Questions

1. Compare the views in Sources 6 and 8 on the extent of the influence of religion on Gladstone's political career. (15)
2. 'The impact of religion on Gladstone's ideas and policies was both consistent and beneficial.' How far do Sources 5 to 8, and your own knowledge, support this view? (30)

Total (45)

3

SOCIAL, ECONOMIC AND INSTITUTIONAL REFORMS

BACKGROUND

Disraeli served as Prime Minister in 1868 and again between 1874 and 1880. Gladstone presided over four governments all together: 1868–74, 1880–5, February to August 1886, and 1892–4. They were both responsible for a substantial number of Acts of Parliament which were aimed at reforming Britain's institutions and relieving social problems. Although their overall emphasis varied, some of their measures were complementary, promoting a period of progress which was significantly more rapid than earlier decades of the nineteenth century.

One of Disraeli's most important measures was guided through Parliament while he was still Chancellor of the Exchequer under Derby. This was the 1867 Reform Act, which doubled the electorate by extending the vote to the top layer of the working class (see Chapter 4). This did not, however, prevent Disraeli, now Prime Minister, losing the 1868 general election by 271 seats to the Liberals' 387. Clearly the new voters were looking to the Liberals rather than the Conservatives to provide a reforming impetus.

Gladstone's first ministry is seen as one of the great reforming governments of the nineteenth century. It started with the Irish Church Act (1869) which meant that Anglicanism was no longer the official state religion of Ireland and followed up with another measure to try to reduce disturbances – the Irish Land Act (1870). The same year saw the introduction of Forster's Education Act, setting up School Boards which would ensure non-denominational religious education in their schools, although voluntary schools were to retain their existing rights. In the University Tests Act (1871) Gladstone withdrew the exclusive right of Anglicans to teach, administer or hold scholarships at the Universities of Oxford and Cambridge. Central administration was overhauled by the civil service reforms (1871), which established the principle of competitive recruitment and promotion. Industrial relations were covered by two measures in 1871 – the Trade Union Act, which recognised trade unions as legal bodies, and the Criminal Law Amendment Act, which banned picketing as an accompaniment to strike action. The year 1872 saw a variety of measures. The Public Health Act divided England and Wales into health authorities, each of which was to appoint a medical officer; the Ballot Act reduced the opportunity for electoral intimidation by introducing the secret ballot; and the Licensing Act gave magistrates control over the issue of licences to public houses, prescribed closing times and forbade the adulteration of beer. In the following year the Judicature Act (1873) consolidated the existing seven courts into the Supreme Court of Judicature and removed the power of the House of Lords as the final court of appeal. Finally, at various stages during Gladstone's ministry, Cardwell's reforms modernised the British army. Commissions were to be earned through merit, not bought, flogging was abolished, and the length of service overseas was reduced from 12 to 6 years abroad and 6 years in the reserves at home. Much-needed administrative reforms extended the centralising control of the War Office, brought the Commander-in-Chief under the Secretary for War, and divided the country into sixty-nine districts – each with a regiment.

Despite the scope of these reforms – and because of the contro-versial nature of many of them – Gladstone alienated a sufficiently large proportion of the voters to lose the 1874 general election by 251 seats to Disraeli's 342. Measures of the subsequent Conservative government were also varied, although they possibly showed a greater focus than Gladstone's on social issues. This applied particularly to 1875. The Public Health Act made it compulsory for local authorities to provide adequate drainage and sewerage and to monitor and control infectious disease and offensive trades. More specific regulations were provided in the Sale of Food and Drugs Act (1875), which dealt with the longstanding problem of deliberate contamination, and the Artisans' Dwellings Act (1875) which gave local authorities the power to undertake slum clearance. Disraeli's government also involved itself in the increasingly controversial area of industrial relations. The Conspiracy and Protection of Property Act (1875) removed Gladstone's prohibition on picketing, while also making trade unions liable to being charged with conspiracy should picketing be used to excess. The Employers and Workmen Act (1876) placed employers and employees on the same level in the event of breach of legal contract: instead of being subject respectively to civil and criminal law, both were under civil law. Meanwhile, Sandon's Education Act (1876) set up local School Attendance Committees and encouraged parents to ensure regular attendance by their children. In the same year, two measures achieved an early form of environmental control. The Enclosures Act (1876) prevented landowners from acquiring common land and introduced the idea of green-belt protection from building. Another measure in the same year prevented the tipping of solid industrial waste and poisonous liquids into rivers. Finally, measures were also introduced to regulate certain types of working practice. The Factory Act of 1874 reduced the maximum working day to ten hours and raised the minimum age for full-time employment to 14 years, while the 1878 Factory and Workshops Act shifted the duty of factory inspection from local authorities to central government. A particularly hazardous form of work on board unseaworthy vessels was at least partly dealt with by the Merchant Shipping Act (1876) which insisted on the painting of a 'Plimsoll' line on the hull of all merchant ships to prevent deliberate overloading.

During the last three years of Disraeli's second ministry there was a noticeable switch in attention from domestic reform to foreign and imperial issues (see Chapters 5 and 6). This gave Gladstone the opportunity to return to the offensive in the highly effective Midlothian campaign of 1879. As a result, Gladstone won the 1880 election by 353 seats to Disraeli's 238. The expectation of the electorate was another six years of domestic reform. But, like Disraeli (who died in 1881), Gladstone faced serious complications abroad, especially in east, west and southern Africa (see Chapter 6). The reforming impetus did not dry up altogether. The Married Women's Property Act (1882) removed a longstanding anomaly and restored to married women the property rights they had possessed when single. The Corrupt and Illegal Practices Prevention Act (1883) placed a limit on the expenditure on the election of candidates to Parliament; the 1884 Representation of the People Act further enlarged the electorate (see Chapter 4); and the Redistribution of Seats Act (1885) reformed an antiquated system by ending most of the two-member constituencies.

In addition to having to deal with unwelcome diversions abroad, Gladstone also spent much of his second ministry trying to resolve an increasingly desperate situation in Ireland (see Chapter 7). Unsuccessful with his Coercion Act (1881) and Second Irish Land Act (1881), he began to consider Home Rule as the only feasible solution. This became official Liberal policy in his third ministry (1886) but the effort involved in the unsuccessful attempt to secure the passage of the First Home Rule Bill in 1886 virtually destroyed the possibility of any other reforms and badly split the Liberal party in the process. His fourth and final government (1892–4), which was elected partly on the basis of widespread reforms promised in the party's Newcastle Programme, secured the passage of the Second Home Rule Bill through the Commons, only to have it vetoed by the Lords. Again, other initiatives were squeezed out, the only significant reform being the Local Government (Parish Councils) Act of 1894; this provided for the subdivision of county councils into urban and rural districts and enabled married and single women to vote in local elections.

But the overall trend towards single-issue policies during Gladstone's last two ministries eventually persuaded his successors to refocus on multiple reform. Gladstonian Liberalism was to be replaced by 'New' Liberalism under the leadership of Campbell Bannerman and Asquith. Disraelian Conservatism, by contrast, experienced a rather smoother passage into the twentieth century.

ANALYSIS 1: COMPARE THE CONTRIBUTIONS OF GLADSTONE AND DISRAELI TO THE DEVELOPMENT OF THE BRITISH ECONOMY.

Gladstone and Disraeli both influenced a variety of nineteenth-century developments, including the reshaping of political parties and the introduction of institutional and social reform. But a particularly important part of their overall contribution was to Britain's economic development – through policies which were both deliberate and reactive, during periods as Chancellor of the Exchequer or Prime Minister or, in Gladstone's case, both. Although there were periodic differences between the two, there was also an underlying continuity: both aspects need to be included in any comparison between their contributions to underlying economic policy and to more detailed financial management. The criteria could be their attitude to protectionism and free trade, their development of budgetary policies, their contribution to the whole principle of responsible government expenditure, and their response to the intrusion of external economic crises.

During the 1830s Gladstone and Disraeli, then in the same party, were staunch protectionists and were opposed to any extension of the free-trade measures introduced in the 1820s by 'liberal' Tories such as Huskisson and Robinson. During the 1840s, however, things changed. Gladstone moved over to free trade, convinced partly by the arguments of Robert Peel (Prime Minister 1841–6) and partly by his own experience as President of the Board of Trade (1843–5). His change amounted to a total conversion and he invested his new economic ideas with a strong moral emphasis; he wrote in 1894: 'For my part I am a Free Trader on moral no less than on economic grounds: for I think human greed and selfishness are interwoven with every thread of the Protective system.'[1] Disraeli, by contrast, remained an equally ardent protectionist, articulating the argument that the landed and agricultural classes would be ruined with the removal of tariffs. Hence the two were on opposing sides when Peel introduced the repeal of the Corn Laws in 1846 – although Disraeli eventually abandoned protectionism in 1848. During the following decade both Gladstone and Disraeli played an important role in re-educating their respective parties to new attitudes. As he became increasingly involved with the Whigs, through Russell and Palmerston, Gladstone brought a Peelite vision of free trade which became increasingly ambitious in its scope: the 1860 Cobden Treaty with France, for example, added an internationalist dimension. Disraeli, for his part, persuaded the Conservatives (including their leader, Derby) to drop protection after 1852. His main argument was political – that free trade was a *fait accompli* which the Conservatives would have to accept if they ever hoped to win a future general election.

As Chancellor of the Exchequer, both Gladstone and Disraeli became skilled in devising budgets, although Gladstone had less trouble in securing parliamentary assent. By contrast, Disraeli's 1852 budget, which sought to help the agricultural interest by lowering the malt tax, was defeated by 305 votes to 286. Yet once Disraeli had taken the plunge to accept the principle of *laissez-faire*, there was a strong degree of continuity between his measures and Gladstone's. Both believed in reducing income tax and cutting government expenditure. Both had similar targets here – control of defence expenditure, the reduction of waste. The idea was that taxation could be steadily reduced because revenue would be increased through economic growth and through increased consumption of those luxury items on which duties were still levied. Disraeli's 1858 budget took advantage of a surplus to reduce income tax from 7d to 5d in the pound and hoped to abolish it completely by 1860 (the date which Gladstone had set for the same thing in his first budget of 1853). Gladstone tried consistently to eliminate income tax, promising its abolition in the 1874 election campaign. Although he never managed this, he did bring it down to 4d in the pound by 1865 and to 3d in 1868. Disraeli preferred to keep income tax as a permanent form of revenue, although at the lowest possible level: during his second ministry, Disraeli's Chancellor, Northcote, managed to reduce income tax to 2d in the pound.

Both Gladstone and Disraeli emphasised the need for strict financial management. Gladstone acknowledged his debt to Peel for 'financial strictness' and 'loyal adherence to the principle of public economy'.[2] He also believed that wealth was a 'trust' which should be increased so that it could 'fructify in the pockets of the people'.[3] Disraeli used the argument that 'A good management of the finances is the only thing which really will get the country with us.'[4] Both resisted pressures for further expenditure. This severely restricted the scope of social reform by either leader and undermines any claim to the extensive benefits of Tory Democracy. It also explains why most of Disraeli's social reforms were permissive rather than mandatory. Cross, for example, defended his Artisans' Dwellings Improvement Bill in 1875 on the grounds that it did not 'infringe the laws of political economy'.[5] It also accounts for Gladstone's unwillingness to compete with the Conservatives in this area.

There were occasions when both Gladstone and Disraeli had to respond to externally imposed crises – with varying success. With the onset of depression at the end of the 1870s Disraeli took the decision not to respond to the pressure of the agricultural interest and introduce protection. This was in direct contrast to other European states, including Germany, which experienced a revival of tariffs. Nor did Disraeli's government have any realistic measures to deal with the growing distress in Ireland. Northcote, as Chancellor of the Exchequer, argued that nothing should be done to relieve the situation, since this might set a bad precedent for the future. His 'wait and see' approach became a permanent characteristic of British economic policy. Gladstone was no different in principle, although he was outraged by some of the measures of detail, such as Northcote's borrowing in 1879 through the issue of exchequer bonds and his decision in 1880 to raid the Sinking Fund which had been set up to reduce the national debt. But what did Gladstone do to meet the pressures of the depression? Like Disraeli, he opposed tariff reform, and his solution to distress in Ireland was Home Rule. Indeed, part of the reason for the latter was to reduce the financial burden on central government through the devolution of political power. If this was the case, then the economic policy pursued by the Liberals was actually very similar to that of the Conservatives. The competition was not so much on which party had the better overall strategy to create an appropriate economic environment, but rather which was more adept at controlling expenditure and therefore being able to reduce taxation.

Did Gladstone and Disraeli make much difference? Both contributed to the development of *laissez-faire*, even if there was a difference in their motives for doing so. Both can be credited with sound financial management and the sort of budgetary control which was considered essential to good government. Both managed to limit government expenditure (although not all governments would agree that that was necessarily a good thing). Both contrived to reduce the burden of taxation, although later politicians were to argue that it was not much of a burden anyway. Disraeli, however, had a permanent influence upon his party's approach to economic policy and the finances in the future, whereas Gladstonian Liberalism, with its emphasis on low taxation, was to give way at the turn of the century to the 'New' Liberal policy of redistributive taxation and higher levels of public expenditure.

Questions

1.   Who did more for the British economy: Gladstone or Disraeli?

ANALYSIS 2: HOW HAVE HISTORIANS VIEWED THE ECONOMIC, SOCIAL AND INSTITUTIONAL REFORMS OF GLADSTONE AND DISRAELI?

Chapter 2 examined the ideas of Gladstone and Disraeli. The extent to which ideas were behind the changes actually made is the main issue in this analysis.

Economic policy

The first major political office held by both men was that of Chancellor of the Exchequer. They both also retained a strong influence over the direction of economic policy as Prime Minster; indeed Gladstone sometimes doubled up the two offices (1873–4 and 1880–2). Each has attracted a wide diversity of interpretation, although there seem to be three broad trends.

The first is the neo-Marxist view that Gladstone and Disraeli were at the mercy of longer-term economic trends and could do little more than respond to them in line with the demands and needs of the classes which they represented. According to Hobsbawm, political action during the period between the 1840s and the 1870s was dominated by the economic infrastructure and by the need for free trade. This 'seemed indispensable, for it allowed primary producers overseas to exchange their products for British manufactures, and thus reinforced the symbiosis between the United Kingdom and the underdeveloped world on which British economic power essentially rested'.[1] Britain's needs were, however, different from those of the countries which had industrialised more recently, in the sense that they rested more directly on trade, manufacturing and the exploitation of other areas through imperialism. This meant that free trade was seen as the only viable policy to pursue, even with the arrival of the Great Depression in the late 1870s. Hence 'Britain was the only country in which even Conservative statesmen, in spite of the ancient commitment of such parties to protection, were prepared to abandon agriculture.'[2] This approach allows for no distinction between the policies pursued by Gladstone and Disraeli: in each case, policy is seen as the practical expression of the economic needs of the ruling classes. Both leaders represented the same classes, even if they belonged to opposing political parties and there was a conflict of interest between the agricultural and industrial sectors. Such differences were incidental to the overall relationship between politicians and the stratum of society they served.

A second, and contrasting, approach is to allow for much more individual influence from the politicians, whose decisions did have a direct impact. This much is directly assumed, although there is some controversy as to whether their policies were projective or reactive, systematic or opportunist.

This is particularly the case with Disraeli. Some historians have maintained that he was deliberate in the changes he brought and the financial policies he sought to implement. Ghosh, for example, believed that *all* of Disraeli's policies were underpinned by an economic approach which was intended to extend the future appeal of the Conservative party. Even though it was defeated, his 1852 budget was 'a principled and coherent measure' and 'a remarkable attempt to secure the approval of a moderate majority and yet to reconcile this with the prejudices and interests of the landed men who sat behind Disraeli'.[3] It also showed the way in which he had managed at last to come to terms with the economic legacy of Robert Peel.

On the other hand, Disraeli could be seen more in the light of an improviser. Jenkins argued that 'Disraeli's willingness to jettison protection betrayed the fundamentally opportunistic nature of his attachment to the agriculturalists' cause in 1846'. Far from his political approach being influenced by a conversion to Peelite economics, his political attack on Peel delayed his acceptance of the inevitable. Hence his earlier commitment to protection had always been 'based far more on the condemnation of Peel's treachery to his party than on any defence of the Corn Laws per se'.[4] Nor, it has been argued, was the opportunist as clever as he thought in manipulating the finances for political purposes. Smith considered that Disraeli's 1852 budget had two 'fatal flaws'. The first was that he had to compensate for halving the malt tax by lowering the exemption limit of income tax and house tax, while also doubling the rate of the latter. This 'made it easy to represent his proposals as paying for the concessions of the farmers out of the pocket of the urban property-owner'. Disraeli laid himself open to attack also on the precariousness of the difference between earned and unearned income. Hence the budget was 'a setback' but 'Disraeli meant to go on infringing the patent of the men opposite'.[5]

There is an equivalent divergence of opinion over Gladstone. Some historians have attributed to him a clear vision of an economic policy. Biagini, in fact, pointed to a fundamental distinction between the financial strategies of Gladstone and Disraeli. They differed, for example, over income tax: 'while Disraeli wanted to turn income tax into a permanent feature of the British fiscal system, Gladstone saw it as a dangerous incentive to government financial irresponsibility and a warlike foreign policy'.[6] This was very much in line with Gladstone's Liberalism. 'Technically, Gladstone's financial approach was a further development of his Peelite creed: its ingredients were a balanced budget, regular surpluses and a careful consideration of the social and political implications of the various taxes.'[7] It has also been argued that Gladstone's principle was to remove the tax burden on those who were not enfranchised by lowering indirect taxation. Matthew, for example, maintained that Britain's Parliament comprised 'a self-taxing class of income-tax paying electors'.[8] This was the price to be paid for reducing indirect taxation. However,

Gladstone always saw it as a temporary expedient and tried to repeal it in 1873. Although overtaken by the general election, this was more than mere political opportunism. According to Biagini, 'Had he won – even with a reduced majority – he would have been able to rule from Number 11 as well as from Number 10 through the financial restraints implied in his manifesto, a sort of "fiscal constitution".'[9] Thus, in the totality of his economic vision he was actually well ahead of his time. Jenkins, too, saw financial and economic policies and issues as the catalyst for Peel's political change – 'Free Trade provided the essential link between Gladstone and Liberalism', while 'its wider policy implications also assisted in his general political conversion'.[10] Not only, therefore, did Gladstone have a direct impact on the British economy; his economic ideas helped shape his political ones.

The emergence of one from the other has some overlap with the approach of Hobsbawm. The crucial difference, however, is that the interplay between the economic and political is individual rather than infrastructural, personal rather than impersonal. On the other hand, the individual might be given too much credit for developing his *own* system. Gladstone – like Disraeli – could be seen as an opportunist, lacking an overall economic plan while possessing a strategy to deal with the political implications of economic problems. This restores the influence of the economic infrastructure while, at the same time, giving the politician more of a role than merely the leader of an inert superstructure.

It is even possible for an individual to react differently to the influences of the economic infrastructure, depending on the political circumstances. Again, this allows for the practical impact of political decisions made by the individual. Disraeli, who conceded the triumph of free trade in the mid-century, decided in 1852 that the Conservatives should go with it and abandon protectionism. Yet, when the agricultural depression affected Britain in the late 1870s, he took the reverse decision – which was to do nothing. This could be attributed to his unwillingness to risk alienating the urban-based voter, to whom a free market for exports and cheaper food were both vital – a contrast to his tendency to take the support of the landed interest for granted. Hence, although he dithered in terms of an economic strategy, he did have a political one and adopted the exact opposite of the approach of Bismarck in Germany. Sometimes statesmen go with a trend not because they feel compelled by it but because they do not wish to find an alternative. It may be that there is none (because the economic policy is itself a strategy) or, alternatively, that the political strategy suggests inaction. Either way a decision has been made; indecision is itself a decision.

'Gladstonian Liberalism' and 'Tory Democracy' in practice?

The other reforms, mainly of the 1870s and 1880s, have often been associated with Gladstonian Liberalism and Tory Democracy. The basic ideas connected with these are covered in Chapter 2. This section focuses on whether the institutional and social reforms introduced during the ministries of Gladstone and Disraeli depended in any way upon theory – or whether they were a pragmatic response to contemporary political or economic needs.

There has always been support for the view that Gladstone acted in accordance with his ideas. Earlier historians adopting this line included Morley and Hammond, followed during the 1960s by Magnus, who stressed the importance of Gladstone's religious background. More recently, the list has come to include Biagini and Feuchtwanger. The former maintained that 'Gladstonian Liberalism had a remarkable "ideological" cohesion, greater than that of any continental Socialism.'[11] Feuchtwanger agreed: 'The abolition of privileges, the removal of barriers to advancement by merit and the establishment of full civic equality were part of the philosophy of Gladstonian Liberalism and consequently the government [of 1868–74] to make merit and expertise rather than patronage the basis of recruitment to the civil service.'[12] It is not hard to see the reason for this continuity in approach. Gladstone was both academic in his interests and receptive to the ideas he encountered. His psychology therefore made considerable use of his intellect, especially since he was inclined to rationalise conceptually rather than to conceptualise the rational – which was more Disraeli's method.

The alternative approach is to emphasise that Gladstone's commitment to reform has been overstated. According to Adelman, Gladstone did not have a series of policies in his first ministry; nor did these amount to a coherent programme. 'With the exception of one or two Irish reforms, Gladstone had no great personal commitment towards them.' Some reforms were institutional: 'Here the aim was primarily efficiency and economy.' Other reforms 'were already in the pipeline when Gladstone took over as Prime Minister'.[13]

A parallel debate rests on whether Disraeli gave the Conservatives a reforming and social emphasis through 'Disraelian Conservatism'/ 'Tory Democracy'. Disraeli's own words would suggest so. He seemed to give a high priority to social reform, arguing that 'the first consideration of a Minister should be the people's health. Pure air, pure water, the inspection of unhealthy habitations, the adulteration of food, these and many kindred matters may be legitimately dealt with by the legislature.'[14] Historians of the early twentieth century gave Disraeli considerable credit for social change. Wilkinson, for example, maintained that 'Throughout his career in Parliament he consistently supported all measures of social reform'[15] and that this added up to the distinctive brand of 'Tory Democracy' that he used as the title to his book.

Some historians consider that Disraeli *did* have a commitment to Tory Democracy which, although it 'was not a programme of political action' was, nevertheless, 'more than a political slogan'. Disraeli's 'belief in Tory Democracy' helps explain the confidence with which he pressed for parliamentary reform in 1867 and at least some of his social reforms.[16] This was particularly the case with his trade union legislation. Also, 'it is possible that Disraeli was at his most sincere when he was at his most visionary and idiosyncratic'.[17] But his successors were less interested in the working classes, and the rise of new unionism and labour had the reverse effect. Hence 'Disraeli may well have believed in "Tory Democracy", and the legislation of his second ministry did something to make a reality of the promise of his rhetoric: but in the evolution of the Conservative Party social policy towards the working classes, it represents not a beginning but a dead end.'[18] Tory Democracy was therefore started by Disraeli – but did not survive him. This is an interesting contrast to the more common approach, which sees 'Tory Democracy' as a description applied to Disraeli's reforms retrospectively by Lord Randolph Churchill, Balfour and Lord Salisbury. Like Disraeli himself, it became part of the mythology of the Conservative party – lacking in any real substance but with an increasingly attractive image. Far from being a 'dead end', therefore, Tory Democracy provided a vista for the future – even if it was not an entirely realistic one.

Many views have actually been quite negative about the theoretical background to Disraeli's social reforms. Adelman claimed that 'Tory Democracy' was little more than 'windy rhetoric',[19] while Machin went so far as to say that 'it is spurious' to attempt to 'elevate and dignify' Disraeli's social reforms by the attribution of a philosophic approach.[20] Smith argued that Disraeli's social reforms cannot be viewed 'as the embodiment of any social "policy"'. Instead, 'it was empirical, piecemeal reform, dealing with problems as and when they were pushed into prominence by their inherent size and urgency'.[21] Very much the same point was made by Feuchtwanger: Disraeli and his ministers 'were not motivated by any clear social philosophy and proceeded cautiously and empirically'.[22] Blake attributed to Disraeli an ability to counter-attack the real policy-maker, Gladstone. 'Gladstone's great reforming ministry frightened the forces of property, landed or otherwise, even as the Whig–Liberal alliance had frightened them in the 1830s. Disraeli exploited this situation with cautious adroitness, mending the party machine, waiting shrewdly upon events, and above all attacking Gladstonianism for its radical implications.'[23]

In a way, much of the debate about whether Disraeli had specific plans for social reform begs the question: why should we actually expect Disraeli to have had a carefully worked out legislative programme? According to Jenkins, Gladstone had produced an unexpected general election in 1874 and 'it was not accepted practice at this time for party leaders to issue detailed manifestos, listing their plans of action: if anything at all was specified, the emphasis tended to be placed on a single issue, like the income tax, while broad statements of intent were added in the hope of setting a certain tone to the election campaign'.[24] Disraeli's message was that 'the Conservatives would give the country a rest from harassing legislation'. Hence his immediate priority was 'to pay off certain election debts' such as to the licensed victuallers – which explains his Intoxicating Liquors Bill.[25] 'Certainly there was no question of the Conservatives embarking on a systematic exercise in paternalistic social reform, inspired by the sort of "One Nation" principles that Disraeli had laid down in his Young England days.'[26] He was therefore 'faithful to his stated view that useful, non-contentious social reform measures were an appropriate form of action for the Conservatives as an antidote to the Liberal Party's obsession with attacking national institutions like the Church and the House of Lords'.[27]

While, therefore, we should avoid reading too much influence from nineteenth-century ideas and ideologies on to the political policy of Gladstone and Disraeli, we should also be wary of attributing twentieth-century party organisation and campaigning to their political action.

The personal involvement of Gladstone and Disraeli in the reforms of their ministries

Whether or not their reforms were based on programmes is distinct from the issue of the personal interest and commitment shown by Gladstone and Disraeli in their actual preparation. Not surprisingly, there is some controversy here as well.

Gladstone has been depicted as directly involved in a surprisingly wide variety of reforms. According to Feuchtwanger: 'The Irish Church Disestablishment and Irish Land Bills were the work of Gladstone' both in principle and in detail. He showed a particular command of detail 'in personally conducting most of the consultations necessary, in drafting these bills and piloting them through the House of Commons'.[28] Disraeli's style as Prime Minister was very different. 'He could not compete with his rival in grasp of detail or powers of work, but he may well have excelled him in his ability to direct the strategy and to impose his will where it really mattered.'[29] Biagini provided a similar picture of Gladstone, as a Prime Minister who was energetic and versatile – but selective. He saw the major issue as Ireland, to which he gave his personal attention through Disestablishment. Elsewhere, bills were sometimes drawn up by others, and he even disapproved of the Ballot Act, moving behind it only when it was rejected in the House of Lords. 'In contrast to the view that he focused his mind and attention on only one issue at a time, he was in fact able to divide his energy among most of the many Bills, projects and proposals which the government and leading backbenchers produced between 1868 and 1874.'[30]

Jenkins was less convinced by this. 'It would be a mistake to suppose that the legislation passed by Gladstone's government was all part of a programme inspired and masterminded by the Prime Minister.'[31] Quite often his approach was opportunist, based on the need to secure the support of different parts of the party. This, for example, explains his adoption of the principle of the secret ballot – to gain the support of the Radicals. In any case, the reforms of Gladstone's first ministry did not lead to any great changes or upward mobility for the lower orders. Civil service reform and the changes made to the army by Cardwell only marginally affected promotion. 'Meritocracy within the existing elite, rather than a more general equality of opportunity, was the keynote of the Liberal reforms.'[32]

Parry went very much further than this with an iconoclastic and original revision of Gladstone's reputation both as a reformer and as a personal influence on his government. Gladstone may have 'condoned' most of the Liberal agenda. But, Parry maintained, 'hardly any of it was his. It arose from the Whig–Liberal tradition, updated to cope with political needs after 1867. In essentials, Gladstone's aims remained conservative.'[33] Even in the 1870s, 'before Irish obstruction became serious, his legislative record was actually less effective than Palmerston's or even Russell's, because too much of it was too controversial'. Parry provided a revealing statistic (interestingly, relegated to a footnote) in an analysis of government bills introduced in four sessions. Russell's government introduced 195 in the 1847–8 session and 159 in 1849–50, Palmerston's ministry 178 in 1863–4 and Gladstone's 152 in 1871–2, of which the percentage actually making it through were 83.3, 75, 86 and 72.4 respectively.[34] Parry's whole argument was based on the premise that Gladstone provided neither the reforming impetus nor the unifying influence within the Liberal party. On the contrary, he damaged the earlier liberal achievements of the Whigs and Radicals.

Disraeli is often seen as personally uninterested in the details of legislative reform. Many historians have quoted the view of Richard Cross on Disraeli's failure to provide any real leadership or guidance when the cabinet came to discuss the Queen's speech in 1874: 'I was, I confess, disappointed at the want of originality shown by the Prime Minister. From all his speeches, I had quite expected that his mind was full of legislative schemes, but such did not prove to be the case: on the contrary, he had to rely on the various suggestions of his colleagues, and they themselves had only just come into office.' Suddenly, therefore, 'there was some difficulty in framing the Queen's Speech'.[35] With this later indictment by one of Disraeli's main lieutenants, it is hardly surprising that the Prime Minister's role in the 1874–80 government has been put into perspective. Some historians have taken the logical next step, attributing much of the influence for Disraeli's reform to Cross who, according to Watts, 'was highly competent' and 'a good administrator' with 'a grasp of practical affairs'.[36] This was much needed, since 'Disraeli's own attention was largely focused elsewhere, mainly in foreign affairs.'[37] The same point was made by Jenkins, who argued that Cross and other colleagues were committed 'to an active policy in the belief that the State had the power to do good in certain areas'.[38] On the other hand, Disraeli did much to provide an appropriate overall atmosphere in which such purposeful activity could take place. Jenkins aptly summarised Disraeli's contribution in providing the 'impetus for a constructive Conservative policy through his general assertions of the party's intention to devote its energies to social legislation, even if it never specified what that social legislation was going to be'.[39]

Ultimately, the line taken on the personal involvement of the Prime Minister in government will depend on how the historian balances the different sources available. In this instance these are substantial, ranging from the diaries and personal correspondence of both Gladstone and Disraeli to subsequent accounts provided by cabinet ministers such as Cross, Sandon and Adderley (Conservatives) and Granville, Chamberlain and Hartington (Liberals). The overall balance on the Prime Minister's involvement might, however, depend on a steer given by the apparent direction taken by the government as a whole. Ministerial recollections could well attribute excessive interference or withdrawal by the Prime Minister in one area because of a personal grievance against similar action in another. The same might well apply to the overall judgement arrived at by historians. For example, if the view is that Gladstone wrecked a consensus that had grown up amongst Liberals, two alternatives are possible about his involvement in the details of government. One is that he interfered excessively in the day-to-day details; the other that he ignored the normal functions of multiple reform to focus on single-minded crusades. If Disraeli managed to *retain* a Conservative consensus, it could be because he knew when to act in his cabinet to see the implementation of his 'Tory Democracy', or – more likely – because his interests were more in the area of party politics and foreign policy, meaning that he was more inclined to delegate on social reform. These are only a few amongst the numerous possibilities which can only serve to keep alive the whole debate on precisely what Gladstone and Disraeli did and did not do.

Questions

1. Consider the view that, because they were products of the Victorian economy and society, Gladstone and Disraeli did very little to change either.
2. 'Disraeli came closer than Gladstone to implementing his concepts of reform.' Do you agree?

SOURCES

1. DISRAELI'S SOCIAL REFORMS

(Time allowed: 60 minutes)

Source 1: A cartoon from *Punch*, 6 March 1875. The caption has been slightly adapted.

See Figure 3.

Source 2: From a speech by Disraeli at Crystal Palace in 1872.

Gentlemen, another great object of the Tory Party, and one not inferior to the maintenance of the Empire, or the upholding of our institutions, is the elevation of the condition of the people. . . . It must be obvious to all who consider the condition of the multitude with a desire to improve and elevate it, that no important step can be gained unless you can effect some reduction in their hours of labour and humanize their toil. . . . I ventured to say a short time ago, speaking in one of the great cities of the country, that the health of the people was the most important question for a statesman. . . . What is the opinion of the great Liberal Party – the party that seeks to substitute cosmopolitan for national principles in the government of this country – on this subject . . . ? A leading member . . . denounced them the other day as 'policy of sewage'.

INJURED INNOCENTS

BUNG (to BUMBLE, *owner of Unwholesome Dwellings*): 'Talk of harassing legislation! It was our turn last session: now it's yours!'

BUMBLE: 'A regular Cross, I call it. Might just as well have the other lot back again!'

Figure 3.

Well, it may be a 'policy of sewage' to a Liberal Member of Parliament. But to one of the labouring multitude of England, who has found fever to be one of the members of his household . . . it is not a 'policy of sewage', but a question of life and death.

Source 3: From a speech in the House of Commons by Richard Cross, Home Secretary, in February 1875. Cross was introducing the Artisans' Dwellings Bill.

I take it as a starting point that it is not the duty of the Government to provide any class of citizens with any of the necessaries of life, and among the necessaries of life we must include that which is one of the chief necessaries – good and habitable dwellings. That is not the duty of the State, because if it did so, it would inevitably tend to make that class depend, not on themselves, but upon what was done for them elsewhere, and it would not be possible to teach a worse lesson than this – that 'If you do not take care of yourselves, the State will take care of you.' Nor is it wise to encourage large bodies to provide the working classes with habitations at greatly lower rents than the market value paid elsewhere. Admitting these two principles of action, there is another point of view from which we may look, and another ground upon which we may proceed. No one will doubt the propriety and right of the state to interfere in matters relating to sanitary laws. Looking at this question as a matter of sanitary reform, there is much to be done by the Legislature, not to enable the working classes to have houses provided for them, but to take them out of that miserable condition in which they now find themselves – namely, that, even if they want to have decent homes, they cannot get them . . .

Source 4: From Richard Cross, *A Political History*, published in 1903. Cross is describing a cabinet meeting at the beginning of Disraeli's second ministry in 1874.

I was, I confess, disappointed at the want of originality shown by the Prime Minister. From all his speeches, I had quite expected that his mind was full of legislative schemes, but such did not prove to be the case; on the contrary, he had to rely on the various suggestions of his colleagues, and they themselves had only just come into office.

Questions

1. Explain the references in Source 1 to 'Unwholesome Dwellings', 'harassing legislation' and 'A regular Cross'. (20)
2. Compare Sources 2 and 3 as evidence for Conservative social policy in Disraeli's second ministry. (40)

3. 'There was nothing distinctive about the policy on social reform between 1874 and 1880 to identify it as Disraeli's policy.' How far do Sources 1 to 4, and your own knowledge, agree with this view? (60)

Total (120)

2. INTERPRETATIONS OF THE REFORMS OF GLADSTONE'S FIRST MINISTRY (1868–74) AND DISRAELI'S SECOND MINISTRY (1874–80)

Source 5: Disraeli answers criticism of his legislation in the House of Commons, 24 June 1875.

Disraeli: It may be all very well for hon. and right hon. Gentlemen to treat with affected contempt the notion that our legislation should be founded on permission, but permissive legislation is the characteristic of a free people. It is easy to adopt compulsory legislation when you have to deal with those who only exist to obey; but in a free country, and especially in a country like England, you must trust to persuasion and example as the two great elements, if you wish to effect any considerable change in the manners and customs of the people.

Source 6: From T.A. Jenkins, *Disraeli and Victorian Conservatism*, published in 1996.

Certainly, there was to be no question of the Conservative embarking upon a systematic exercise in paternalistic social reform, inspired by the sort of 'One Nation' principles that Disraeli had laid down in his Young England days. Disraeli may still occasionally have used language reminiscent of his earlier views – for instance, his assertion in 1872 that the 'condition of the people' was the issue of prime importance for politicians – but in reality his government's response to such matters was influenced by the prevailing doctrines of political economy. A generation of Conservative administrators had grown up – men like Northcote and Cross, who were imbued with the teachings of mid-Victorian laissez-faire Liberalism – and there is little to suggest that Disraeli dissented from such thinking.

Source 7: From L.C.B. Seaman, *Victorian England*, published in 1973.

The important domestic legislation of the Gladstone–Disraeli years may therefore be legitimately considered as a whole and to a great extent without reference to either of them. Both have had their names attached to reforms which owed little to their initiative and not much to their encouragement. Entirely without a sense of proportion, Gladstone absorbed himself to the exclusion of all else in whatever at any given time ministered to his passion for conducting a great moral crusade; while Disraeli devoted the best of his now limited energies to the task of presenting himself as an overdressed and vulgar reincarnation of Palmerston at his least likeable. The conventional contrast between the legislative sterility of the twenty years before 1867 and the great burst of reforms that followed it owes more than is realized to the Victorian taste for melodrama. In most respects, the legislative activity of the period from 1868 to 1885 was the culmination of the process of gradual reform that had gone on since 1846. Gladstone and Disraeli produced little that was new.

Source 8: Two extracts from Eugenio F. Biagini, *Gladstone*, published in 2000.

Extract 1

There were lofty expectations as to what the first Parliament elected by borough household franchise would do. Different sections of the Parliamentary party and Liberal movement in the country wanted different things, though all agreed on the basic underlying philosophy. In home affairs, the issues which demanded legislative intervention included the abolition of university tests, reform of the civil service, trade union law, primary education, the ballot and Ireland, which was a bundle of unsolved problems. Of these areas only the last one commanded Gladstone's unqualified support, while some of the others he regarded with caution, if not open aversion.

Extract 2

[Gladstone] presided over the drawing of other important Bills, and loyally supported his ministers in Parliament and in the country. In contrast to the view that he focused his mind and attention on only one issue at a time, he was in fact able to divide his energy among most of the many Bills, projects and proposals which the government and leading backbenchers produced between 1868 and 1874.

Questions

1. To what extent are the views expressed on Disraeli in Source 6 borne out in Disraeli's speech in Source 5? (15)
2. 'The reforms of Gladstone's first ministry and Disraeli's second were extremely limited and entirely unoriginal.' Comment on this view, using Sources 5 to 8 and your own knowledge about historians' views. (30)

Total (45)

4

CONSTITUTIONAL REFORM

BACKGROUND

There have been three key constitutional issues in the modern United Kingdom. These are the representative nature of the House of Commons (through the extent of the franchise and the size of the constituencies); the legislative power of the House of Commons in relation to the House of Lords as a blocking mechanism; and the right of parts of the United Kingdom to a measured form of autonomy or devolved power. The following broad outline is intended as an overall perspective to the periods before, during and after the careers of Gladstone and Disraeli.

The House of Commons: the franchise and seat redistribution

Pressures to make the House of Commons more representative went back well into the eighteenth century. But it was the Whigs, under Earl Grey, who prepared specific measures and forced them through, first the House of Commons and then the House of Lords, in a bitter campaign. As a result of the 1832 Reform Act the county franchise in England included 40-shilling freeholders, £10 copyholders and £50 leaseholders, while the borough franchise was extended to £10 householders. In all, the electorate increased from 478,000 to 813,000. Parliamentary seats were also redistributed, although the total number of 658 remained unaffected. Fifty-six boroughs, each with fewer than 2,000 voters, lost 2 members, while 31 boroughs with between 2,000 and 4,000 each lost one member. This made a total of 141 available seats. Of these, 65 went to previously unenfranchised boroughs, 65 to the counties, 6 to Scotland and 5 to Ireland. Although seen as a 'final settlement' at the time, the 1832 Reform Act was soon being criticised for its inadequacies. The Chartists pursued a radical objective which would have included universal suffrage, equal constituencies and annual elections; their petitions were, however, rejected by Parliament in 1839, 1842 and 1848. Much more modest proposals for reform were unsuccessfully put forward by the Conservatives in 1858 and by the Whigs and Liberals in 1851, 1852, 1854 and 1860.

The climax came in 1866 and 1867, in which both Gladstone and Disraeli were involved (although in charge of their parties in the Commons, they were still subordinate to the overall leadership of Russell and Derby in the Lords). In 1866 Russell's Liberal government introduced a bill to enfranchise £7 householders in the boroughs and £14 tenants in the counties. The Conservatives, under Disraeli and Derby, formed an alliance with the right-wing Liberals (nicknamed the 'Adullamites') to wreck the bill. Following Russell's resignation, Derby established a minority Conservative government. Disraeli then proceeded to introduce a minimalist measure to avoid provoking a split with the right-wing Conservatives. When the Liberals threatened to reject this, in the process rediscovering their unity, Disraeli changed the terms to produce a bill which was even more radical than the original Liberal measure. After a number of Liberal amendments, this was eventually enacted in August 1867.

The Second Reform Act made all householders and £10 lodgers eligible to vote and extended the county franchise to £12 ratepayers, £5 copyholders and £5 leaseholders. Forty-five seats were removed from boroughs with a population of under 10,000: of these, 15 were given to boroughs which did not yet have an MP, 25 went to the counties, one each to Manchester, Liverpool, Leeds and Birmingham, and one to the University of London.

Predictably, there was soon to be pressure for further reform. Gladstone's initial priority, however, was to minimise disruption to the existing franchise through intimidation and corruption. The 1872 Ballot Act substituted secret voting through the ballot box for open voting at the hustings. The Corrupt and Illegal Practices Act (1883) defined a range of campaign offences for which the penalties were fines or imprisonment. Then, in 1884 Gladstone's government introduced another measure to extend the franchise. This passed through the Commons but was blocked in the Lords by the Conservatives. Their leader, Lord Salisbury, came to an agreement with Gladstone that there should be an accompanying measure to redefine constituencies. There were therefore two separate pieces of legislation. The Franchise Act (1884) gave the vote to all householders in the counties, which now achieved uniformity with the boroughs and doubled the electorate from 2.5 million to just under 5 million. The Redistribution Act (1885) removed both members from boroughs with a population of under 15,000 and one from those with fewer than 50,000. A major change was that all but 23 constituencies (647 out of 670) were now single-member.

Three further changes occurred during the twentieth century. Following pressure from women's suffrage movements and the democratising experience of war, Lloyd George introduced the Representation of the People Act (1918). This enfranchised all men over 21 and those women over 30 who were householders, were married to householders or were university graduates. This remaining qualification barrier was removed by Baldwin, whose Equal Franchise Act (1928) extended the vote to all women between 21 and 30 and also eliminated any remaining property qualifications. The voting age, both for men and women, was lowered by Wilson in 1969 to its current level of 18. Over the later period the size of constituencies was decided by regular boundary commissions rather than in redistribution acts.

The House of Lords: the veto and delaying powers

Throughout the nineteenth century the Lords took an active part in legislation and a number of Prime Ministers (for example, Grey, Russell, Derby, Palmerston, Salisbury and Rosebery) were based in the upper House. Being unelected, it had a permanent Tory/Conservative majority. This usually meant that Conservative governments faced fewer obstacles than Whig/Liberal ones to their legislative proposals. There were periodic high-profile clashes between the Commons and Lords over, for example, the Reform Bill of 1832, the Irish Church Act (1869), the Franchise Bill (1884) and the Second Home Rule Bill (1893). Gladstone was a major victim of the Lords' power of veto, although he was unable to do much about it. In two conflicts (in 1832 and 1911) a Whig and a Liberal government secured the agreement of the King to create sufficient new peers to pass their bills, at the threat of which an entrenched Tory and a Conservative majority backed down.

It was not until 1911 that the powers of the House of Lords were reduced. Following the budget crisis of 1909, and two general elections in 1910, Asquith's Liberal government passed the 1911 Parliament Act which reduced the Lords' veto to a delaying power over three successive sessions. This was further reduced to one year by Attlee in the Parliament Act of 1949.

Devolved power to the regions

The United Kingdom comprised four main parts. England and Wales had been effectively united since the reign of Edward I (1272–1307). The thrones of England and Scotland had been linked from the accession of James I in 1603 and Scotland had been fully integrated with England by the Act of Union (1707), while Ireland was brought in by the 1800 Act of Union. The last of these connections proved the most problematic and the main priority of Gladstone's later career was to find a solution. His proposal for Home Rule (or devolution) was, however, defeated in the House of Commons in 1886 and vetoed by the House of Lords in 1893. The measure was revived by Asquith in 1912 as the Third Home Rule Bill but was suspended because of the outbreak of war in 1914. Following extensive disruption and the threat of full-scale civil war, Ireland was given independence as the Irish Free State in 1921; the North (comprising six counties of the province of Ulster) remained part of the United Kingdom, although with its own parliament at Stormont. The period of disturbances in the North from 1969 saw the suspension of this autonomy until the revival of the Northern Ireland Assembly over thirty years later. In the meantime, Scotland and Wales achieved devolution in 1998, with their own assemblies in Edinburgh and Cardiff. Because of its disproportionate size and influence, England has not so far been accorded devolved powers, although schemes have been suggested for 'regional councils'.

Since its accession in 1973 to the European Community (now the European Union) the United Kingdom has also become accustomed – if reluctantly – to supra-national as well as intra-national institutions.

These two levels now exist alongside the more traditional national sovereignty of the United Kingdom itself.

ANALYSIS 1: COMPARE THE ATTITUDES AND POLICIES OF GLADSTONE AND DISRAELI ON THE REFORM OF PARLIAMENT.

Politicians often move towards the right as they age. This is one stereotype which neither Gladstone nor Disraeli fits. On the other hand, nor was there any great conversion to sweeping reform and democracy. They did, however, make important contributions to the whole process of parliamentary reform between the 1850s and early 1880s, in ways which were similar and yet different – and sometimes surprising.

Although neither had yet become an MP, both had strong views on the 1832 Reform Act, the starting point of nineteenth-century parliamentary reform. Disraeli welcomed it as something which would facilitate his career in politics, while Gladstone roundly condemned it in a debate in the Oxford Union. Both subsequently favoured a further extension of the franchise, although from different parties and standpoints. Disraeli introduced an unsuccessful bill in 1859, while Gladstone's attempts came in 1854 and 1860. During this period of their lives Disraeli favoured a relatively limited increase in enfranchisement, while Gladstone preferred a broader approach, believing that 'every man who is not presumably incapacitated by some consideration of personal unfitness or of political danger is morally entitled to come within the pale of the Constitution'.[1] Indeed, 'I do not admit that the working man, regarded as an individual, is less worthy of the suffrage than any other class.'[2]

Yet, in the hectic competition to take control of the reform issue between 1866 and 1867, it was Russell and Gladstone who adopted the limited measure (which would have enfranchised £7 householders in the boroughs and £14 tenants in the counties) and Derby and Disraeli who went somewhat beyond that by giving the vote to all householders and £10 lodgers in the boroughs, along with £12 ratepayers and £5 copyholders in the counties. Although this was almost certainly influenced by pragmatic considerations of Conservative needs (see Analysis 2) it is certainly true that Disraeli extended the vote well down below the top layer of the working class originally targeted by Gladstone. This was because he knew that the well-to-do worker, probably unionised, would be more likely to vote Liberal; on the other hand, there could well be a blue layer below the gold. It was this gamble which induced Disraeli to 'dish the Whigs', 'shoot Niagara' and take 'a leap in the dark' all in the same mixed metaphor. Gladstone was more restrained when his turn came to expand the electorate. He resisted his earlier hints at universal suffrage, settling instead for enfranchising all householders in the counties, thereby expanding the electorate from 3.7 million to 5.7 million. This, however, still excluded one in three adult males from the vote, leaving a huge gap in the male vote which was not filled until Lloyd George's Representation of the People Act in 1918.

Omitted from the Reform Acts of both 1867 and 1884 was the enfranchisement of women. Disraeli was not fundamentally opposed to this. He had argued that 'in a country governed by a woman' and which allowed women to be peeresses in their own right, 'I do not see on what reasons she has not the right to vote.'[3] He was less forthcoming, however, when an amendment was proposed to his 1867 Reform Bill to change 'man' to 'person'. For the sake of the unity of the party, rather than from any strong conviction, Disraeli joined the majority in rejecting the amendment. The 1884 Act might have extended the franchise to women. This time, however, it was Gladstone who refused to make the necessary changes, arguing that it would alter the whole nature of the bill and make it liable to rejection by the House of Lords. In any case, his line had always been to 'take no step in advance until I am convinced of its safety'.[4] The difference between the two men, therefore, was that Disraeli expressed progressive views but found reasons for not acting on them, while Gladstone found reasons for avoiding the issue altogether.

Accompanying the extension of the franchise was a parallel scheme for seat redistribution. These were part of the same measure in 1867 but separated out in 1884 and 1885. Both were instigated by the Conservatives to minimise the damage which might be done to them through a broader franchise. Hence Disraeli was reducing his own risk in 1867, while Salisbury was able to pin Gladstone down in 1884. The redistribution component of the 1867 Act affected 45 seats, while the separate measure of 1885 dealt with some 142. The latter measure also ended almost all of the two-member constituencies, ending the practice of fielding both a Whig and a Liberal in the same constituency. As a result, the Whigs, who had been 'dished' in 1867, became virtually extinct by the turn of the century. Gladstone was never able to do the equivalent to the aristocratic section of the Conservatives.

In addition to franchise measures and seat redistribution, parliamentary reform also encompassed measures against intimidation and corruption. These mattered rather more to Gladstone than to Disraeli, partly because of his instinctive loathing for any form of corruption or waste, partly because the Liberals were less adept at manipulation. Or perhaps it was that Disraeli was more interested in the positive approach to presentation than in the negative concept of corruption. It was, therefore, Gladstone who secured the Ballot Act (1872) and the Corrupt and Illegal Practices Act of 1883.

Within the House of Commons itself, there was a more even-handed contribution to removing anomalies and ending exclusions. Gladstone and Disraeli both voted in favour of admitting Jews to the Commons in 1847, although for different reasons. Disraeli saw it as a religious issue: he considered that Christianity was Judaism 'fully completed' (which justified his own conversion). Hence, as he said in the debate in 1847, it was 'as a Christian' that he could not support the exclusion of 'those who are of the religion in the bosom of which my Lord and Saviour was born'.[5] Gladstone made it an issue of religious toleration, although a greater test for him was his support for the right of the newly elected MP Charles Bradlaugh not to take a religious oath of allegiance in 1885 – since he was an atheist.

Gladstone was always conscious of a great weight which bore down on any reforming Liberal government from on high – the House of Lords. Disraeli had no such impediment, which meant that the upper House was much more compliant to his reform of 1867 than to Grey's in 1832 or Gladstone's in 1884. As the Earl of Beaconsfield, Disraeli eventually immured himself within it. Gladstone, by contrast, continued to fight it, especially over Home Rule, and included its reform in the Liberal party's Newcastle Programme. By this stage, however, the Liberal impetus was slowing down in the House of Commons, paralleled by the approaching end of Gladstone's own political life.

Questions

1. Who did more for the reform of Parliament: Disraeli or Gladstone?
2. 'In the reform of Parliament, Gladstone completed what Disraeli had started.' Do you agree with this view?

ANALYSIS 2: EXAMINE THE VIEWS OF HISTORIANS ON GLADSTONE, DISRAELI AND THE REFORM ACTS OF 1867 AND 1884.

Both Disraeli and Gladstone played a key part in the evolution of the franchise during the second half of the nineteenth century, along with changes to the distribution of parliamentary seats. In each case, however, there is a range of views about their motives and the effectiveness of their reforms – introduced respectively in 1867 and 1884.

Views on Disraeli and the 1867 Reform Act

The debate on Disraeli hinges on the apparent anomaly that a Conservative orchestrated successful opposition to a Liberal franchise measure in 1866, before going on, in 1867, to introduce one which was even more radical. This is explicable in terms of genuine commitment or opportunist manipulation, depending on the political or historical perspective used.

One is a Conservative myth which was popularised by Monypenny and Buckle,[1] the original biographers of Disraeli. This claimed that Disraeli aimed from the outset to create a much larger electorate in the belief that it was likely to be fundamentally Conservative. Indeed, he was really preparing his party and the country for his own vision of democracy. This view retained a few influential advocates, including Himmelfarb,[2] who argued that Disraeli was firmly wedded to the concept of Tory Democracy and that the Conservative party was far more attuned to the needs and aspirations of the working class than were the Liberals. On the other hand, such an approach has been extensively criticised, not least by the modern biographer, Blake: Disraeli 'was never a Tory democrat' and, in any case, he did his best to neutralise the effect of household suffrage 'by redrawing the county and borough boundaries'.[3] Whatever Disraeli's motives were, he cannot be seen as 'a far-sighted statesman, a Tory democrat or the educator of his party'.[4]

At the other end of the scale is the Liberal myth that the working man owed the vote less to Disraeli than to the constant pressure exerted by Gladstone throughout 1867 after the Conservatives had defeated Russell's measure in 1866. The new electorate subsequently acknowledged the real source of their extended franchise by voting the Liberals into power in the 1868 general election. This interpretation now has very few adherents since it does not really hold water; although in favour of a measure of reform, Gladstone had never wanted household suffrage and had consistently voted against the 1867 bill for that reason. Although he did show progressive ideas at various stages in his career, the parliamentary events in 1867 made him look more like an obstacle to action than an agent for it.

If Disraeli did not submit to Liberal pressure, perhaps he was affected by the threat of action from below and feared that this might get out of hand. In July disturbances occurred in Hyde Park, during the course of which a 1,400-yard stretch of railings was pulled down and destroyed. This was less violent than the events in Bristol and Nottingham in 1831. But, as with the First Reform Act, the *threat* of violence has been seen as a significant factor in forcing the pace; history, in other words, was repeating itself. This was certainly the line taken by the original biographer of Gladstone, John Morley. He argued that the House of Commons which passed the 1867 Act had actually been elected 'to support Palmerston' and that the reason for its reversal 'would seem to be that the tide of public opinion had suddenly swelled to flood'; particularly important were the Hyde Park riots and huge demonstrations and open air meetings held in Glasgow, London, Birmingham and elsewhere.[5] Trevelyan agreed with this line, referring to the solidarity between the middle and working classes which characterised 'the agitation in the country over which Bright presided in the autumn of 1866'.[6] More recently, Harrison claimed that historians have underestimated the fears of revolution among contemporaries. The Hyde Park demonstration appeared menacing and politicians were ready to concede limited measures at this stage to avoid having to grant universal suffrage in the future. The Conservatives were, therefore, pushed by the disturbances into picking up reform again.[7]

This type of argument has certain merits. It restores to the people an element of control over events: the intervention of the crowd is a theme much used by historians, like Trevelyan, with a particular interest in social history or, as in the case of Harrison, in the development of the working class. Morley arrived at his view under a different influence. Late, in 1884, he felt that Gladstone was not sufficiently responsive to public opinion and may well have allowed his political inclinations then to influence his historical perspective of the masses in 1867.

There are, however, anomalies in the view that pressures were operating from below. For one thing, there was a time-lapse of six months between the disturbances and the introduction of the Conservative reform bill. Since such bills could be – and were – drawn up at very short notice, this scarcely indicates a knee-jerk reaction by the government. The alternative argument is therefore that public opinion was not as significant a factor as in 1832. As Cowling stated: 'The passage of the Reform Act in 1867 was effected in a context of public agitation: it cannot be explained as a simple consequence.' He also maintained that 'There was no "capitulation" to popular pressure.'[8] 'The final verdict', said Feuchtwanger, 'must be that the public reform movement did not do much more than act the part of the chorus in this play.'[9]

More likely than any of the views so far provided is the emphasis on pragmatic considerations. In the words of Walton: 'The nature of the Act was determined by the exigencies of party strife in a complex and fragmented political system.'[10] This was also the position of Blake, who maintained that Disraeli and Derby 'had the wide franchise of 1867 forced on them as the price of staying in power'. Disraeli realised that he had to adapt to new circumstances – and he was better at doing this than most. 'It was like a moonlight steeple-chase. In negotiating their fences few of them saw where they were going, nor much cared so long as they got there first.'[11] Cowling went further, stressing the importance of cynical party politics. Disraeli moved towards household suffrage not through principle or through careful calculation about his party's future, but rather because of the pressure of events. He added: 'Disraeli's was a policy of consistent opportunism.'[12] The actual methods involved were aptly summarised by Feuchtwanger: 'In the session of 1867 Disraeli practised the tactics he had so often since he became leader of his Party, the attempt to link up with any available group to secure a majority.'[13] An even more calculating Disraeli was presented by Machin. Disraeli used the Reform Bill as a means to 'divide and weaken Liberal forces'. By 1866, 'The prospect was opening for Disraeli of resuming his tactics of dividing one Liberal section from another and using the Liberal opposition to Reform to defeat a Liberal bill on the subject.'[14]

Pragmatic actions usually involve some form of a risk. The year 1867 was an exception, since Disraeli took measures to control the effects of franchise changes. 'There was no point in Disraeli's gaining a great parliamentary triumph and new prestige among his fellow-Conservatives if the result was simply to give the Liberals a larger majority.'[15] This explains why the Redistribution Bill was also passed in 1867, which transferred only 52 seats (half to the counties and only 9 to the cities). 'This was the smallest transfer of seats in any of the three Reform measures in the nineteenth century.'[16] 'Further evidence that party interest rather than principle was behind the Reform can be found in the establishment of a government Boundary Commission filled with Conservative landowners.' The intention was to transfer 'suburb-dwelling county voters' to the boroughs. This would ensure that the counties would remain Conservative, while adding at least a proportion of Conservatives to the normally Liberal boroughs.

A synthesis might be developed to include at least some of these arguments. Having turned Russell and Gladstone out of power in 1866, the Conservatives had no option but to introduce their own measure of parliamentary reform. Disraeli deduced from the experience of 1832 that the party which took the initiative could frame the details of the franchise extension, whereas the party opposing reform could expect only a period in political exile. But he could hardly expect the Liberals to support a new measure close to Russell's bill in 1866. A Conservative bill would have to be substantially different, going either above or below the Liberal baseline of 1866. Since the Conservatives were in a minority, Disraeli had to keep his own party together and, in addition, get some support from the Liberals. The former could be accomplished by a mild measure, pitched somewhere above the Liberal baseline. But when Disraeli tried this in order to appease Cranborne and the Conservative right, he quickly realised that there would be no chance of any Liberal support. Such backing would only come if the proposals were sufficiently progressive. Disraeli therefore opted for a bold stroke to take the enemy completely by surprise. In 1867, as at other times in his career, he delivered a tactical *coup*. Yet he could not afford to be entirely cynical. Public opinion could not be ignored, especially if it threatened to turn nasty. It would be far better to make a positive statement to the working class by enfranchising the layer below the £7 householders target of Russell's bill. The well-to-do section of the working class had already established contacts with the Liberals through reform associations. But by enfranchising *all* householders and, in addition, £10 lodgers, Disraeli might be opening up a new layer of Conservative support for the future. Finally, if he did not do this, the Liberals would almost certainly introduce a more radical measure once they returned to power in the future.

This approach places the main emphasis on Disraeli's political calculation – while also allowing for Liberal pressures, progressive Conservative influences and at least a glance at the state of public opinion. Historical interpretation generally does involve a combination of ingredients: the question is what proportions these should take.

Views on Gladstone and the 1884 Reform Act

Gladstone introduced a bill to extend the franchise in 1884; this passed through the Commons, which had a Liberal majority. It was, however, rejected by the House of Lords, which demanded the inclusion of a redistribution bill to counterbalance the increase in the electorate. At this point the controversy became increasingly public, with mass demonstrations in Hyde Park. Gladstone made an agreement with Salisbury to secure the passage of the Reform Act in December 1884 and of a Redistribution Act the following June.

The debate on Gladstone and the 1884 Reform Act has fewer major contrasts than that on Disraeli and the 1867 Act. The developments were apparently less complex, with fewer opportunities for detailed controversy. Even so, Gladstone's role in all this has been variously interpreted.

Perhaps the most obvious line was that Gladstone was the driving force behind this further extension of the franchise. Gash, for example, argued that Gladstone was projecting himself increasingly as a populist politician and wanted to 'round off his term of office on a creditable reforming note'[17] and partly to compensate for the government's unpopularity over Egypt. In support of this it might also be argued that

Gladstone was moving towards a broader view of parliamentary reform which would soon come to include Home Rule for Ireland. Gladstone was therefore in the most reforming phase of his career and brought to the cause a passion which was unmistakable in Parliament.

This can be seen also in the results of the reform settlement, since it forms a continuity with earlier measures. Biagini was in no doubt as to the importance of the Acts of 1883, 1884 and 1885: 'Together, these three electoral reforms brought about the greatest restructuring of the British representative system in the nineteenth century.'[18] The main impetus behind this was always Gladstone, 'who devoted much care and attention to the details of electoral reform, and ensured its difficult passage through Parliament'. In response to Conservative opposition and stalling in the House of Lords, Gladstone 'conducted a vigorous campaign of public speeches around the country'.[19] He also made 'a huge diplomatic effort to persuade the recalcitrant Whigs', conducting 'vast correspondence' with, for example, Hartington and Spencer. This view of an energetic Gladstone seeking to take his party with him over franchise reform would certainly be in line with the Gladstone about to launch a much more radical policy on Ireland. It might even be that he saw parliamentary reform as a dress rehearsal for devolution.

There is, however, an alternative perspective. The reforms of 1884 and 1885 were, in fact, a shared achievement – a compromise between Gladstone and Salisbury. This was because Gladstone could not get his own way and was forced to come to terms with a resolute opponent; the alternative would have been stalemate. Jenkins maintained that Salisbury did rather well out of the process. Indeed, in an interesting twist, it seems that it was Salisbury who wanted the change – not the proposed increase in the franchise but the seat redistribution which he insisted must accompany it. Salisbury felt no commitment to the electoral system produced by Disraeli which (apart from 1874) 'had produced decades of Liberal majorities'. He therefore pressed for the redistribution of seats and, in particular, the creation of single-member constituencies, 'both of which worked against the Liberals' own interests'. Salisbury was also thinking of future advantages and was 'well aware of the possibilities offered by the growth of what he called "Villa Toryism" in the suburban areas'.[20] Gladstone fell for the apparent concession offered on franchise reform, without realising the potential danger of seat redistribution. He therefore arranged an agreement with Salisbury and the Lords, despite the misgivings of both the Whigs and the Radicals within his party. Jenkins therefore provides a fascinating picture of a leader pursuing one objective (franchise reform) despite extensive misgivings within his party that he might actually be playing into the hands of the Conservatives.

This is a less impressive Gladstone, certainly – but one which can also be squared with the Gladstone preparing for a greater confrontation and a more obvious risk over Home Rule.

There is another way in which Gladstone is perceived to have handed the initiative to Salisbury. Despite being a man of the people – 'the people's William' – he was careful not to use public opinion as pressure behind his argument for franchise reform. In this he was out of line with the Radicals in his party who, according to Abbott, were intending to promote a campaign to 'stir up the passions of the country'.[21] Some historians have taken this argument further. Their target was the Conservative-controlled House of Lords, which was preventing the passage of franchise reform without an accompanying redistribution bill. Morley, a member of Gladstone's government as well as his future biographer, was certainly in sympathy with the Radicals over this, as were many others of more centrist Liberal views. Instead of targeting this pressure on to the Conservatives, as they wanted, Gladstone hastened to make terms with Salisbury to ensure the bills for franchise reform and redistribution both went through before public pressure could increase. Gladstone, in other words, sided with Salisbury and the status quo against his Radicals and the people. This approach might be seen as a little harsh. After all, Gladstone had always opposed demagoguery and it could be argued that the Radicals were playing a dangerous game, especially if we accept the view of Hayes that popular pressures were already intense. 'At bottom the course of events in mid-November reflected the importance of the battle out-of-doors, and more broadly, demonstrated the critical role played by popular opinion in the making of the Third Reform Act.'[22] Perhaps the critics of Gladstone have gone too far in the direction of arguing that he should have done more manipulation of his own to prevent himself from being manipulated.

Still, one can question the extent to which the measures of 1884 and 1885 were a victory for progressive change. They do not necessarily show that Gladstone capitulated to Salisbury. But nor do they show a decisive victory on Gladstone's part. Just as the seventeen years following Disraeli's Reform Act were to be dominated by the Liberals, so the twenty-two after 1884 were predominantly a period of Conservative government. This may well have been due to the split in the Liberal party over Home Rule. But the worrying feature for Gladstone was that, despite an electorate which had been enlarged in 1884, the Liberals lost 5 per cent of their support from the working class between 1884 and 1892. This seems to suggest that the Conservative party under Salisbury was better prepared at this stage than the Liberals under Gladstone to provide a mass appeal, an issue which is dealt with in the next chapter.

Questions

1. Does the outcome of the 1867 and 1884–5 constitutional changes suggest that Disraeli and Gladstone both miscalculated?
2. 'Historians tend to see opportunism as a strength in Disraeli but as a weakness in Gladstone.' Is this true of the historiographical debate on the reform of Parliament in 1867 and 1884–5?
3. What relative importance have historians given to the franchise and to seat redistribution in 1867 and 1884–5?

SOURCES

1. GLADSTONE AND PARLIAMENTARY REFORM

(Time allowed: 60 minutes)

Source 1: A cartoon from *Punch*, 5 August 1871.

See Figure 4.

Source 2: From a speech made by Gladstone in the House of Commons, February 1884.

Is there any doubt that the peasantry of the country are capable citizens, qualified for enfranchisement, qualified to make good use of their power as voters? This is a question which has been solved for us by the First and Second Reform Bills; because many of the places which under the name of towns are now represented in this House are really rural communities, based upon a peasant constituency. For my part, I should be quite ready to fight the battle of the peasant upon general and argumentative grounds. I believe the peasant generally to be, not in the highest sense, but in a very real sense, a skilled labourer. He is not a man tied down to one mechanical exercise of his physical powers. He is a man who must do many things, and many things which require in him the exercise of active intelligence.

Source 3: From a speech by Joseph Chamberlain in January 1885.

Next year two millions of men will enter for the first time into the full enjoyment of their political rights. These men are for the most part your fellow-workers in factory and in field, and for the first time the toilers and spinners will have a majority of votes, and the control, if they desire it, of the Government of the country. To-day parliament is elected by three millions of electors, of whom, perhaps, one third are of the working classes. Next year a new House will come to Westminster elected

BRITISH VOTER OF THE FUTURE

'Now, what more <u>can</u> we do to protect him?'

Figure 4.

by five millions of men, of whom three fifths belong to the labouring population. It is a revolution which has been peacefully and silently accomplished. The centre of power has been shifted, and the old order is giving place to the new.

Source 4: From Justin McCarthy, *A History of Our Own Times from 1880 to the Diamond Jubilee*, published in 1897.

The government, although evidently weakened and sinking, did not go out of office without having done some good and substantial work for the constitution and for the country.... There were two distinct problems to be dealt with: first, the question of franchise, and next, the question of redistribution of seats.... With regard to the distribution of seats, the most flagrant anomalies and injustice were still existing. In some cases pitiful little boroughs with only a few hundred inhabitants returned as many representatives as some great and important counties.... Mr. Gladstone ... divided his great reform scheme into two separate portions; that is to say, into two separate bills.

Questions

1. Using Sources 2 and 3, explain the terms 'peasantry' (Source 2) and 'fellow-workers in factory and in field' (Source 3). (20)
2. Compare Sources 2 and 3. To what extent did Chamberlain agree with Gladstone about the priorities of parliamentary reform? (40)
3. Using Sources 1 to 4, and your own knowledge, consider the view that, by the end of his second ministry, Gladstone had addressed all the remaining issues of parliamentary reform. (60)

Total (120)

2. INTERPRETATIONS OF DISRAELI AND THE 1867 REFORM ACT

(Time allowed: 45 minutes)

Source 5: From a speech made by Disraeli in the House of Commons in March 1867.

Our Bill is not framed, as was the one of last session, to enfranchise a specific number of persons. We do not attempt that. We lay down a principle and let that principle work; but if you ask us what will be the result of its working, we say – although we do not wish to found our policy upon it – that we do not apprehend the number that will be admitted to the enjoyment of the franchise will exceed the number contemplated by the Bill of last session . . . the proposition that we make is founded upon a principle that is not liable to alteration.

I hear much of the struggle of parties in this House, and I hear much of combinations that may occur, and courses that may be taken, which may affect the fate of this Bill. All I can say on the part of my colleagues and myself is that we have no other wish at the present moment than, with the co-operation of this House, to bring the question of parliamentary Reform to a settlement. . . .

Generally speaking, I would say that, looking to what has occurred since the Reform Act of 1832 was passed – to the increase of population, the progress of industry, the spread of knowledge, and our ingenuity in the arts – we are of opinion that numbers, thoughts and feelings have since that time been created which it is desirable should be admitted within the circle of the Constitution.

Source 6: From a speech made by Disraeli in Edinburgh after the passage of the Reform Act in 1867.

I had to prepare the mind of the country, and to educate – if it be not arrogant to use such a phrase – to educate our Party. It is a large Party, and requires its attention to be called to questions of this kind with some pressure. I had to prepare the mind of Parliament and the country on this question of Reform. This was not only with the concurrence of Lord Derby, but of my colleagues.

When you try to settle any great question, there are two considerations which statesmen ought not to forget. First of all, let your plan be founded upon some principle. But that is not enough. Let it also be a principle that is in harmony with the manners and customs you are attempting to legislate for. . . . In a progressive country change is constant; and the great question is not whether you should resist change which is inevitable, but whether that change should be carried out in deference to the manners, the customs, the laws, the traditions of the people, or in deference to abstract principles and arbitrary and general doctrines. The one is a national system; the other, to give it an epithet, a noble epithet which perhaps it may deserve, is a philosophic system. Both have great advantages; the national party is supported by the fervour of patriotism; the philosophical party has a singular exemption from the force of prejudice.

Source 7: From Robert Blake, *Disraeli*, published in 1966.

It is often believed that Disraeli, infinitely more discerning than the dull squires who followed him, had long perceived that household suffrage would enfranchise a class basically more Conservative than the electorate created in 1832; that he aimed throughout at this objective, carrying Derby with him and educating the rest of the Party in the process. . . .

It is probably true that the Reform Bill did in the end enfranchise a class which for a number or reasons tended to vote Conservative rather than Liberal. It is also true that Disraeli, more than any other statesman of his day, had the imagination to adapt himself to this new situation and to discern, dimly and hesitatingly perhaps, what the artisan class wanted from Parliament. . . . But there is nothing – or very little – to suggest that he had any such awareness in 1867. The importance of that period in his life is quite different. In the course of two years from the summer of 1865 he transformed his position in the Conservative Party. It was his sparkling success in the session of 1867 which made him, as he had by no means been before, Derby's inevitable successor. . . .

For what he did in 1867 he deserves to go down in history as a politician of genius, a superb improviser, a parliamentarian of unrivalled skill, but not as a far-sighted statesman or the educator of his party.

Source 8: From P. Smith, *Disraeli: A Brief Life*, published in 1996.

If Disraeli was guided by no concealed purpose to launch his party on 'Tory Democracy', he was certainly operating with a conception of Toryism which made it easy and in a sense obligatory to trust the political reliability of the people to any extent necessary to pass a Conservative reform bill.

What impact the electorate he was calling into being would have on Conservative fortunes, Disraeli could know no better than anyone else. Reassuring Derby on 28 February, he wrote: 'What are called the "working classes" in the small boroughs are those who are under the patronage of the Upper Classes and depend on them for employment and existence. In great towns the "working classes" are powerful trades formed into Unions and the employers are dependent on them.' The comment tends to substantiate the view . . . that, when Disraeli weighed the electoral implications of various reform proposals, he thought in terms of the politics he had known all his life, in which Toryism was based on the management by traditional methods of the counties and small towns, and had largely resigned itself to the predominance of the Liberals in the great centres of industry and commerce.

Source 9: From Paul Adelman, *Gladstone, Disraeli and Later Victorian Politics*, published in 1970.

The motives that now governed the Conservative leaders, and the tactics that were pursued by Disraeli especially, in the twelve months down to the passing of the final Act, have been analysed in almost microscopic detail by a group of recent historians. . . . As a result, a whole mythology has been virtually destroyed. It is now clear that Disraeli's attitude during the Reform crisis was purely opportunist. He neither sought to 'educate his party', nor displayed either firmness or consistency of purpose in his support for 'democracy'. Indeed, during these months Disraeli had only one major aim: to destroy Gladstone's leadership over a united Liberal Party, and, by seizing the initiative in reform himself and promoting a Reform Bill, to consolidate his own leadership of the Conservative Party. . . .

To many contemporaries, both of Left and Right, the Second Reform Act seemed to be an essentially democratic measure which gave effective political power to the working class. Superficially this appeared to be true. Nearly a million new voters were added to the electoral list, and the increase was widest in the great cities where working-class voters now became a majority. But the position in the counties was very different, and does much to justify Mr Cowling's remark that Disraeli 'was prepared to let Radicals have their way in the boroughs, so long as he had his to some extent in the counties'.

Questions

1. Compare Sources 5 and 6 as Disraeli's explanations for the introduction of the 1867 Reform Bill. How would you explain any differences? (15)
2. 'Disraeli's motives for introducing parliamentary reform in 1867 were muddled.' Do sources 5 to 9, and your own knowledge, support this view? (30)

Total (45)

5

FOREIGN POLICY

BACKGROUND

The scope of 'foreign' policy differs from that of 'imperial' policy, although there are clearly occasions where they overlap. They are therefore covered separately, with additional consideration of any relevant interconnection. 'Foreign' policy would have been the responsibility of the Foreign Office. It would have been concerned with relations with other governments over issues involving British interests – but not necessarily over British possessions (the initial responsibility for which would have been the Colonial Office with a particular focus on 'imperial' policy).

Both Gladstone and Disraeli played a very active role in foreign policy, completely overshadowing their respective Foreign Secretaries. This was partly because they both had strong views about Britain's priorities and partly because the rise of Germany and the revival of Russia greatly affected Britain's role in Europe (see Analysis 1). It was no longer possible for Britain to exercise the kind of influence as had been the case under Palmerston (Prime Minister 1855–8 and 1859–65).

During his first ministry (1868–74) Gladstone had to adjust to the reality of pressures from both Germany and Russia. Indeed, the unification of Germany was completed during this period, with the defeat of France by Prussia (1870–1). This involved Gladstone in three ways. First, he tried diplomatically to remove any pretext for war between France and Prussia by trying to neutralise the issue of the Spanish candidature (which involved France's objection to the claim of Prince Leopold of Hohenzollern-Sigmaringen to the Spanish throne). Gladstone failed, however, to prevent Bismarck from provoking Emperor Napoleon III into declaring war on Prussia in 1870. Second, he did succeed in preventing British involvement while, at the same time, securing a guarantee from both sides that Belgian neutrality would not be violated. He was, however, less successful in his attempt to persuade Bismarck not to inflict a punitive settlement on France by annexing Alsace-Lorraine to the newly victorious German Reich. He experienced similar difficulties with Russia. He had hoped to submit to international arbitration Russia's repudiation of the Black Sea clauses of the 1856 Treaty of Paris. Instead, at the London Conference (1871) he had to accept the action as a *fait accompli*, adding a face-saving device that nations should not in future take unilateral action on what had been agreed multilaterally. Gladstone also had to eat 'humble-pie' over an issue concerning the United States. He accepted international arbitration, reached in Geneva, that Britain should pay £3.25 million in compensation to the United States for damage caused during the Civil War by a warship, the *Alabama*, which had been built in Britain and mistakenly allowed by Palmerston's government to join the Confederate side. By 1874, foreign policy had become an embarrassment to Gladstone and, although it is unlikely to have been the main cause of Liberal defeat in the general election, it could well have increased the size of Disraeli's majority.

The main focus of Disraeli's foreign policy between 1874 and 1880 was the Eastern Question. Previously there had been a broad consensus between political parties about the need to maintain the territorial integrity of Turkey as a barrier to the expansion of Russian power and influence into the Balkans: the Crimean War had been fought partly on this issue. Such agreement, however, dissolved into direct confrontation between Disraeli and Gladstone concerning Turkey's repressive rule over the Christian provinces of Serbia, Montenegro and, above all, Bulgaria, which experienced a series of massacres at the hands of Turkish irregular troops. Disraeli tried to contain anti-Turkish feeling in Britain, while Gladstone detailed the atrocities committed and called for immediate Turkish withdrawal from the 'province they have desolated and profaned'. Disraeli's concern was that Russia would take advantage of the unstable situation in the Balkans to establish direct influence over any new Balkan states and to annex Turkish territory. When Russia went to war with Turkey in 1877, it seemed that these fears would be realised, especially when, in 1878, Russia forced Turkey to sign the Treaty of San Stefano. In addition to recognising Serbia, Montenegro and Romania as independent states, this established a substantial and independent Bulgaria. Fearing that 'Big Bulgaria' would soon become a Russian puppet, Disraeli accepted the offer of the German Chancellor, Bismarck, to act as 'honest broker'. At the Congress of Berlin (1878) Disraeli played a major role in revising San Stefano somewhat less in Russia's favour and, in particular, trisecting 'Big Bulgaria'. This saved Turkish Macedonia and prevented Russian access to a port on the Aegean coast. Gladstone was outraged and attacked Disraeli's record over the Eastern Question as 'immoral' and 'iniquitous'. His Midlothian campaign at the end of 1879 did much to set up a Liberal victory in the 1880 general election and Gladstone's return to power.

During his second and third ministries (1880–5 and 1886) Gladstone was more immediately concerned with imperial issues than with foreign policy as such – although there were often implications for Britain's relations with other powers. For example, the British occupation of Egypt (1882) alienated France for the rest of the century, while fears of Russia were aggravated by developments in Afghanistan and the north-west frontier of India. But there was minimal involvement in Europe – as the focus of diplomatic intrigues was firmly on Bismarck's construction of the Triple Alliance (1882) between Germany, Austria-Hungary and Italy, a follow-up to the Dual Alliance with Austria (1879). There was a dangerous recurrence of the Eastern Question and the threat of another Balkans crisis from 1885 but the climax occurred during Salisbury's second ministry (1886–92). Indeed, it was Salisbury, not Gladstone, who dominated British foreign policy in the second half of the 1880s and the 1890s. He, not Gladstone, shaped Britain's response to the emergence of a counter-alliance system, based on France and Russia, and the policy usually referred to as 'Splendid Isolation'. Whether Salisbury's approach to foreign policy was actually a continuation of Disraeli's is considered in Analysis 2.

ANALYSIS 1: COMPARE THE AIMS OF GLADSTONE AND DISRAELI IN THEIR FOREIGN POLICIES BETWEEN 1868 AND 1885.

For much of the period between 1815 and 1868 British foreign policy had been based on a broadly agreed priority, which was to maintain the balance of power in Europe and uphold the Vienna settlement of 1815. Between 1868 and 1885, however, there was much more debate on fundamental issues and practical diplomacy. The rivalry of Gladstone and Disraeli can be assessed through their basic approach to diplomacy, their conception of 'Europe', their contrasting aims in the 'Eastern Question' and their use of conferences and congresses.

Neither Gladstone nor Disraeli had previously had any connection with the Foreign Office. But once they became Prime Minister, they took over the key decision-making role: their Foreign Secretaries – Granville, Derby, and Salisbury – were pushed into the background. This was partly because Gladstone and Disraeli were both aware that Europe had been made potentially more dangerous from 1870 by the rise of Germany and the revival of conflict between Russia and Turkey, and partly because each had a strongly individual approach. Disraeli preferred to project British power forcefully and decisively, in the Palmerstonian tradition. He said in 1879: 'So long as the power and advice of England are felt in the councils of Europe, peace, I believe, will be maintained, and for a long period.'[1] He preferred this to be in the form of unilateral or bilateral action, whereas Gladstone emphasised the importance of multilateralism in which British action would be within the context of concert diplomacy and international law; an example of his approach was the London Conference, called in 1871 to deal with Russia's repudiation of the Black Sea clauses of the 1856 Treaty of Paris.

Underlying their contrasting approaches to diplomacy were two different perceptions of Europe. Disraeli was the more insular, viewing Europe with suspicion and making his calculations on the assumption that there were no underlying moral principles to observe or values to uphold. Gladstone, by contrast, had a deep attachment to Europe as a cultural ideal. He frequently visited Europe and, as well as being a classicist, spoke German, French and Italian. He considered that Britain had a spiritual and cultural role in Europe, along with an obligation to protect the weak and vulnerable rather than aggressively pursue Britain's own interests. He considered that Disraeli's foreign policy threatened 'all the most fundamental interests of Christian society'.[2]

The differences were sharpest over the Eastern Question between 1875 and 1879. Indeed, the two statesmen pursued policies which were diametrically opposed. Gladstone condemned the Turkish atrocities of 1876 in his pamphlet *The Bulgarian Horrors and the Question of the East* and called for immediate diplomatic pressure to secure the autonomy of the Christians of Bulgaria, Macedonia and Serbia, all of whom were being repressed by a corrupt regime. Disraeli, who at the time held office – and therefore the initiative – was much more concerned about maintaining the territorial integrity of Turkey against an expansionist Russia intent on gaining influence over a series of new Balkan states. This explains his refusal to associate Britain with the Berlin Memorandum (1875) or to condemn the Bulgarian massacres. While Gladstone was actually encouraging Russia to expel the Turks from Bulgaria, Disraeli dispatched a British fleet to Constantinople to warn the Russians not to press the military victory they had achieved by the beginning of 1878. While Gladstone anticipated the disintegration of Turkish rule in the Balkans, Disraeli used the Congress of Berlin in the summer of 1878 to reassemble it by unpicking the Treaty of San Stefano which had been forced on Turkey by Russia in March. Whereas Gladstone could only deplore this policy in his Midlothian campaign, Disraeli claimed success at Berlin for his objectives of preventing Bulgaria from displacing Turkish rule; by helping restore Turkish sovereignty to Macedonia, he reinforced the traditional British strategy of blocking the advance of Russian hegemony towards the eastern Mediterranean. The moral and diplomatic implications of all this are considered in Analysis 2.

It might be argued that Gladstone was less realistic than Disraeli in his view of what was possible in foreign policy. His vision was not only more idealistic; it was also more extensive, involving multilateral relationships rather than specific constraints on potential opponents. His diplomacy in 1870–1 first to prevent, and then contain, the Franco-Prussian War was hardly likely to succeed, given the determination of Bismarck to exploit the Hohenzollern Candidature and crush France militarily. Disraeli recognised this when he said in 1871 that, as a result of 'the German revolution', the balance of power had been 'entirely destroyed' and 'the country which suffers most, and feels the effects of this great change most, is England'.[3] Gladstone's response to the changed international situation was to seek international accord through conferences, which explains his unsuccessful attempt in London in 1871 to get Russia to withdraw its repudiation of the Black Sea clauses. Disraeli drew a different deduction – the single-minded pursuit of the national interest. Superficially, the Congress of Berlin (1878) seemed to epitomise multilateralism. In reality, however, most of the issues there were settled by behind-the-scenes bilateral manoeuvring. Interestingly, Bismarck had some respect for Disraeli (once he had swallowed his racial prejudice), while Gladstone he denounced as a dangerous idealist.

Yet, from another perspective, there is a case for saying that Gladstone read the long-term situation more effectively than Disraeli. Analysis 2 considers the possible links between Bismarck, Disraeli, the Congress of Berlin and the descent of Europe into chaos by 1914. Disraeli's solutions were immediate, while Gladstone's would have had a deferred impact. Immediate solutions can, however, generate their own problems. Salisbury later admitted that he and Disraeli had 'backed the wrong horse' at the Congress of Berlin, while Gladstone's assessment of his rival was that he was 'clear-sighted' but 'short-sighted'.

ANALYSIS 2: HOW HAVE HISTORIANS INTERPRETED THE INVOLVEMENT OF GLADSTONE AND DISRAELI IN THE EASTERN QUESTION BETWEEN 1870 AND 1885?

The 'Eastern Question' concerned the future of that area in the Balkans which was still under the control of the Ottoman Empire after the Treaty of Paris (1856). During Disraeli's second ministry (1874–80) the Balkans erupted in a series of revolts by Christian sub-nations and Turkish retaliation. Complicating the whole issue were the very different percep-tions held by Gladstone and Disraeli as to what was the real issue – and where the priorities lay for Britain. The differences between Gladstone and Disraeli over this are obvious and powerfully documented. The implications and results of their policies have, however, developed a considerable historiography. This is considered in connection with the Bulgarian Horrors and the ensuing crisis, the Congress of Berlin and its results, and the way in which the Eastern Question affected domestic issues.

Attitudes behind the Eastern Question

There is no doubt about one point. Gladstone and Disraeli were in fundamental disagreement over how Britain should respond to the crisis in the Balkans: indeed, Gladstone emerged from his retirement as Liberal leader to attack the policy of Disraeli's government in 1876. He was incensed at Disraeli's apparent support for the Ottoman Empire despite the latter's record of brutal repression in its Christian provinces in the Balkans. Disraeli, by contrast, focused on the strategic problem of how British interests would be affected in the Near East and the Indian sub-continent should Russia be given a chance for further expansion through the collapse of Turkey.

The debate is centred rather on how this disagreement was expressed. It became particularly emotive after the Bulgarian massacres in 1876, to which Gladstone responded in his pamphlet on *The Bulgarian Horrors and the Question of the East*, while Disraeli accused Gladstone of over-reacting to evidence which had, in any case, been exaggerated. Early comments immediately gave Gladstone the moral high ground, Morley for example insisting that Gladstone's approach was principled and Paul arguing that his reaction was based on sound common sense and judgement. 'He was not for peace at any price. He was for prompt and immediate action, not alone, but in alliance with the other civilised Powers of Europe.' Gladstone 'knew the British nation' and 'saw that the best way of guiding public opinion was to strike the iron where as well as when it was hot'.[1] Hammond and Foot attributed to Gladstone a firm belief in national self-determination and in the virtues of 'nations struggling rightly to be free', whereas 'Disraeli repudiated all this'.[2] Biagini also saw Gladstone as principled, although he emphasised the importance of Christian influences behind Gladstone's thinking. As a 'High-Churchman' Gladstone 'recognized the Eastern Orthodox Church as a legitimate "national" branch of the universal Church of Christ'. If there should be cooperation between the various churches, it followed that the powers should take concerted action on their advice.[3]

Disraeli, by contrast, emerges as pragmatic, even ruthless. To some extent this is the result of his unguarded response to Gladstone's pamphlet. Smith, for example, felt that 'He was incautious and provocative in dismissing the early reports of massacres on insufficient information, and he inflamed matters by his off-hand cynicism about Turkish methods of dealing with rebels.'[4] Hammond and Foot extended this into a broader criticism of Disraeli's approach to self-determination in the Balkans. 'The only nationalism with which he sympathised was English nationalism. This was in no way incompatible with being singularly un-English himself. All other nationalities he suspected or ignored.' They also pointed to his ruthlessness and pragmatism: 'He believed in *Realpolitik* and the use of power. This is why he got on so well with Bismarck.'[5]

Although the Bulgarian massacres do tend to polarise perceptions of Balkan policies, Disraeli's reaction might be considered from another perspective. Gladstone was renowned for his anti-Turkish views, whereas Disraeli had rather more of an understanding of Turkish culture. He was also aware that Turkish rule had been considerably more tolerant than Europe's Christian regimes to Jewish minorities. This is considered by Smith, but dismissed as an influence on Disraeli's policy: 'the evidence is not strong enough to support an interpretation of his policy as funda-mentally inspired, rather than marginally reinforced, either by Semitic exaltation or by Turkish delight'.[6] Disraeli was influenced by English interests (and he had, of course, accepted conversion to Christianity). But this does not mean that Disraeli was entirely opportunist and amoral in his attitude to atrocities in the Balkans. It could well be that he had another perspective which, while not being at the forefront of his mind, at least enabled him to be less concerned about what he considered to be atrocity propaganda.

There was also an unsavoury element about the Bulgarian Horrors publicity. This was not of Gladstone's making, since his objective was to draw attention to the persecution of helpless minorities. The issue was, however, given an antisemitic twist, aimed directly at Disraeli. The historian E.A. Freeman maintained in 1877 that 'Turk and Jew were in league against the Christian' and that Disraeli was sacrificing 'the policy of England to Hebrew sentiment'.[7] Thus the Balkans crisis brought out the best – and worst – in public opinion and, in the words of Chamberlain, 'touched deep nerves in the Victorian psyche'.[8]

The handling of the crisis 1875–8

There has been more controversy over Disraeli's handling of the pressure on Turkey than over his reaction to the massacres in Bulgaria. A typical argument is that his diplomacy between 1875 and 1877 exacerbated the problem. Seaman argued that Disraeli lost the opportunity to influence Turkey when it mattered most. 'On balance, the crisis in the Near East from 1875 to 1878 may be said to have been to a great extent created by Disraeli's initial abandonment of concerted action when refusing to associate England with the Berlin Memorandum.'[9] Davis attributes this lack of cohesion to Disraeli having his own agenda. 'Disraeli's desire to make a grand stroke helps to explain his government's skepticism of the continental powers' attempts to associate Britain in urging reforms on the Turks, and its great reluctance to join in a proposal that was therefore drawn up without its being consulted.' The same applies to the decision to send the navy to Besika Bay in 1876. 'Both these actions strengthened the Turks in setting their faces against reform.'[10] This line of argument can even lead to establishing an indirect responsibility for the massacres which followed.

There is, however, an alternative approach. Disraeli, it has been argued, was doing nothing new. He was merely following a traditional line on foreign policy which went back, through Palmerston and Canning, to the Younger Pitt. Russia had been seen by both political parties as a key threat to British strategic interests and Turkey had been given full military support during the Crimean War (1854–6) despite its abiding reputation for corruption and repression. If Disraeli was dismissive about reports of atrocities in 1876, he was therefore following well-established precedents. Nor was he necessarily being arrogant. As Feuchtwanger pointed out, he consulted his cabinet and 'ducked and weaved between the constantly shifting positions of his colleagues'. This was not inappropriate to the circumstances; he listened to advice and his 'awareness that he derived his power from party' made Disraeli 'a modern politician'.[11] He was also a statesman of his own time. Smith acknowledged that criticisms of Disraeli's inconsistency are 'not unfair', but they do 'ignore the possibility that Disraeli's politics of gesture, improvisation and waiting on events were peculiarly appropriate to the situation he found in 1875–8'.[12]

Gladstone's alternative to Disraeli's unilateral action is also controversial. Lloyd posed the possibility that his schemes for concert diplomacy really did fit the needs of Britain and Europe, rather than the more self-interested policies of men like Disraeli and Bismarck. Of course, Lloyd acknowledged, 'the case for Gladstonianism does owe a great deal of its strength to the fact that Bismarckianism is blamed for two destructive wars that might have taken place even in a world less committed to the politics of power. Even if the policy of the Concert of Europe was the best policy for everyone in the late nineteenth century, it could be argued that following the policy at a time when the rest of Europe was behaving differently was not necessarily the second-best policy that Britain could have followed.'[13] The case for Gladstone is not, in other words, proven. It should not, however, be dismissed as irrelevant or anachronistic.

A more hard-headed argument might be that Gladstone was simply out of touch with the realities of the international situation in the 1870s. Europe then was very different to that of the 1840s and 1850s, having had to adjust in the meantime to the rise of Germany and to the ultimate practitioner of *Realpolitik* – Bismarck. There is no evidence to suggest that Gladstone would have managed to contain the situation more effectively than Disraeli. Indeed, according to Medlicott, Gladstone's multilateral approach was made obsolete by Bismarck's more ruthless diplomacy, especially during the 1880s. In any case, Bismarck regarded Gladstone as a dangerous ideological threat to Germany: his liberalism influenced Crown Prince Frederick, heir to the German throne. Since one of his domestic priorities was to neutralise German liberalism, Bismarck was hardly likely to be receptive to Gladstonian diplomacy. Disraeli, on the other hand, earned Bismarck's grudging respect. He also succeeded in getting a Congress out of him – even if it was not the type that Gladstone had wanted.

The Berlin Settlement 1878

The Congress of Berlin was one of the diplomatic highlights of the nineteenth century and has been associated with a very wide range of – usually – incompatible consequences.

The most positive argument is that Disraeli contributed to a lasting diplomatic stability. He claimed on his return from Berlin that he had accomplished 'Peace with Honour'. With this *The Times* agreed: 'He has, at all events, averted a terrible war; he has, at the same time, maintained the dignity and authority of his country; and he has in all probability established affairs in the East upon a basis on which a really stable edifice may be erected.'[14] Some historians also consider that Disraeli achieved something remarkable – in dismantling the Treaty of San Stefano and frustrating Russia's attempt to dominate the Balkans through an enlarged Bulgaria. Had San Stefano stood, the resentment of the other Balkan peoples, especially the Serbs and Greeks, would have been transferred from Turkey to Bulgaria and its protector, Russia. Turkey, meanwhile, would have collapsed in Europe, with the other states fighting each other for the remains. As it was, the aspirations of the Balkan states were partly met, through the acknowledgement of Romanian, Serbian and Bulgarian independence, while the attempt made at San Stefano to truncate Turkey-in-Europe was reversed by the trisection of the enlarged Bulgaria. Russia was placated by the transfer of Bessarabia, while Austria-Hungary was satisfied by the earmarking of Bosnia-Herzegovina. Britain, of course, had managed to block the expansion of Russian influence in the Balkans. From this perspective it is hardly surprising that the Treaty of Berlin should be seen as a major accomplishment of Disraeli and as a contribution to future stability. According to Blake, it was 'followed by almost as long a period of peace between the European great powers as the interval separating the Crimean War from the Congress of Vienna. As one of the two principal plenipotentiaries at Berlin, Disraeli must share with Bismarck some of the credit.'[15]

The negative views on Disraeli's policy are more numerous – and more varied. The first of these is that whatever *was* achieved at Berlin was not Disraeli's doing. Davis argued that the credit should be given to Salisbury, who had replaced Derby as Foreign Secretary. The trisection of Bulgaria was 'in fact a modified policy of partition, against which Disraeli had always contended, at least in public'.[16] It was also Salisbury who was behind Britain's main acquisition, Cyprus, made by separate agreement with Turkey before the Congress. The impression from Davis is that Salisbury gave clarity to Disraeli's scheme to prevent Russia from expanding. Beyond that, Disraeli 'never had a policy',[17] even though he did make 'a tremendous impression' and give 'a great and glorious performance'.[18] Shannon looked elsewhere for a source of the success at Berlin. Disraeli 'was rescued from the consequences of his persistent application of a bankrupt policy by the brokerage of Bismarck'. Indeed, Disraeli did 'nothing serious personally at the Congress except to be the gratified recipient of Bismarck's heavy flattery'. Harsher was still to come: 'Beaconsfield's empty role at Berlin symbolized the speciousness of his ultimate achievement in foreign affairs.'[19] It is true that Turkey in Europe had been saved, but the threat to its existence would not have arisen had Disraeli gone along earlier with the Berlin Memorandum and the Constantinople Conference.

A slightly different approach is to criticise Disraeli on the grounds that he did too little to press the advantage which Britain held in 1878. According to Herbert Paul, writing in 1905, Disraeli 'must be held to have thrown away a magnificent opportunity'. His reasoning was as follows. Bismarck, normally 'unscrupulous', showed at Berlin a 'pene-trating and impartial spirit'. His aim was 'the peace of Europe' and he identified Egypt as the 'place most likely to disturb it', especially because of its serious misrule by 'a rapacious tyrant'. Bismarck privately suggested that Britain should annex Egypt but Disraeli refused because 'it would have impaired that sacred principle, the integrity of the Ottoman Empire'. Because of a misguided attachment to Turkey, Disraeli therefore missed the opportunity of placing Egypt under the 'one Power' with a 'capacity for governing Eastern races'.[20] Paul's imperialist focus prevented him from appreciating the problems which fell to Gladstone, who did annex Egypt five years later.

A broader criticism is applied to both Disraeli and Bismarck on the grounds that they set up the lines of conflict which eventually led to the outbreak of the First World War. The Berlin Settlement, it has been argued, was short-sighted and stored up major problems for the future over Bulgaria, Macedonia and Bosnia-Herzegovina.

The case for the dangers posed by the treatment of Bulgaria was put by Morgan, who argued that the trisection frustrated Russia to such an extent that the latter did everything possible to undermine Bulgaria in the future.[21] One instance of this was the Bulgarian crisis of 1885, which caused the Bulgarian government to look to Austria and Germany for protection against Russian encroachment. This meant that Turkey gradually moved away from a pro-British stance and became a German satellite. Arguably, German influence in the Balkans posed a greater threat than Russia could ever have done. A.J.P. Taylor, by contrast, maintained that the real danger was the decision to allocate Bosnia-Herzegovina to Austria-Hungary, which 'contained the seeds of future disaster', leading to the spiral which included the annexation of 1908 and the assassination of the Archduke Franz Ferdinand in June 1914. Ensor's perspective was, again, slightly different. While acknowledging that the transfer of Bosnia-Herzegovina to Austria-Hungary was one of the 'especially bad' features of the Berlin Settlement, he considered that there was no one who 'could stop Andrassy' achieving this. The trisection of Bulgaria 'did no great harm nor good in the sequel; it was ended within eight years'. The real mistake, he concluded, was the return of Macedonia to Turkey, which 'ushered in thirty-four years of misrule'.[22] Stavrianos managed to combine all of these factors into the broadest view of all. 'The direct and logical outcome of the Berlin settlement was the Serbian–Bulgarian War of 1885, the Bosnian crisis of 1908, the two Balkan Wars of 1912–13, and the murder of the Archduke Francis Ferdinand in 1914.'[23]

Could Gladstone have done any better? Davis seemed to think so. 'Britain would', he argued, 'have been much better advised to have put her faith in Balkan, and particularly Bulgarian nationalism as a bar to the advance of the great neighbour to the north rather than trying to shore up a despotic and corrupt power to the south. Gladstone had some perception of this fact.' Gladstone's failing, however, was that he 'put his advice in such emotional terms as to be unintelligible to the great majority of responsible politicians'.[24]

This is an attractive argument and seems to be backed by long-term events. But it should not be assumed that Disraeli had given no thought to the issue of Balkan nationalism. Shannon and Smith have shown that Disraeli had views as strong as Gladstone's. While Gladstone looked to the development of independent states in the Balkans as the best safeguard against Russian advance, Disraeli had always distrusted 'this modern, new-fangled sentimental principle of nationality'.[25] He had criticised Britain's naval intervention on the side of Greece against Turkey in 1829 as a 'bloody blunder' and was highly critical of 'autonomy for Bosnia, with a mixed population'.[26] Hard-headed, perhaps; unsentimental, certainly; but Disraeli was hardly ignorant of the issues. Gladstone can be justified to an extent by the eventual achievement of national self-determination in the Balkans. But with the bloodshed following the collapse of Yugoslavia in the 1990s, who can say that Gladstone was entirely right and Disraeli entirely wrong?

Comments

The Eastern Question, which so tested Disraeli and incensed Gladstone, was a highlight in nineteenth-century British policy which has attracted an unusual spread of controversy.

This is partly because it had a particular dramatic intensity. It burst on the scene through news of appalling atrocities committed in Bulgaria, which acquired unprecedented notoriety in the nineteenth century. In actual fact, there were other comparable events which escaped a similar reaction. What made the difference in this case, to provide so much focus – both at the time and retrospectively? One factor was Gladstone's sudden re-emergence from retirement as Liberal leader. This involved a new beginning and a new cause – the impact of which is still being analysed. The intensity of his attack on a bemused Disraeli was bound to have a powerful impact on the population – and to inspire views on mass politics. Gladstone's emotive writing, liberated by his being in opposition, can be contrasted with the more cautious response of a government forced to prevaricate; this provides ample material for criticism and defence from many different angles. Above all, the conflict between moral issues and strategic issues, expressed in writing through pamphlets and orally in Parliament, has the potential to move historians to make their own judgements or, conversely, to take particular care to avoid making them; either approach will strongly influence their style of writing.

Interpretations of the events leading up to the Congress of Berlin will inevitably be shaped by different considerations of the contributions made by specific *people*. The contest between two individuals has always been an appealing subject. In the nineteenth century it was especially so and the political debate frequently overlapped with the historical one. 'Politics' were then closer to 'history' than they are today. The exposition of the politician was then more reasoned and at greater length, while the scope of the historian was broader and often more polemical. Hence historians frequently polarised round their political subjects. More recent attitudes have altered so that it is no longer 'good history' to show partisan support for one individual or the other – except through an occasional aside or parenthetical comment. Instead, the main differences are taken for granted, while the subtleties are given greater attention. Disraeli may well have been an opportunist and he certainly downplayed the sheer nastiness of the Bulgarian massacres. But might his perspective not also have been partially influenced by a knowledge that the Ottoman Empire had been less antisemitic than Christian states? By making this point the intention is not to justify or vilify Disraeli – but rather to explain him. Similarly, it is difficult to challenge Gladstone's righteous indignation against the Turkish atrocities in Bulgaria – but it does no harm to point out the advantage taken of this by parasitic antisemitism aimed, for political reasons, at Disraeli.

There are also reasons for the wide spread of interpretations of the

Treaty of Berlin. More than any other topic in this book, the assessment of the Berlin Settlement depends on the *perspectives* used. Perspectives, in turn, change in accordance with the *vantage points* selected. This applies especially to the connection between the settlement and subsequent developments in the Balkans. The vantage points of Blake and Stavrianos seem directly opposite to each other. This might perhaps be due to their contrasting purposes: to provide a biography of the man directly connected with the settlement, as opposed to a more general history of the Balkans explaining the impact of an externally imposed solution to an internal problem. Most historians aim to consider this longer perspective. Some, however, tend to concentrate on two points: the immediate issue under discussion, and a future one which is considered to be directly related to it. The first will be seen as making a direct contribution to the second and, quite possibly, as a 'turning point' which leads straight towards it. This is very much the approach of Ensor and of Taylor. It is, however, possible to take a very different 'time-stream' approach; here the flow of the original influence is progressively diluted by the infusion of other tributaries, with which it becomes so intermingled that it loses its separate identity. Historians like this in theory, because it is complex. In practice, however, they tend to remain faithful to the paramountcy – if not uniqueness – of the influence on the future of their particular topic. It is more difficult to justify a detailed study of an issue for which no direct influence can be claimed.

A final thought. Historians value complexity – but also clarity. Each tries to present the former through the latter. Multiply this by the number of historians covering the same area and the result is a criss-cross of clear complexities. But while they remain individually clear, when overlapped they become blurred. This invites new attempts at clarification which will lead, in turn, to further complexity. The scope for reinterpretation is therefore infinite.

SOURCES

1. THE 'BULGARIAN HORRORS'

Source 1: A cartoon from *Punch*, August 1876.

See Figure 5.

NEUTRALITY UNDER DIFFICULTIES
Dizzy: 'Bulgarian atrocities! I can't find them in the official reports!!!'

Figure 5.

Source 2: From Gladstone's *The Bulgarian Horrors and the Question of the East*, 6 September 1876.

We now know in detail that there have been perpetrated, under the immediate authority of a Government to which all the time we have been giving the strongest moral, and for part of the time even material support, crimes and outrages, so vast in scale as to exceed all modern example, and so unutterably vile as well as fierce in character that it passes the power of heart to conceive, and of tongue and pen adequately to describe them. These are the Bulgarian horrors.

Source 3: Extracts from a speech made by Disraeli in the House of Commons, 11 August 1876.

We are always treated as if we had some peculiar alliance with the Turkish Government, as if we were their peculiar friends, and even as if we were expected to uphold them in any enormity they might commit. I want to know what evidence there is of that, what interest we have in such a thing. We are, it is true, the Allies of the Sultan of Turkey; so is Russia, so is Austria, so is France, and so are others . . .

What our duty is at this critical moment is to maintain the Empire of England. Nor will we ever agree to any step, though it may obtain for a moment comparative quiet and a false prosperity, that hazards the existence of that Empire.

Source 4: From B.H. Abbott, *Gladstone and Disraeli*, published in 1972.

Gladstone's campaign in the autumn of 1876 sabotaged Disraeli's policy. By dividing British public opinion and sanctifying Russia's pretext for intervention, Gladstone effectively destroyed Disraeli's freedom of action. Lord Salisbury was sent as British delegate to the Constantinople Conference, which recommended an armistice with the Serbs and a programme of reforms for Turkey – all with Russia's agreement. The Turks, however, would not accept, believing that Russia would shrink from war, and that Salisbury's threat to leave Turkey to her fate was an idle one. This was largely Disraeli's fault in refusing Salisbury's request to remove the pro-Turkish Elliot from Constantinople. Discussions were continued and another protocol was issued, but Turkey obdurately refused to give way. In April 1877 Russia declared war on Turkey. Disraeli declared Britain's neutrality, though warning Russia of the inviolability of Constantinople and the navigation of the Straits, and added to these old demands the maintenance of free communication through the Suez Canal and the exclusion of Egypt from military operations. The effect of Gladstone's intervention in weakening Disraeli's hand cannot be denied.

Questions

1. Briefly explain the meaning of the cartoon in Source 1, including the caption. (20)
2. Compare the views expressed in Sources 2 and 3 on the policies being followed by the British government. (40)
3. Using all the sources, and your own knowledge, comment on the view expressed in Source 4 that 'Gladstone's campaign in the

autumn of 1876 sabotaged Disraeli's policy' over the Eastern
Question. (60)

Total (120)

2. INTERPRETATIONS OF DISRAELI AND THE TREATY OF BERLIN (1878)

Source 5: From *The Times*, 17 July 1878.

In Dover and in London the return of Lord Beaconsfield and Lord Salisbury won a
popular ovation. The London, Chatham and Dover twin steamer . . . in which Lord
Beaconsfield and Lord Salisbury travelled, put alongside the Admiralty Pier at 2.40.
There was a large crowd which cheered heartily, and a local band struck up 'Home,
Sweet Home'. The town and the shipping in Dover harbour were decorated. . . . The
following address, which was very beautifully illuminated, was presented to Lord
Beaconsfield . . . 'May it please your Lordship – We, the members of the Dover
Workingmen's Constitutional Association, humbly bid your Lordship a cordial
welcome to our shores on your return from that Congress at whose deliberations,
by the blessing of God, you have, by your great intellect and firm demeanour, added
so materially to the restoration of the peace of Empires and the assertion of
England's might and position among nations. . . . '

Lord Beaconsfield, in reply, said – 'I do not like to go away without thanking you
for the very kind manner in which you have received me and my colleague Lord
Salisbury. We have brought a peace, and we trust we have brought a peace with
honour.'

Source 6: From Robert Blake, *Disraeli*, first published in 1966.

Judged by the criteria of tactical skill and achievement of objectives, Disraeli's
foreign policy was an undoubted success. As for the Berlin settlement, of course it
was not perfect. No treaty ever is. But it was followed by almost as long a period of
peace between the European great powers as the interval separating the Crimean
War from the Congress of Vienna. As one of the two principal plenipotentiaries at
Berlin Disraeli must share with Bismarck some part of the credit.

Source 7: From R.W. Davis, *Disraeli*, first published in 1976.

He had been determined from the beginning that Russia should not have her own
way, and she had not got it.

Beyond that, however, he had never had a policy; and the policy that triumphed
at Berlin was not really his, but that of the once skeptical Salisbury, who had
succeeded Derby as Foreign Secretary. It was in fact a modified policy of partition,

against which Disraeli had always contended, at least in public. So far as Britain was concerned, the most important modification of San Stefano was the vast reduction of Bulgaria. An autonomous Bulgaria was now to have the Balkan Mountains as its southern boundary. The territory to the south, to be known as Eastern Rumelia, was to have a special organization, but to remain part of Turkey. Macedonia was to enjoy certain reforms, but was to be returned to Turkey without other restrictions. Thus a Turkish buffer in Europe was to be retained. Salisbury, however, had little faith in Turkey's long-term prospects. He therefore proposed that Britain should annex Cyprus in return for a guarantee of Asiatic Turkey. Disraeli had, it is true, long had in mind the acquiring of some place of arms; and in the course of the past several years his fertile imagination had run from the Black Sea, to the Persian Gulf, to spots all over the eastern Mediterranean, including Cyprus. Salisbury, however, certainly had more notion of what he wanted to do with it, though Disraeli was quite willing to assure the Queen that 'Cyprus is the key to Western Asia.' It was therefore acquired, by a separate agreement with Turkey before the Congress met.

Source 8: From R. Shannon, *The Crisis of Imperialism*, first published in 1974.

Thus Beaconsfield was rescued from the consequences of his persistent application of bankrupt policy by the brokerage of Bismarck rescuing the Russians from the consequences of succumbing to their pan-Slav temptations. Beaconsfield achieved nothing serious personally at the Congress except to be the gratified recipient of Bismarck's heavy flattery. There was really nothing for him to do. The logic of the situation was quite clear and everything depended on Bismarck's seeing it through. Salisbury admirably sustained Beaconsfield in this hollow role, much as Shuvalov on the other side sustained the senile Gorchakov. Salisbury had abated nothing of his original conviction that the Palmerstonian policy was clearly at an end; but he was, after all, a comparatively young man, and could afford to wait. Beaconsfield's empty role at Berlin aptly symbolized the speciousness of his ultimate achievement in foreign affairs. Turkey-in-Europe was saved; but more of it could have been saved at the Constantinople Conference at the beginning of 1877, and more of it still at the time of the Berlin Memorandum. The division of the two Bulgarias in any case lasted only until 1884. Otherwise, nothing substantial was achieved except perhaps to please the 'national' public. Above all, the re-imposition of a Palmerstonian European credit was not attained. Berlin, far from inaugurating a new era of concert politics, in fact inaugurated, in 1879, the first of the alliances – the Austro-German alliance – which indicated definitively the direction in which the post-concert system of Europe would henceforth find its logical expression. But it would be Salisbury's task to cope with that situation, not Beaconsfield's.

Questions

1. Which of Sources 6, 7 and 8 comes closest to the view expressed in Source 5? (15)
2. 'A hollow achievement.' To what extent do Sources 5 to 8, and your own knowledge, support this view of Disraeli's performance at Berlin in 1878? (30)

Total (45)

6

IMPERIALISM AND EMPIRE

BACKGROUND

The distinction between 'foreign' and 'imperial' policies was established in Chapter 5. 'Imperial' policies relate directly to colonial issues within or adjacent to the British Empire, although these may have a direct impact on 'foreign' policy since they affect relations between the European powers involved. 'Imperialism' can be seen as momentum towards spreading influence into undeveloped areas. Colonial acquisitions were relatively limited in the mid-nineteenth century and few politicians openly favoured imperialism. However, between 1874 and the end of the century colonisation steadily accelerated, reaching its peak in the 1890s. Any comparison between Gladstone and Disraeli brings out a paradox: Gladstone, in theory opposed to imperialism, presided over more colonial additions than Disraeli, who was an ardent imperialist (see Analysis 1).

The first governments of Disraeli and Gladstone (1868 and 1868–74) saw a resolution of older issues rather than the beginning of new ones. Derby and Disraeli approved the new Dominion of Canada, to which Manitoba was added in 1870, British Columbia in 1871 and Prince Edward Island in 1873. Similar consolidations occurred in the Cape Colony, which was granted responsible government in 1872.

A turning point in British imperialism occurred when, in 1875, Disraeli purchased from the bankrupt Egyptian Khedive a majority holding in the Suez Canal shares. This gave Britain a permanent strategic interest in the eastern Mediterranean and Indian Ocean, with considerable knock-on effects in northern and southern Africa. Analysis 2 explores the possible connection between concern about the Suez Canal and a whole range of future developments, such as the annexation of the Transvaal in 1877 and, in 1878, of Walvis Bay and Cyprus. Disraeli was quick to take advantage of any positive image offered by imperialism, especially when, in 1876, the Royal Styles and Titles Act made Queen Victoria 'Empress of India'. But imperialism also brought problems and embarrassment to Disraeli's government. The worst of these were the British military defeat by the Zulus at Isandhlwana (1879) and the unsuccessful British campaign in Afghanistan (1879–80).

Gladstone's second and third ministries (1880–5 and 1886) may have been a less eventful period in terms of foreign policy, but the same could hardly be said of imperial commitments. In a period of particularly hectic activity, Gladstone was drawn into one crisis after another. The First Boer War, which included further British defeat at Majuba (1881), forced Gladstone to restore independence to the Transvaal by the Convention of Pretoria. In the following year British interests were threatened in Egypt by the revolt of Arabi Pasha against the Egyptian Khedive. To protect the Suez Canal, Gladstone felt obliged to send British troops. The result was the defeat of Arabi Pasha at Tel-el-Kebir and the establishment of a British protectorate over the whole country. Gladstone tried to avoid being drawn further up the Nile as a result of the revolt of the Mahdi in the Sudan against the Khedive's rule – and hence British influence – from Egypt. Instead, he dispatched General Gordon to organise the evacuation of the Egyptian garrison from Khartoum, which was threatened by the Mahdi's forces. Gordon, however, disobeyed orders and tried to organise the defence of the city instead. Gordon paid with his life as the Mahdi sacked Khartoum, and Gladstone suffered considerable political fallout and public condemnation in England. Even Afghanistan erupted again, this time because Russian forces occupied Penjdeh, a disputed boundary region between Russia and Afghanistan. Perhaps the one positive event of Gladstone's administration was British involvement in the Berlin Conference (1884–5) which was intended to bring some sort of order to the scramble for colonies – especially in Africa – by the powers. It was certainly more in keeping with

Gladstone's supposed preference for multilateral agreement rather than the unilateral action he had been undertaking.

Gladstone is remembered for the extent of his imperial involvements rather than for their successful outcome. Unlike Disraeli he was always reluctant to take the imperial solution. His successor, Lord Salisbury (1885–6, 1886–92 and 1895–1901), was perhaps partway between the two. While more prepared than Gladstone to take forceful action, he was less convinced than Disraeli about the principle of Empire itself.

One final point is worth making: the growing, if misleading, connection between imperialism and Ireland. Gladstone saw Ireland as a domestic issue requiring a domestic solution, eventually in the form of devolved power, or Home Rule. The opponents of Home Rule, however, always used a double argument against Home Rule. One was that it would destroy the United Kingdom, the other that it would threaten the integrity of the Empire. Partly responsible for this approach was Disraeli who applied the imperial connection even before Gladstone's conversion to Home Rule. His Conservative party remained convinced that imperialism and unionism were integral to Britain's future, and it was this combination which persuaded a number of Liberal imperialists (such as Joseph Chamberlain) to defect from Gladstone and plunge the Liberal party into crisis. Imperialism was therefore the bridge crossed by some Liberals to Conservatism.

ANALYSIS 1: COMPARE THE RECORDS OF GLADSTONE AND DISRAELI ON IMPERIAL ISSUES.

A comparison of the imperial policies of Gladstone and Disraeli could be made under three main criteria: what they *made* of imperialism (their ideas and the ways in which they adapted to it); what they *did* (their actions, successes and failures while in office); and where they *left* it (their influence on future policies and developments).

What they *made* of imperialism

For a substantial period – between the 1820s and the 1860s – both of the major parties considered that adding to the Empire already in existence would be unnecessary and financially counterproductive. This applied to the Whigs under Russell and Palmerston as well as to the Conservatives under Peel and Derby. Disraeli certainly seemed to reflect the prevailing view when he said in 1852 that colonies were a drain on Britain's resources, even a 'millstone round our necks'.[1] Yet, by 1870, he had changed his approach, claiming that 'England is no longer a mere European Power; she is the metropolis of a great maritime empire, extending to the boundaries of the farthest ocean.'[2] Gladstone underwent no such conversion. In 1872 he considered that Britain's Empire was 'satiated'.[3] In *England's Mission*, published in 1878, he argued that the main concern of the government should be to take care of 'her own children within her own shores'.[4] He added in 1881, 'Nothing will induce me to submit to these colonial annexations.'[5] Gradually, however, even he came to accept that imperialism exerted a powerful appeal. 'The sentiment of Empire may', he acknowledged, 'be called innate in every Briton.' Hence it was 'part of our patrimony' and was 'interwoven with all our habits of mental action upon public affairs'.[6]

Thus, whereas Disraeli was a willing convert to imperialism, Gladstone remained nothing more than a reluctant imperialist. Gladstone was outspokenly critical of Disraeli's 'false phantoms of glory' and 'mischievous and ruinous misdeeds'.[7] He also accused Disraeli of undermining the constitutional system in Britain – by his purchase of the Suez Canal shares, without reference to Parliament, and by upgrading the title of Britain's head of state to Empress of India. For his part, Disraeli accused Gladstone of wishing to break up the Empire by aiming for inappropriate measures of self-government: in this case, irresponsibility meant negligence and abandonment. Perhaps these criticisms reflect the way in which each adapted to imperialism, whether willingly or unwillingly. Disraeli used 'Empire' to underpin the values of the Conservative party. Imperialism became part of a triple appeal to the electorate: in 1872 he said that Conservative policy must be 'to maintain the institutions of the country, to uphold the Empire of England, and to elevate the condition of the people'.[8] Gladstone was less opportunist – he could never weave imperialism into the fabric of Liberalism, but he did develop a way of looking at it positively as having the potential for a larger community of sovereign states. This was, however, more in keeping with deconstructing colonial rule rather than extending its scope. Ironically, it was the latter with which Gladstone was more associated in practice.

What they *did* with imperialism

There was a surprising degree of continuity between the actual developments under the two leaders, especially between Gladstone's first ministry (1868–74), Disraeli's second (1874–80) and Gladstone's second (1880–5). Although the most extensive acquisitions came under Gladstone, they were often the result of actions initiated by Disraeli. The continuity is especially apparent in Egypt. In buying Suez Canal shares dumped on the market in 1875 by the bankrupt Khedive, Disraeli provided Britain with a longstanding interest in the region. This was subsequently extended by the occupation of the whole country by Gladstone in 1882. There are also links elsewhere in Africa. Under Disraeli the Transvaal, an independent Boer Republic, was brought under British rule, although the First Boer War (1880–1) resulted in the restoration of its autonomy by Gladstone through the Convention of Pretoria. Gladstone was, of course, accused of incompetence here. Earlier, Disraeli had claimed the credit for the subduing of the Ashanti at Kumasi in West Africa in 1874, although Wolseley's expedition had actually been sent by Gladstone the year before.

There were similar overlaps in Asia and the Pacific. In 1873, for example, Gladstone's government secured from the Rajah of the Malay states the right to appoint British Residents or advisers. Disraeli subsequently claimed the credit for this as well as for the security of the British naval base at Singapore. Similarly, a delegation sent to Fiji in 1873 to improve relations ended up by annexing it in October 1874. Afghanistan was more of a problem. Both Gladstone and Disraeli were aware of the expansion of Russian interests in central Asia and it appeared that Afghanistan might go the same way as Turkestan and Uzbekistan. This would bring the Russian frontier up against British India. Gladstone preferred negotiation for neutrality (1873) but during Disraeli's ministry military action was taken, which, again, continued after the return of Gladstone to power in 1880. Elsewhere the momentum seemed to increase after Disraeli's death (1881), with the annexation of half of New Guinea in 1884 and Upper Burma (1885).

There appears to be some inconsistency in the 'convert' to imperialism actually contributing fewer territories to the Empire than the 'reluctant imperialist'. There is, however, a logical explanation. Disraeli's aim was specifically to develop the commercial and strategic empire, with the focus on the East rather than in Africa where most of the annexations under Gladstone occurred. Disraeli also made a direct link between his imperial policy and his foreign policy, where he concentrated most of his efforts, especially in the Balkans and eastern Mediterranean. To protect the Suez Canal he involved Britain in schemes to prevent the collapse of Turkey (which would destabilise Egypt) and the expansion of Russia, which would threaten British imperial interests both in the Near East and in central Asia. The Suez Canal was the key to the economic viability of the Empire, and the security of Constantinople would guarantee that of Suez.

The problems of this approach fell to Gladstone. Disraeli's foreign policy may have helped prolong Turkey's presence in Europe, but it could not prevent its collapse in Africa. Nor could the Egyptian Khedivite prevent internal chaos. The revolt of Arabi Pasha threatened the Canal which Disraeli had delivered to Britain in 1875, and Gladstone saw the solution in Cairo, not in Constantinople. He therefore broke the link which Disraeli had established with the Eastern Question and, instead, became heavily involved in Africa. The starting point was the occupation of Egypt in 1882, following the naval bombardment of Alexandria and the military defeat of Arabi Pasha by Wolseley at Tel-el-Kebir. Gladstone's motive was always defensive: he later said in the House of Commons, 'I affirm . . . that the situation in Egypt is not one which we made, but one that we found.'[9] But it was no less entangling for that, leading to further involvement in the Sudan in response to the Mahdist threat of the early 1880s. Had Disraeli lived longer than 1881, it would have been interesting to see whether he handled the situation any differently.

Turning to specific characteristics of policy, Disraeli is usually credited with a greater ability than Gladstone to take swift and decisive action. There are two examples of this. One is the Abyssinian campaign (1866), which Disraeli authorised to release the British consul and other hostages held by the Emperor Theodore of Ethiopia. This resulted in Napier's victory at Magdala and the release of the hostages – but no territorial annexation. The other example is the purchase of the Suez Canal shares, with the use of a loan from Rothschilde ('What is your security?' 'The British Government!' 'How much do you require?') There is a certain ruthlessness here, which did not escape Gladstone's attention, since it involved bypassing normal Treasury, let alone parliamentary, controls. But the gamble worked and Disraeli was able to inform the Queen: 'It is settled: you have it, Madam. The French Government has been out-generalled.'[10] The nearest Gladstone came to a decision like this was the bombardment of Alexandria in 1882. This was, however, a considered response to a crisis and was authorised after discussion in the cabinet. Important though it was, it was not a *coup* in the same sense that Disraeli's action had been in 1875.

Both Gladstone and Disraeli tasted the bitterness of failure – and of disaster. Disraeli had to explain the crushing defeat of a British army by the Zulus at Isandhlwana (1879) and the massacre of the British legation at Kabul in the same year. Gladstone's equivalent was the death of General Gordon in the defence of Khartoum against the Mahdi in 1884: this outraged public opinion more than any other event in Gladstone's long career. Although very different in their origins, each of these crises revealed a problem which affected the governments of both men – an ineffective control of subordinates. In Disraeli's case, loose government was shown over events in Zululand and Afghanistan, where Sir Bartle Frere and the Earl of Lytton (respectively High Commissioner of the Cape and Viceroy of India) involved Britain in two unnecessary wars. Disraeli commented that, if Viceroys disobeyed orders, 'they ought at least to be sure of success in their mutiny'.[11] Similarly, Gladstone lost control over General Gordon, who was sent to evacuate Khartoum but ended up trying to defend it. Gordon wrote in his diary, 'I own to having been insubordinate to Her Majesty's Government.'[12] Although both Gladstone and Disraeli faced problems of communication, the way in which the initiative was seized at local level does surely indicate some lack of central government direction.

Where they *left* imperialism

According to Rubinstein, 'Disraeli's government actually annexed relatively few new areas to the Empire, but was largely responsible for a profound long-term alteration in the way the Empire was viewed.'[13] It could certainly be argued that Disraeli made imperialism an integral part of the Conservative ethos. It was also important in strengthening the Conservative stand on Ireland. It reinforced their argument against Home Rule and enticed a number of Liberal imperialists out of Gladstone's camp. The emphasis on imperialism, established by Disraeli, therefore strengthened the appeal of unionism, developed by Salisbury, Balfour and Lord Randolph Churchill. Home Rule was the issue which drove Chamberlain and others from the Liberal party; imperialism was the appeal which pulled them over to the Conservatives.

Gladstone left no such legacy to the Liberals, despite adding substantially to the British Empire. Imperialism never became for the Liberals what it was for the Conservatives, especially after the departure of the Chamberlain Radicals and the Hartington Whigs. The Irish issue saw to that. The nearest Gladstone came to leaving a policy to the Liberals was a long-term anticipation of self-government, which was essentially post-imperialist. In the period immediately after Gladstone it was clear that imperialism would play no major part in Liberal policy or Liberal values. Rosebery (1894–5) made a half-hearted effort in that direction but the subsequent leaders – Campbell-Bannerman and Asquith – placed the focus very much on reinvesting British resources in internal reform and the beginnings of a welfare state.

Questions

1. Who contributed more to the development of the British Empire in the 1870s and 1880s: the Liberals under Gladstone or the Conservatives under Disraeli and Salisbury?
2. 'Neither Gladstone nor Disraeli was influenced by ideas or principles connected with Empire; they reacted only to events and opportunities.' How far do you agree?

ANALYSIS 2: CONSIDER THE RANGE OF HISTORICAL VIEW-POINTS ON THE REASONS BEHIND THE IMPERIAL POLICIES OF GLADSTONE AND DISRAELI.

The three main approaches considered in this analysis include the whole range of interpretations, from direct individual responsibility for the growth of British imperialism at one end to the operation of impersonal, infra-structural, influence at the other. Between the two is a third possibility – the response, especially of Gladstone, to local crises in Africa.

Interpretations based on the influence of politicians

Most historians have seen the expansion of the British Empire as directly connected to policies and decisions made by Gladstone and Disraeli as Prime Ministers, whether these were willing or unwilling, consistent or sporadic. With Disraeli the debate centres on whether he was a genuine imperialist or a convert; if the latter, how fundamental was the conversion? In Gladstone's case it is generally accepted that he was suspicious of imperialism *per se* but arguments have been presented to show how he was able to justify his involvement all the same.

There is a consensus that Disraeli showed increasing enthusiasm for imperialism during the late 1860s and 1870s, expressing open commitment in his 1872 Crystal Palace speech. But how genuine was this? One approach is to connect Disraeli's commitment to imperialism with his perception of Conservative needs. According to Smith, 'There was nothing original in what Disraeli said about empire in 1872. What was novel was his promoting empire to the centre of the Conservative platform which he was constructing, not only as an issue on which the Liberals seemed vulnerable, but as one which could perform a vital integrating function in providing for all classes a common symbol of national stature, a common source of national prosperity, and a common object of national pride and endeavour.'[1] Blake followed a similar line. Disraeli saw imperialism as 'probably a bigger electoral asset in winning working-class support during the last quarter of the century than anything else'.[2] Gann and Duignan emphasised the importance of imperialism in consolidating loyalty to the party within Conservative associations, clubs and officers' messes.[3] Eldridge attributed to Disraeli a wider perspective: he was using imperialism as an agent in British power as well as Conservative appeal. It was a 'visible expression of the power of England in the affairs of the world'. Disraeli pursued 'policies of prestige, policies which played an equal stress on the display of power and force as on their possession'.[4]

While emphasising the importance of imperialism in Disraeli's party politics and foreign policy, some historians point to an absence of any programme as such. Machin emphasised Disraeli's opportunism: 'He carried out imaginative and popular strokes of policy which acknowledged the current importance of Empire but did not represent any systematic, long-term plan of colonial expansion on his part.'[5] This explains why Disraeli did not add significantly to the extent of the British Empire. It could be argued that Disraeli the opportunist established a broader justification for empire without having ambitious aims for its expansion. Perhaps imperial policy was even subordinated to the needs of the economy and to foreign policy. He envisaged what was essentially a commercial empire, based on India and its approaches, while specific imperial decisions were always taken with a view to Britain's relations with other powers, whether France in 1875 or Russia in 1878. Where initiatives did occur, they were sometimes the result of loss of control rather than the exercise of it. Smith maintained that 'The forward movements of empire were the result, not of Disraeli's imperialism, but his excessively loose control of the cabinet.'[6] The developments during his second ministry bear this out, since his problems in South Africa and Afghanistan were both the result of overactive subordinates.

Gladstone is also seen as being of huge personal importance in the development of the British Empire, not least because his second ministry (1880–5) saw considerably more territory added than Disraeli's second (1874–80). It has even been argued that the occupation of Egypt in 1882 was one of the key factors in starting the Scramble for Africa. The debate focuses not so much on whether he was important to the development of British imperialism as on whether his role was negative and reactive or, in some way, positive and formative. The former argument is based on a literal interpretation of Gladstone's anti-imperialist statements: that he was opposed to imperialism in any form and was forced into making annexations he deeply disliked. Most historians, however, consider this approach lopsided. For one thing, he was never a pacifist in the way that the Cobdenite Radicals were; nor was he against intervention on principle where British interests were involved. There was certainly an element of reluctance and there is no equivalent to the exuberant way in which Disraeli pounced on the Suez Canal shares in 1875. Yet Gladstone became aware of the importance of Empire and managed to square it with his principles. The interesting element here is the way in which historians have explained this last point.

The counterpart to Disraeli's opportunist use of imperialism is Gladstone's attempt to shape it into a long-term vision. This is the line taken by Shannon, who believes that Gladstone used his Midlothian campaign of 1879 to bring colonial and foreign policy within the scope of a moral crusade and to denounce 'Beaconsfieldism' as a distortion.[7] Gradually Gladstone was able to construct a positive image of Empire as 'a community held together by loyalty to British culture and by shared economic interests in a free-trade world'.[8] His organic conception of the Empire was influenced by Edmund Burke and involved a degree of self-government. What it did not mean was self-sustaining expansion and he stood against 'the rising tide of militant jingoism'. In some ways the way in which he adapted imperialism anticipated a 'proto-Commonwealth'. For example, his solution for South Africa was to allow for the autonomy of the Boers. This was in line with a greater degree of local initiative in India under Lord Ripon as Viceroy, which was 'the context in which the first Indian National Congress (1883–5) was established as an organization basically inspired by the ideals of Gladstonian Liberalism'.[9]

So far, the emphasis has been on both Disraeli and Gladstone coming to terms with imperialism in their own individual ways and influencing the shape taken by the British Empire accordingly. There is, however, another line which acknowledges the importance of personal influences – but operating from Berlin rather than from London. A.J.P. Taylor argued for the centrality of Bismarck, not Gladstone or Disraeli, in the growth of empires during the 1870s and 1880s. The German Chancellor was so concerned that France might try to build an alliance against Germany, before launching a war of revenge to regain Alsace-Lorraine, that he sought to bring the Third Republic under his influence. This meant distancing both France and Germany from Britain. Hence 'Bismarck quarrelled with England in order to draw closer to France.' The method of quarrel was 'the deliberately provocative claim to ownerless lands, in which the German government had hitherto shown no interest'. French and German expansion, in turn, provoked Britain into her own bout of colonisation in West, East and southern Africa. The theme of great-power rivalry is extended by other historians. Fieldhouse believed that 'imperialism may be seen as the extension into the periphery of the political struggle in Europe'.[10] Thomson used a similar analogy: 'The naked power politics of the new colonialism were the projection, on to an overseas screen, of the inter-state frictions and rivalries of Europe.'[11] These views take the focus off Gladstone and Disraeli, moving it instead to statesmen on the Continent. The 'diplomatic view' of imperialism does rather make Germany (Bismarck) the schemer, France the accomplice and Britain (especially Gladstone and Salisbury) the dupe.

Interpretations based on infrastructural factors

A very different explanation for the spread of British imperialism is based on the influence of forces operating through the economic infrastructure. This was first advanced by the Liberal writer J.A. Hobson whose *Imperialism: A Study* was published in 1902. He maintained that industrialisation in Britain had generated enormous amounts of 'surplus capital' which could not 'find investments within the country', and therefore sought outlets overseas. Consequently, Britain and other industrial powers had to 'place larger and larger portions of their economic resources outside the area of their present political domain, and then stimulate a policy of political expansion so as to take in the new areas'.[12]

Hobson therefore considered imperialism an assertive force, an overflow of productive capitalism. A variation on the theme of infrastructural influences was provided over half a century later by Hobsbawm. The essence of his argument was that imperialism was a defensive reaction to threats to British economic interests which appeared with 'the defaults of their foreign debtors in the 1870s – for example the collapse of Turkish finance in 1876'. These crises 'mobilised those militant consortia of foreign bondholders or governments acting for their investors, which were to turn nominally independent governments into virtual or actual protectorates and colonies of the foreign powers – as in Egypt and Turkey after 1876'.[13] Britain was especially affected by this wave of imperialism because her relatively unsophisticated economy was based on earlier industrialisation than her rivals. 'She was too deeply committed to the technology and business organisation of the first phase of industrialisation, which had served her so well, to advance enthusiastically into the field of the new and revolutionary technology and industrial management which came to the fore in the 1890s.' As a result, Britain had only one way out – a traditional one which involved 'the economic (and increasingly political) conquest of hitherto unexploited areas of the world. In other words, imperialism.' Imperialism was by no means new for Britain. 'What was new was the end of the virtual British monopoly in the undeveloped world, and the consequent necessity to mark out regions of imperial influence formally against potential competitors.' From the 1880s, therefore, Britain 'exchanged the informal empire over most of the under-developed world for the formal empire of a quarter of it, plus the older satellite economies'.[14]

It is significant that neither Hobson nor Hobsbawm made any reference to the governments of the 1870s, 1880s or 1890s, let alone to any influence exerted by individuals like Gladstone or Disraeli. The broadstream of economic change seems to have carried along governments, leaders and politics with an irresistible – perhaps inevitable – momentum.

Interpretations based on the interaction between strategic and local factors

Imperialism has also been seen as the interaction between central decision-making and local forces. They may well have started with individual strategic decisions, taken at government level, but then began to assume a momentum of their own, driven by local reactions. These two elements – strategic and local – are central to the arguments of Robinson and Gallagher. These restore to Gladstone and Disraeli their capacity to make vital decisions without, however, letting them remain in control of the subsequent developments.

According to Robinson and Gallagher, Britain was drawn into Africa through 'the persistent crisis in Egypt' and the threat posed to British interests by the Boer Republics in South Africa. Britain's main concern, the argument goes, was to protect sea routes to India, the most valuable part of the British Empire, through the Suez Canal and round the Cape of Good Hope. Unfortunately, local problems made the northern and southern tips of Africa very unstable. The Egyptian Khedive was threatened, in 1881, by a major revolt led by Arabi Pasha, who aimed at freeing Egypt from all European influence. The British occupation of 1882 was not the end of the matter, for the great Islamic revolt in the Sudan against Anglo-Egyptian rule necessitated military action by Kitchener, culminating in the Battle of Omdurman in 1898. British rule was dragged further up the Nile and into East Africa by the need to outflank the Islamic threat and to counter the moves of France and Germany. 'From start to finish the partition of tropical Africa was driven by the persistent crisis in Egypt. When the British entered Egypt on their own, the Scramble began.'[15]

Similarly, the Boer Republics of the Transvaal and the Orange Free State were threatening the long-term British scheme for a loose feder-ation of South African states which would also incorporate the Cape and Natal. The alternative could well be a United States of South Africa, dominated by a republican Transvaal and bitterly hostile to any British influence. Again, therefore, the British government was receptive to pressure to acquire territory as a means of outflanking or isolating the challenge, in this case promoting the colonisation of Bechuanaland on the western border of the Transvaal, and the Rhodesias to the north. The overall result of the two separate processes of expansion was a stretch of territory from the Cape to the Mediterranean broken only by German East Africa.

Although this interpretation encompasses the whole period from 1870 to 1900, both Gladstone and Disraeli are involved at crucial stages. Gladstone inherited the consequences of Disraeli's decision in 1875 to purchase the Suez Canal shares and, in 1882, authorised the occupation of Egypt to defend British interests in the Canal from local insurrection and chaos. Gladstone especially had to deal with the interaction between strategic concerns and local threats to these. A key feature of the argument is that Africa was far from being an inert target for British attention, as the other two approaches tend to suggest. Instead, politicians in London were having to respond to the actions of the likes of Arabi Pasha in Egypt, Muhammed Ahmed in the Sudan and Paul Kruger in South Africa; before Gladstone's preoccupations with these there was also Disraeli's preoccupation with Cetewayo in Zululand. An additional complication was the growing business and commercial interest – although this operated not at an impersonal level but through specific individuals, often in league with local officials and administrators. Africa's pull began in the late 1870s, intensified in the 1880s and climaxed in the 1890s during the premiership of Lord Salisbury.

Comments

Imperialism and colonisation have been regarded as negative words for over half a century. Each is associated with exploitation and the aggressive imposition of power, culture and ideas. Modern use of the terms is therefore derogatory and possibly ideological. The terms are, in short, 'loaded'. Whether this has a direct effect on the approach taken to nineteenth-century developments depends very much on underlying assumptions. It is unlikely to affect *detailed* studies of Gladstone and Disraeli since most historians go to considerable lengths to avoid value judgements, especially if these are seen to be anachronistic ones. They are much more likely to identify attitudes of the time and to consider policies in the light of other influences – whether political, economic or ideological. Historians have, after all, made a case for the positive as well as negative impact of the slave trade on West Africa; a 'value-free' assessment of late nineteenth-century imperial policies should be no more difficult than this. On the other hand, the negative reputation of imperialism may well affect more overtly economic interpretations and lead to sympathetic reconsideration of Marxist views and of the arguments of Hobson.

There is always likely to be a divergence between an infrastructural approach and one based more on the direct influence of the individual statesman. There are, however, problems with each which help to promote variations *within* each. Where, for example, does the infrastructural approach allow for decision-making channels? What is the mechanism by which long-term economic developments convert into specific events? When does the impersonal become personal? There is a multiplicity of possible answers to these questions, which ensures that Marxist history-writing maintains a diversity that seems to belie any monolithic base: there are, for example, considerable differences between explanations advanced by Lenin and Hobsbawm. A similar diversity exists when assuming a top-down approach, attributing changes to key decisions made by individual politicians. What are their motives – and how do these relate to longer-term trends and influences? Does policy-making mean imposing their stamp on a situation or making the best of a confusing set of options? Or could there be a mixed approach, allowing for the complex interaction of infrastructural forces and political responses, with the individual able to influence both?

A particular strength of the method used by Robinson and Gallagher is that the 'pull' of local factors (such as proto-nationalism in Egypt and South Africa, fundamentalism in the Sudan, and capitalist enterprise everywhere) can be identified with particular representatives acting as outlets (Arabi Pasha, Kruger, the Mahdi, Rhodes and many others). These forces – and individuals – in turn affected national governments, with individuals like Disraeli and Gladstone reacting to local threats in a way which would, they hoped, protect Britain's key trade routes and strategic interests. 'Top-down' and 'bottom-up' exert a mutual influence in a variety of ways which have already led to Robinson developing several different lines of argument in a reconsideration of his own work. Historiography, therefore, is not based just on the way in which one historian, or 'school', revises the work of another. It can also include a trend which is beginning to expand: internal revisionism. The historian's right to rethink is therefore becoming as firmly established as the right to original hypothesis.

Questions

1. 'Beyond their control.' Is that how historians have seen 'imperialism' during the era of Gladstone and Disraeli?
2. Which is considered the more genuine: Disraeli's 'imperialism' or Gladstone's 'anti-imperialism'?

SOURCES

1. PROBLEMS IN THE EMPIRE

Source 1: A cartoon from *Judy* (sister paper to *Punch*), 1879. The caption (not included) reads: 'If they will irritate him, they must take the consequences'.

See Figure 6.

Source 2: From Edgar Feuchtwanger, *Disraeli*, published in 2000.

Disaster first struck in South Africa, the defeat and destruction at Isandhlwana of Lord Chelmsford's force of 1200 men in January 1879. . . .

Then, on 3 September, disaster also struck in Afghanistan, with the slaughter of the British mission under Sir Louis Cavagnari. Lytton, exceeding his orders from London, had forced his mission on the amir. Disraeli criticised him in private, but fully backed him in his Guildhall speech in November 1879. Disraeli felt that situations had been allowed to arise in South Africa and Afghanistan which he had not intended and which could not be fully controlled from London. His style of government was to set general orientations and let his subordinates get on with it.

Source 3: From a private letter from Disraeli to Lord Cranbrook, Secretary of State for India, 26 September 1878.

I am not satisfied with the position, as nothing could justify Lytton's course except he was prepared to act, and was in a situation which justified the responsibility of disobeying the orders of HM Government.

He was told to wait until we had received the answer from Russia to our remonstrance. I was very strong on this, having good reasons for my opinion. He disobeyed us. . . . He was told to send the Mission by Candahar. He has sent it by the Khyber, and received a snub, which it may cost us much to wipe away.

When V-Roys and Comms-in-chief disobey orders, they ought to be sure of success in their mutiny. Lytton, by disobeying orders, has only secured insult and failure. . . .

Figure 6.

Source 4: From a speech made by Disraeli (now Earl of Beaconsfield) in the House of Lords, 10 December 1878.

What was our difficulty with regard to Afghanistan? We could gain no information as to what was going on beyond the mountain range or what was preparing in the numerous valleys of Afghanistan. What we wanted, therefore, was eyes to see and ears to hear, and we should have attained our object had the Ameer made to us those concessions which are commonly granted by all civilised States, and which even some Oriental states do not deny us – namely, to have a minister at his capital – a demand which we did not press – and men like our consuls-general at some of his chief towns. That virtually would have been a rectification of our frontier, because we should have got rid of those obstacles that rendered it utterly impossible for us to conduct public affairs with any knowledge of the circumstances with which we had to deal as regarded Afghanistan. . . .

Source 5: Extracts from the speeches of Gladstone's Midlothian campaign, 1879.

We have made war on the Zulus. We have therefore become responsible for their territory; and not only this, but we are now, as it appears from the latest advices, about to make war on a chief lying to the northward of the Zulus; and Sir Bartle Frere . . . has announced in South Africa that it will be necessary for us to extend our dominions until we reach the Portuguese frontier to the north. . . .

Well, and as if that were not enough, we have, by the most wanton invasion of Afghanistan, broken that country into pieces, made it a miserable ruin, destroyed whatever there was in it of peace and order, caused it to be added to the anarchies of the Eastern world, and we have become responsible for the management of the millions of warlike but very partially civilised people whom it contains. . . .

Source 6: From a speech made by Liberal MP Sir Wilfred Lawson, in July 1882, criticising Gladstone's policy in Egypt.

He [Lawson] always thought that the present Government had been put in power to alter the Tory policy, and now the argument was that they must go the same way as the Tories began.

Questions

1. Explain the significance of the cartoon and caption in Source 1. (3)
2. Use your own knowledge to explain why Gladstone was attacking Disraeli's imperial policies in 1879 (Source 5). (5)

3. How far does the information in Sources 3 and 4 confirm the view expressed in Source 2? (5)
4. Compare Sources 5 and 6 in terms of their value in the study of the imperial policies of Gladstone. (5)
5. 'In reality, there was very little difference between the imperial policies of Disraeli's Conservatives and Gladstone's Liberals.' How far do Sources 1 to 6, and your knowledge, confirm this view? (12)

Total (30)

2. INTERPRETATIONS OF MOTIVES FOR EMPIRE

Source 7: From an article by Gladstone, 'England's Mission', written in 1878.

Between the two parties in this controversy there is a perfect agreement that England has a mighty mission in the world; but there is a discord as fundamental upon the question what that mission is.

With one party, her first care is held to be the care of her own children within her own shores, the redress of wrongs, the supply of needs, the improvement of laws and institutions. Against this home-spun doctrine, the present Government appears to set up territorial aggrandisement and the accumulation of a multitude of fictitious interests abroad, as if our real interests were not enough.

Source 8: From a speech made by Disraeli at Crystal Palace in 1872.

If you look at the history of this country since the advent of Liberalism – forty years ago – you will find that there has been no effort so continuous, so subtle, supported by so much energy, and carried on with so much ability and acumen, as the attempts of Liberalism to effect the disintegration of the Empire of England. And, gentlemen, of all its efforts, this is the one which has been the nearest to success. It has been shown . . . that there never was a jewel in the Crown of England that was so truly costly as the possession of India. How often has it been suggested that we should at once emancipate ourselves from this costly incubus.

Source 9: From Denis Judd, *Empire: The British Imperial Experience, from 1765 to the Present*, published in 1996.

Supported by many elements within Egyptian society, from constitutional liberals to landlords, and including Muslim traditionalists and the long-suffering peasantry, Urabi Pasha and his junta of colonels continued to wring a series of constitutional concessions from the newly appointed Anglo-French puppet Khedive, Taufiq. When, in 1882, Urabi became Minister for War, and one of his supporters Prime Minister, Anglo-French interests were faced with a thorny choice.

The recently elected Liberal administration in Britain, led by Gladstone, vacillated as to the best response. The Prime Minister himself was genuinely ambivalent in his attitude. On the one hand, he recognised the strength of Egyptian nationalist sentiment; on the other, he felt bound to uphold British interests in the Suez route. It is, however, worth noting that Gladstone, like many in his party – the prominent Radical M.P. Henry Labouchere, for instance – had a private financial interest to consider as well as the well-advertised public ones. Some 37 per cent of the Prime Minister's investment portfolio was sunk in Egyptian shares. Although initially his Cabinet seemed dangerously divided on the issue, it is therefore perhaps not surprising that the interventionists, strongly and perhaps unexpectedly supported by the extreme Radical Joseph Chamberlain, soon gained the upper hand.

When Anglo-French diplomatic pressure and a naval demonstration off Alexandria failed to overawe the Urabi government, the propaganda machines of both countries began to paint a lurid and misleading picture of what they perceived as the 'Egyptian crisis'. It was asserted, despite the lack of concrete evidence, that the Suez Canal was unsafe in Egyptian hands. When rioting in Alexandria in June 1882 resulted in the death of some forty Europeans, British and French newspaper reports produced horrendous and largely fictitious accounts of violent disorders that had allegedly left up to three hundred Europeans dead.

Its collective mind now made up by reports of the Alexandria riots and by the pressure and clamour of alarmed British investors and Suez Canal Company shareholders, the Gladstone Cabinet decided on military intervention.

Source 10: From R. Robinson and G. Gallagher, *Africa and the Victorians*, published in 1961.

Until the Eighteen eighties, British political expansion had been positive, in the sense that it went on bringing valuable areas into her orbit. That of the late-Victorians in the so-called 'Age of Imperialism' was by comparison negative, both in purpose and achievement. It was largely concerned with defending the maturing inheritance of the mid-Victorian imperialism of free trade, not with opening fresh fields of substantial importance to the economy. Whereas the earlier Victorians could afford to concentrate on the extension of free trade, their successors were compelled to look above all to the preservation of what they held since they were coming to suspect that Britain's power was not what it once had been. The early Victorians had been playing from strength. The supremacy they had built in the world had been the work of confidence and faith in the future. The African empire of their successors was the product of fear lest this great heritage should be lost in the time of troubles ahead.

Because it went far ahead of commercial expansion and imperial ambition, because its aims were essentially defensive and strategic, the movement into Africa remained superficial. The partition of tropical Africa might seem impressive on the wall maps of the Foreign Office. Yet it was at the time an empty and theoretical expansion. That British governments before 1900 did very little to pacify, administer and develop their spheres of influence and protectorates, shows once again the weakness of any commercial and imperial motives for claiming them. The partition did not accompany, it preceded the invasion of tropical Africa by the trader, the planter and the official. It was the prelude to European occupation; it was not that occupation itself.

Questions

1. Compare the arguments used by Gladstone and Disraeli in Sources 7 and 8 to attack each other's imperial policies. (15)
2. 'The key factor in the imperial policies of both Gladstone and Disraeli was economic.' How far do Sources 7 to 10, and your own knowledge, support this view? (30)

Total (45)

7

IRELAND

BACKGROUND

Ireland had been connected constitutionally to Great Britain (i.e. England and Wales plus Scotland) by the Act of Union in 1800. In the process she lost her own parliament, instead represented at Westminster through 100 MPs in the House of Commons, along with 28 temporal peers and 4 bishops in the House of Lords. The administration in Dublin was appointed directly by the British government. This raised a number of key problems which in one way or another challenged Gladstone and Disraeli throughout their political careers. The difference in their approaches was that one eventually tried to meet the challenge, while the other consistently avoided it (see Analysis 1). Whether Gladstone's response was entirely altruistic is considered in Analysis 2.

Three main issues emerged from the Act of Union. The first was religious: pressure for Catholic emancipation and for the admission of Catholic MPs into Westminster. The second was political, with the focus on the repeal of the Act of Union. The third was economic, the problem being the poverty of the majority of the population and exploitation by the small landlord elite. Initially distinct from each other, these gradually became intertwined.

The period up to 1830 was dominated by the struggle for Catholic Emancipation. Initially strongly opposed to admitting Catholics to Westminster, the Tory government backed down in response to the escalating campaign of the Irish Catholic leader Daniel O'Connell and the consequent threat of civil war. In 1829 the Catholic Emancipation Act was guided through the House of Commons by Peel (then Home Secretary) and through the Lords by the Duke of Wellington (Prime Minister 1828–30). Gladstone and Disraeli both started their parliamentary careers in the decade after this development (in 1832 and 1837 respectively). Neither, however, showed any sympathy for the further extension of Catholic rights, both supporting the entrenched position of Anglicanism in Ireland.

During the 1830s there was a relative hiatus in the Irish problem, largely because O'Connell's supporters in Ireland allied themselves with the Whig governments of Grey (1830–4) and Melbourne (1835–41) to deliver a series of much needed social and financial reforms. From 1840, however, pressure again began to build up – this time for the repeal of the Act of Union and the re-establishment of an Irish legislature. The backlash of this was felt by Peel (Prime Minister 1841–6), who refused to consider any political change and had O'Connell detained for a year on the charge of conspiracy in 1844. He subsequently moderated his approach and in 1845 sought to mollify Irish opinion by increasing the annual government grant to Maynooth College, a Catholic seminary, from £9,000 to £26,000. At this point Gladstone resigned his post of President of the Board of Trade in protest against the concession. This was to be a defining moment in his career and he later acknowledged that he had been mistaken. Certainly after 1845 Gladstone became more tolerant of other forms of Christianity, including Catholicism.

Part of the reason for this was the rapidly deteriorating economic situation in Ireland. The potato famine, which started in 1845, brought mass starvation. Peel's remedy was to press ahead with the repeal of the Corn Laws in the hope that this would remove 'all impediments' to the import of food. In this he was strongly opposed by Disraeli, who argued that the potato famine was being used as an excuse to push through a policy on which Peel had already decided. Gladstone, by contrast, was sufficiently moved by Ireland's plight to support the repeal and to follow Peel into political exile in 1846. During the period of his political realignment (1846–66) he became increasingly conscious of the need to find a permanent solution to the Irish problem. Disraeli, by contrast, kept the focus on the status quo rather than on reform.

The problem became worse during the late 1850s and the 1860s as opposition to British rule intensified. This now took two forms. One was moderate pressure for land reform in Ireland by, for example, the Irish Tenant League. The other was a new and more radical development – Fenianism – which aimed at nothing less than a complete constitutional break with Britain and the establishment of an Irish Republic. Disraeli condemned both as an attack on British sovereignty; Gladstone showed some sympathy with the moderate objectives while rejecting Fenian aims. His initial focus was on land reform and on the reform of the Irish Church (the Anglican religious establishment in Ireland) rather than on any change in Ireland's constitutional status. His priority was already clear in outline when he was summoned in 1868 to form his first government: his mission, he said, was 'to pacify Ireland'.

Hopeful of cooperation from moderate opinion in Ireland, Gladstone immediately pushed through the Irish Church Act (1869). This disestablished the Anglican Church in Ireland and redirected much of its property into endowing schools, hospitals and workhouses. It was strongly opposed by the Conservatives, Disraeli suggesting as an alternative the concurrent endowment of both Protestant and Catholic churches. Gladstone's second measure was the Irish Land Act (1870), which prevented landlords from charging their tenants 'exorbitant' rents and provided for the payment of compensation to any evicted tenants who had improved their holdings. But, although the provisions of the Act could be referred to the courts, there was some difficulty in their precise definition (see Analysis 1), which resulted in widespread dissatisfaction. The remainder of Gladstone's first ministry saw few further reforms, the emphasis switching to coercion to control violence. Between 1874 and 1880 Disraeli's Conservative government focused on less controversial issues. For example, it provided, from the funds formerly belonging to the Irish Church, endowments for a number of Irish schools and for the Royal University of Ireland. The late 1870s, however, brought economic depression to Irish agriculture – a combination of a potato blight and competition from cheap grain from North America. As a result landlords sought to rationalise their agricultural production, which meant the eviction of more tenants than ever.

By the time that Gladstone returned to power in 1880 powerful pressure was building up from two directions. One was the Land

League which, under Michael Davitt, pressed the claims of the Irish tenants. The other was the Home Rule Party, to which Parnell gave an overtly political agenda. Gladstone's second ministry (1880–5) alternated between attempted reforms, like the second Land Act (1881), and further measures of coercion, including the imprisonment of Parnell and other Irish leaders. By 1885 Parnell had succeeded in uniting the eighty-five Irish Nationalist MPs behind the cause of Home Rule – or devolved power – for Ireland. They showed their collective strength by turning Gladstone out of government.

But not for long. Following a brief Conservative spell, under Lord Salisbury, Gladstone formed his third ministry in 1886. Shortly before his return to power Gladstone took the decision to back the cause of Irish Home Rule and to make it an integral part of future Liberal policy. The reason for this is still open to debate, with explanations ranging from altruistic conversion to opportunist adjustment (see Analysis 2). Whatever the reason, Gladstone pursued his new objective with remarkable energy. The First Home Rule Bill, introduced into Parliament in April 1886, provided for an Irish Parliament in Dublin, along with Irish executive control of all issues except for foreign affairs, external trade and defence. It was, however, defeated in the Commons by 343 votes to 313; although supported by the Irish Nationalists, it caused a major split in Liberal ranks as 93 Liberal 'Unionists' voted alongside the Conservatives to retain British control. The subsequent election brought heavy defeat and six years of Conservative rule. Salisbury's approach to Ireland was a combination of coercion and land reform, along the lines of what Gladstone had already tried and abandoned.

Home Rule was given a further chance in 1892, when Gladstone formed his fourth ministry after the election of 273 Liberals and 81 Irish Nationalists – against 268 Conservatives and 47 Liberal Unionists. The Second Irish Home Rule Bill, introduced in 1893, was energetically pressed by Gladstone, even though he was now 83. It passed through the Commons by 309 votes to 267 – only to be vetoed by the Lords by 419 votes to 41. The impact on the Liberal party was so serious that Home Rule was downgraded in importance. As 'Gladstonian Liberalism' evolved after 1900 into 'New Liberalism', Ireland became one of many issues and took second place to reform. It was not until 1912 that the Gladstonian solution was revived.

ANALYSIS 1: DID DISRAELI GIVE THE CONSERVATIVE PARTY 'A POLICY ON IRELAND'?

During the 1880s and 1890s the Conservative party under Salisbury and Balfour developed a policy over Ireland which was an obvious alternative to that of Gladstone. Whereas the Liberals made Home Rule their target, the Conservative approach was based on maintaining the union between Britain and Ireland while developing local administrative reform and land purchase. Whether this approach was directly inherited from Disraeli is controversial. All of the ingredients would have been known to Disraeli and were partly shaped by him. But the way in which he used them was probably too opportunistic and reactive to enable them to be called a policy. What was really needed to shape them into a policy was the pressure of Home Rule, which Disraeli had anticipated but did not live to see.

The Conservative policy towards Ireland emerged most clearly, from 1885 onwards, as a combination of concessions and firm government. The Crimes Act of 1887 increased police powers to deal with disturbances in Ireland and made possible the suspension of trial by jury. The 1891 Land Purchase Act provided government aid to help peasants buy land. In 1891 the Congested Areas Board was also set up to help finance improvements such as drainage, fencing and farming methods. This was, of course, largely in response to Gladstone's policy of Home Rule. The Conservative response was to maintain the union while increasing the commitment to reform and improvement. It was certainly a departure from earlier opposition to all reform.

Yet there are some traces of Disraeli in all this. Disraeli showed a personal progression from prejudice to a more genuine understanding of the Irish problem, which he bequeathed to his party. The bigotry shown in his attacks on the Irish people in his *Runnymede Letters* (1836) had given way by 1844 to a concern about 'a starving population, an absentee aristocracy, and an alien church, and in addition the weakest executive in the world'.[1] Similarly, he moved from outright opposition to Peel's Maynooth Grant (1845) to acceptance of Bentinck's 1847 scheme for reform based on the endowment of the Catholic Church, compensation to tenants for improvements of land, action to penalise absentee landlords, and improvement of infrastructure. Although Disraeli was not yet ready to risk the fragile unity of the Conservative party by pursuing them, they were ideas which returned in the 1860s, 1870s and 1880s. In 1868, for example, Disraeli opposed Gladstone's bill to disestablish the Irish Church, proposing as an alternative the concurrent endowment of the Catholic Church in Ireland. This became an integral part of later

Conservative policy, although it has to be said that their proposals for land reform were based rather more on the position abandoned by the Liberals in their quest for Home Rule than upon any precedents established by Disraeli.

Disraeli therefore left a fingerprint, rather than a seal, on the Irish policy which emerged during the 1880s. He did, however, provide a strong influence on the strategy of the Conservative party over Ireland, or the policy used by the Conservatives in their struggle against the Liberals. Disraeli made Ireland a key issue in the wake of the 1867 Reform Act and projected the general election of 1868 as 'a great Protestant struggle'.[2] He had calculated that an anti-Irish appeal would be sufficient to win over the new working-class voters enfranchised in 1867 – but it worked only in the Lancashire constituencies and he actually lost the election by 110 seats. He launched a similar offensive before the 1874 election, accusing the Liberals of wanting 'to despoil Churches and plunder landlords, and what has been the result? Sedition rampant, treason thinly veiled.' He was careful to connect this to a broad domestic attack: 'Not satisfied with the spoliation and anarchy of Ireland, they began to attack every institution and every interest, every class and calling in the Country.'[3] This was much more successful, and Disraeli succeeded Gladstone as Prime Minister. By 1880 he had developed another theme, warning the country that the Liberals were about to introduce a policy of Home Rule. This meant that Gladstone would be collaborating with Irish nationalism as part of an attempt to 'enfeeble our colonies by a policy of decomposition'.[4] Although he lost the 1880 election, Disraeli had provided the Conservatives with their key argument against Home Rule. Since he died in 1881, however, he never saw it fully used.

Emphasising that Ireland was an imperial as well as a domestic issue had a double benefit. It reminded the Conservatives that they were a party which would protect the 'Empire' and 'institutions', as well as improving 'the condition of the people'. Churchill, Balfour and Salisbury used Disraeli's combination to appeal directly to dissident Liberals. They continued Disraeli's ideas and reforms as a combination of 'Tory Democracy' and 'unionism'. This exercised a powerful pull on the anti-Home Rulers within the Liberal party, who felt that they were able to go with their political conscience on an imperial issue without entirely abandoning the prospect of social reform. This meant that seventy-seven Liberal Unionists backed Conservative policies after 1886 and that some, like Chamberlain, eventually crossed the floor to join the Conservative party. Salisbury's Conservatives therefore effectively refined a strategy, put together by Disraeli in the pre-Home Rule era, into a policy for the Conservative party *over* Ireland – rather than *for* Ireland.

We should, however, be careful not to attribute *too* much to Disraeli. Although he did pass on strategies on Ireland, these were often negative rather than positive and based on opposition to the ideas of others rather than formulation of his own. His attacks were often vitriolic and destructive, as in the debate on the Maynooth Grant (1845). He could also be dismissive – as in 1846 when he accused Peel of exaggerating the famine in Ireland to secure the repeal of the Corn Laws. He opposed Gladstone's First and Second Land Acts and any measures relating to the Irish Church. Nor was he particularly constructive while in office, considering other priorities to be much more important. Shannon argues that 'In 1874 Disraeli deliberately relegated Ireland to its obscure recess at the back of the political stage whence Gladstone had dramatically removed and spotlighted it in 1868.'[5] Why, it might be asked, did he not use at least some of his time in power (1874–80) to apply some of Bentinck's earlier solutions – with which he had, after all, sympathised? The time would certainly have been appropriate. Ireland was, in the late 1870s, in the grip of depression and a third of the population were severely distressed. Disraeli tended to listen to what he wanted to hear – such as the view of his Chancellor of the Exchequer (Northcote). 'The distress is, I should think, very much exaggerated' and there would no doubt be pressure for 'doing the Exchequer out of some public money'.[6] Pressure was even put on Disraeli's government to start a land purchase scheme: Charles Gordon – later killed at Khartoum – suggested buying up the landlords for £40 million. Land purchase was eventually to be taken seriously by the Conservatives – but not yet. During this government most Conservative ministers favoured either doing nothing at all or providing mild relief measures, using any surplus endowments from 1869. This hardly amounts to a sustained policy.

On the whole, therefore, Disraeli had ideas about Ireland but was less interested in developing them into policies *for* Ireland than in exploiting party differences *over* Ireland. Disraeli's successors equipped the strategy of opposing the Liberals with a policy based on alternatives to Home Rule. Disraeli might well have done this himself had he lived into the Home Rule era. As it was, he left indicators but without directions. This was probably because he was never convinced that Ireland was important in its own right.

ANALYSIS 2: HOW HAVE HISTORIANS INTERPRETED THE REASONS FOR AND EFFECTS OF GLADSTONE'S PURSUIT OF THE POLICY OF HOME RULE FOR IRELAND?

Gladstone opted for Home Rule in 1885, after trying a number of other approaches to the Irish problem, including land reform and coercion bills. Following this, the most important decision of his career, he introduced two Home Rule bills. The first was defeated in the House of Commons in 1886 by 343 votes (cast by Conservatives and Liberal Unionists) to 313 (Liberals and Irish Nationalists). The second passed through the Commons in 1893 but was overwhelmingly rejected by the Lords by 419 to 41. Since the issue dominated party politics for a decade it is hardly surprising that there has been so much controversy about it. This analysis shows a wider range of viewpoints than for any of Gladstone's other policies.

The first explanation of Gladstone's decision to adopt Home Rule as a policy, advanced by both British and Irish historians, can be described as his 'conversion through conviction'. Having tried other measures, he came to the conclusion that a more fundamental solution had to be found to deal with all aspects of the Irish problem. This view is based on the belief that Gladstone had a positive regard for Ireland; according to Hammond, for example, 'what distinguished him . . . was that from first to last he thought of the Irish as a people, and he held that the ultimate test of a policy was whether or not it helped this people to satisfy its self-respect and to find its dignity and happiness in its self-governing life'. Gladstone was convinced that the spirit of Irish nationalism had to be accommodated, a view which was entirely consistent with his earlier sympathies for Italian and Polish nationalism. If, he pointed out, Britain was to avoid the reputation for repression which had attached itself to Austria and Russia, then Ireland must be liberated. This would, in turn, safeguard the future of Britain's wider role in the world. 'Within this vast Empire there is but one spot where the people are discontented with their relation to the central power. That spot is Ireland.' Gladstone arrived at this point of view, Hammond argued, because he was prepared to accept the need for conversion; he 'was the largest-minded man of his age' and his policy over Ireland was 'a superb example of magnanimity'.[1] Despite its record of failure, therefore, the Home Rule policy shows Gladstone at his very best.

To these views can be added similarly favourable comments from Irish writers. O'Hegarty associated Gladstone with Parnell as the twin sources of all that was positive in Britain and Ireland. 'They two dominated the House of Commons while they lived, and they dominate the history of that period now they are dead.' Gladstone knew 'that he was risking his peace of mind, his health, his Party, but only he and Parnell, only they two in Parliament, only they two in these two islands, knew that the moment was pregnant with the fate of Nations'.[2] Mansergh was similarly laudatory: 'Mr Gladstone was the only English statesman of this epoch who made a positive contribution, so ambitious in character as to aim at a final settlement of the Irish Question.'[3]

A second category of explanation, one which perhaps emerges from the first, was Gladstone's conversion through *persuasion*. Again, this has a strong Irish influence. Gladstone still gets much of the credit – but needed to be persuaded that Ireland had been the victim all along. According to MacDonagh: 'Gladstone, the very pivot of mid-Victorian politics, the principal heir of both Cobdenite and Peelite political traditions, and the destined captain of reform for two decades still had to be moved to act, not by direct pressure, but by conviction that he was correcting an original and historical injustice.'[4] Hence it was not a matter of high-mindedness alone, but also a response to pressure. It was Parnell who tipped the scales to Home Rule – through 'the concentration of all nationalist, separatist and Catholic forces upon a single leader'. This was decisive 'in including Gladstone and later the bulk of his cabinet and party to commit themselves to Home Rule'.[5] Caught in a dilemma, argued Foster, Gladstone discovered a justification for something he simply had to do. Hence, 'in full moral cry, he projected a rather unconvincing retrospective continuity, presenting his "mission to pacify Ireland" as consistent since the 1860s. In fact, he had moved through a series of energetic but short-term reactions to immediate political problems.'[6]

There is a third – and very different – explanation. Gladstone was motivated by '*convenience*', rather than by 'conviction' or 'persuasion', into doing something which was essentially pragmatic and opportunist. According to Vincent, 'Gladstone did not idealize the Irish'. Far from adopting a positive and generous view of their needs, he subordinated them to his own political requirement. This was no less than a fundamental realignment of support behind him within the Liberal party. Vincent argued that 'What Gladstone was doing was not passing Home Rule, but carrying out the reorganisation of party structure.'[7] Hamer seemed to go along with this: 'Gladstone's reaction to the growing disorganization of Liberal politics was characteristic: he became increasingly interested in the possibility of discovering a new unifying policy, a policy which would "organize the action of the Liberal Party".' Gladstone therefore believed that what the party needed was 'concentration on a single subordinating issue'. In his analysis, 'it was Ireland that began to emerge as the great cause that might control and subordinate all other political questions and thus create order out of the prevailing chaos'.[8] Little did Gladstone know that his policy was to deepen the very crisis within the party that he was trying to overcome.

The final view is that there was *no real change at all*. Gladstone progressed quite logically from measures aimed to reform land tenure to a policy of Home Rule. According to Loughlin, 'the relationship between the land and Home Rule bills was not haphazard . . . Gladstone conceived both bills as vitally related parts of one comprehensive scheme aimed at solving the Irish problem'. Furthermore, 'Gladstone had been convinced in 1882 that a comprehensive solution to the land question necessitated some kind of local government authority to actually put it into effect.' The combined land and Home Rule schemes, therefore, were designed to achieve a new settlement, based on Irish autonomy and with the 'removal of the land issue as a source of social strife'.[9] This, in Gladstone's mind, would have the additional advantage of restoring the landlord to a fully responsible role within the Irish hierarchy, an indication of the more conservative influences upon his thinking. This argument was supported by Boyce, who maintains that Gladstone's policy 'was shaped by his overall purpose, to restore the Irish gentry to their rightful place in Irish politics'.[10] This would protect the interests of the minorities as well as the rest – but in a social and not a sectarian context.

Biagini pointed to another traditional appeal made by Gladstone – that of 'local patriotism', which was evident in Scotland and Wales as well as Ireland, recognition of which was more likely to hold the United Kingdom together than to break it up. Gladstone therefore 'tried to establish a system which would require no further external intervention and which could be operated by the Irish, for their own benefit, within the British Empire'.[11]

Connected to the motivation for Home Rule is the issue of whether it was actually *realistic*. Two strongly contrasting views are evident here. On the one hand, Feuchtwanger maintained that it was not – because it failed entirely to take into account the influences within Ireland for maintaining the union with Britain. 'Gladstone was hardly aware yet that there was a separate Ulster problem and he was certainly not prepared to accept any Ulster veto on a separate Irish Parliament.'[12] He succeeded only in provoking the organisation of Ulster after 1885 on sectarian lines, a process which was deliberately exploited by Lord Randolph Churchill and the Conservatives who, in Churchill's words, went on to 'play the Orange card'. In contrast to this, Boyce believed that Gladstone actually thought a great deal about the problem of minority opinion in Ireland, although he was unable to resolve it. Gladstone was in a good position to understand the religious uncertainty faced by Irish Protestants in a sea of Catholicism. He had himself rejected in 1874 the Pope's power 'to make any claim upon those who adhered to his communion of such a nature as to impair the integrity of the civil allegiance'.[13] But he believed that Home Rule 'would end the quarrel of centuries'.[14] A key element in this reconciliation would be the recovery by the landed gentry of their responsible 'role in Irish political society'. Thus, 'The lesson from history was plain: create a moderate home rule parliament, possessing moderate powers of self-government . . . and the Irish gentry would find their positive, eighteenth-century role restored, and their future life in Ireland stabilised.'[15] The anti-Home Rulers did not, therefore, know their true interest. Gladstone did consider other options, which included the exclusion of Ulster – or a portion of Ulster – from Home Rule, the autonomy of Ulster, and the reservation of provincial powers on issues such as education. Although he considered none of them to be sufficiently important, he could hardly be said to have ignored the minority issue altogether.

What was the impact of Home Rule?

As in the case of Gladstone's original motives, there is a wide diversity of opinions on the effect of the Home Rule campaign, both on the Liberal party and on Ireland.

The first approach is that it inflicted *massive damage*, especially on the Liberal party. Feuchtwanger acknowledged Gladstone's heroic effort. 'But it was largely due to Gladstone's personality and his handling of the Home Rule crisis that so deep, damaging and lasting a split occurred in the Liberal ranks. In this lay the obverse of his greatness and his genius.' In addition, 'The continuing presence of Gladstone's towering figure until 1894 made the emergence of new leaders and new ideas much more difficult.'[16] Parry painted a picture of similar destruction, although he was more pointed as to where the blame lay. 'Gladstone was fascinated as well as repelled by the power concentrated in the modern state. He had to dominate. His crusades were the product of the clash between his religious conscience and his obsession with power: power to dictate events, power to smash opponents across the floor of the Commons, and power to sway a vast audience. Gladstone could not let power go.'[17] Shannon believed that the result of Gladstone's leadership was the 'ruin of Radicalism'; the Liberal party, with Chamberlain's withdrawal in 1886, was diverted 'from its logical path' which was to be a party 'under predominantly Radical inspiration and control'.[18]

An alternative way of assessing the damage inflicted by Home Rule is to consider its *interaction with other factors*. 'Ireland had become the cuckoo in the nest, crowding out the measures with which Parliament should have been occupying itself at a time when restive social discontent was strongly marked.'[19] This meant that the impetus for social reform passed from the hands of Gladstone to those of Chamberlain. But Ireland intervened again: because of the strength of his views over Home Rule, Chamberlain eventually made common cause with the Conservatives, even joining Salisbury's ministry in 1895 as Colonial Secretary. The Liberal party therefore lost a major impetus to reform and, until the Irish issue was dropped, it proved incapable of making constructive use of what was left of its radical wing. Once Ireland receded in importance, radicalism returned to Liberalism, revitalised it and enabled it to defeat a Conservative party which, in turn, had become divided over the issue of tariff reform. By this argument, therefore, Gladstone diverted his own reforming energies and lost the radicals – both because of his obsession with one issue above all others.

An altogether different approach would be that the Irish issue actually made little difference – because Gladstone was in any case becoming increasingly conservative by comparison with the radical wing of the party. He has been seen by some historians as innately traditionalist in his views and instinctively opposed to the more radical proposals of Chamberlain. His Home Rule solution was in keeping with this conservatism since he expected the Irish landowning class to re-establish itself as the natural ruling elite and for the rest of the Irish population to restore its deferential links with it. Home Rule would force the land-owners to re-examine their attitudes and to justify their political influence, just as the various Reform Acts had forced the British landowning classes to come to terms with an enlarged electorate. But the same principle applied: that enlightened land ownership was a sound basis for order, stability and deference. By this argument, Gladstone's adoption of the single-issue approach did not make a great deal of difference to the Liberal party since he had already moved substantially away from the radical wing on British issues.

So far we have moved across the spectrum of effects from direct damage, through indirect damage to little difference. The fourth position is the opposite of the first: that the impact of the Home Rule campaign, unsuccessful though it proved, was *beneficial* both to the Liberals and to Ireland. Biagini argued that Home Rule acted as a uniting cause as much as a divisive one. In Britain it attracted widespread interest and 'there is evidence to suggest that popular support for Home Rule was culturally deeper, and politically much more significant, than has hitherto been conceded'.[20] For example, most working-class and Lib-Lab candidates endorsed it. It was also popular in Scotland, which had its aspirations for devolution as a prerequisite for social reform. 'Thus, Ireland, far from being regarded as a "special case", became a testing ground for the viability of new reform policies.'[21] There was also a nationalist influence in Wales which showed up strongly in the Liberal organisations. 'In focusing on Home Rule Gladstone provided his Scottish and Welsh supporters with an issue on which "old" and "new" Liberals could combine efforts.'[22] The national and religious influences in the United Kingdom were actually more important than class allegiances, which meant that the Liberals were able to keep a firm grip on the Celtic fringe. As late as December 1910, they still won fifty-eight seats in Scotland (compared with nine Conservative and three Labour). Far from letting Labour in through the Liberal split, Home Rule consolidated the Liberals in the Celtic fringe and held up the rise of Labour by several decades.

The unsuccessful Home Rule campaign also brought benefits to Ireland. According to Eversley (writing in 1912), it established the strongest case 'in favour of conceding autonomy in domestic legislation to Ireland'.[23] When finally accomplished, it would be primarily due to Gladstone's efforts. Thirty-six years later, Hammond made the same point, now in retrospect rather than in anticipation. Gladstone's policy was, he argued, a vital contribution to a long process: 'he used the democratic forces created by the second and third Reform Bills to break down the prejudices that had governed England's treatment of Ireland during two thirds of the nineteenth century'.[24] Boyce's perspective was similar, even though from 2000: 'If politics are about creating new contexts, providing new ways of thinking, then Gladstone was remarkably important in his attitude to Ireland.'[25]

Why have views differed?

Many of the comments made on the historiography of Gladstone in the other chapters would be relevant here as well. But there is a particular challenge in considering Gladstone within the context of Home Rule. Depending on our historian, our eyes are opened to a man of high principles (or low calculation) who chose (or stumbled on) a crusade (or strategy) called Home Rule, with disastrous (or beneficial) effects for the Liberal party and for Ireland – assuming, that is, that he made any impact at all. Which Gladstone are we actually looking at; and which issue – within which context?

The easiest way to explain differences over interpretations concerning Home Rule would be to attribute them to political influences on each side of a very high fence; Anglo-Irish relations are, after all, riddled with conflicting attitudes. This may have been true of the opening decade of the twentieth century and of the period after the establishment of the Irish Free State, but it becomes much less significant by the final third of the century. The strong pro-Gladstone slant shown by Irish writers of the turn of the century – like McCarthy and O'Connor – can to an extent be explained by the prevailing hope for a free Ireland which they clearly shared. Gladstone's campaign would also have been a recent political memory, with the long-term resolution still in the balance. In some cases the political influence would have lasted well beyond the achievement of independence because there was still the unresolved issue of partition. This helps to explain the approach taken by Hegarty, who saw Gladstone as the Englishman standing up to an establishment which eventually left a separate Northern Ireland as a legacy of its blindness. It is also significant that Hegarty was active in Sinn Fein when he wrote his comments.

But establishing 'political' credentials can be *too* easy. In many cases it would be poor historiographical comment on good history-writing. Modern historians go to considerable lengths to avoid polemical approaches based on political stereotypes, fearing perhaps to be connected with the stereotype as much as with polemicism. Current writers on Ireland – whether Irish or British – steer clear of 'value-based' assessments: this applies especially to MacDonagh, Foster, Loughlin and Boyce, all of whom write with edge without grinding an axe.

More significant in their case is the *type* of book they are writing rather than any intended slant. This could, in fact, be seen as another key influence on how Gladstone is assessed. One way of finding a broadstream view of a controversial figure is to see how the figure is handled in a book about something else. Some of the extracts used above were taken from more general histories (such as *Ireland in the Age of Reform and Revolution, Ireland: The Union and its Aftermath* or even *Modern Ireland, 1600–1972*). These are more likely to provide originality through the broad sweep rather than within the individual parts. When the timescale is more limited and the subject more precise, originality comes through more detailed connections being made within the subject. 'Gladstone' is smaller than the 'History of Ireland', but 'Home Rule' is more precise than 'Gladstone' and the implications for the 'landowners' or 'Ulster' or the 'Liberals' more so than 'Home Rule'. This all has a bearing on the contrasting perspectives of the authors.

Or perhaps there is an influence from the prevailing ethos of the age. This is not the same as applying personal polemicism; rather, it is taking a 'modern' view. Provided that it is not actually anachronistic, this can provide 'new' insights. On the other hand, times change;

'modern' becomes 'outdated', 'new' becomes 'older' and 'insights' become 'traditional views'. Hence, Eversley's approach would have reflected the revival of Home Rule from 1911, both as a current issue and as active Liberal policy. Hammond, in *Gladstone and the Irish Nation*, seemed to empathise more than any other historian with Gladstone's views on nationalism. This may well have been because of the inter-war political and international climate in which Hammond was writing: he would have seen first the apparent fulfilment of national self-determination and the emergence of new nations from collapsed empires and then the growing threat of dictatorship and expansionism from the great powers. This combination would have made the Gladstonian approach to nationalism in the Balkans and Ireland appear positive and constructive, and – in the developing storm clouds of the 1930s – an attitude worth remembering and celebrating. Gladstone could be perceived as being ahead of his time over nationalism and Ireland, by contrast with the traditionalism he showed in some other areas. A similar trend emerged, in the era of decolonisation and Commonwealth, to credit Gladstone with foresight in his proposals for self-government within the colonies.

Finally, much of the most recent debate on Gladstone's Irish policy has taken place within a political-party context. This means that the focus is less on Gladstone himself – and sometimes less on Ireland. Instead, it is more on Gladstone's decision to secure a Liberal consensus (or to depart from one which was already there) through a 'crusade'. The point of reference is therefore the development of party politics in the nineteenth century. This would once have been seen as the narrowest possible approach to the issue. Now, however, the development of party politics provides a clear cross-section of the political, economic, social and intellectual developments of the nineteenth century. The term 'political history' has broadened out to include all these other areas, which means that a study of party politics would now include elements which would be sociological, statistical, demographic, regional and cultural – as well as the normal constitutional, political and individual components. To some historians (Hamer and Vincent, for example) the issue of Ireland needs to be seen within the context of Gladstone engaging with other individuals, within a series of cross-currents, for the soul of his party. To others the issue is not so much the damage he did internally as the way in which he was trying to link his party more directly to public opinion as he saw it. Biagini's argument for his success in this is therefore coming at the issue from a different direction. Some of these issues are explored further in Chapter 8.

SOURCES

1. 'IRISH HOME RULE' AND ITS IMPLICATIONS FOR 'EMPIRE'

(Time allowed: 60 minutes)

Source 1: A cartoon from *Punch*, 1885. The horseman is Gladstone and the 'cow-boy' is Joseph Chamberlain.

AT THE CROSS ROADS
Joe (the cow-boy): 'Hoy! – This be your road, Measter!'

Source 2: Extracts from Gladstone's speech in the Commons, 8 April 1886.

Our ineffective coercion is morally worn out. . . . Something must be done, something is demanded from us to restore to Ireland the first conditions of civilised life – the free course of law, the liberty of every individual in the exercise of every legal right, the confidence of the people in the law. . . . The principle I am laying down is not just for Ireland . . . 51 years ago England tried to pass good laws for the Colonies; but the Colonies said – 'We do not want your good laws; we want our own.' We admitted the reasonableness of that principle. We have to consider whether it is applicable to Ireland. We stand face to face with what is termed Irish nationality, which demands complete self-government in Irish affairs. Is this an evil in itself? Is this a thing that we should view with horror? Sir, I believe that it is not.

Source 3: Parnell speaking in favour of Home Rule at Wicklow on 5 October 1885.

We can point to the fact that under 85 years of parliamentary connexion with England, Ireland has become intensely disloyal and intensely disaffected.... We can show that disaffection has disappeared in all the greater English colonies, that while the Irishman who goes to the United States of America carries with him a burning hatred of English rule ... the Irishman ... who goes to one of the colonies of Canada or one of the colonies of Australia, and finds there another and a different system of English rule to that which he has been accustomed to at home, becomes to a great extent a loyal citizen and a strength and a prop to the community amongst whom his lot has been cast....

Source 4: Lord Salisbury (leader of the opposition) speaking against Home Rule at a Conservative party banquet, 18 February 1886.

We are asked to give up to two-thirds, it may be, of Ireland one-third of its inhabitants, landowners, educated men, bankers, merchants, students, men of every class, who have loyally maintained the union, who have acted on the assumption that the Union was to be perpetual, who have avowed English partisanship, have treated it as their greatest honour and trusted in it as their greatest safety, and to whom it will be, if you now abandon them, condemnation to utter and certain ruin [Cheers]....

There are other countries in the world where your Empire is maintained by the faith which men have that those who take your side will be supported and upheld. Whenever the thought crosses you that you can safely abandon those who for centuries have taken your side in Ireland, I beseech you to think of India ['Hear' and cheers]. I beseech you to think of the effect it will have if the suspicion can get abroad there that, should convenience once dictate such a policy, they, like the Loyalists of Ireland, will be flung aside like a sucked orange when their purpose has been fulfilled [Cheers]....

Questions

1. Explain the reference to Joseph Chamberlain in Source 1. (20)
2. Examine Sources 3 and 4. Compare the effects that Parnell and Salisbury feel Home Rule will have on the British Empire. (40)

3. 'Gladstone's policy of Home Rule meant that he was giving up on both Ireland and the British Empire.' Use all four sources and your own knowledge to say whether or not you agree with this view. (60)

Total (120)

2. INTERPRETATIONS OF GLADSTONE AND IRELAND

(Time allowed: 45 minutes)

Source 5: From D. George Boyce, 'Gladstone and Ireland', an essay contributed to a compilation on Ireland published in 1998.

Yet Gladstone and Ireland have made their enduring mark on the politics of the British Isles. If politics are about creating new contexts, providing new ways of thinking, then Gladstone was remarkably important in his attitude to Ireland. If he did not leave behind Home Rule, if he failed to grasp the importance of land purchase to the tenant farmers of Ireland, then at least he left behind some highly charged, ethically focussed phrases: 'justice for Ireland'; 'the government of Ireland by Irish ideas'; 'Ireland stands at your bar expectant, hopeful, almost suppliant', and, above all, his great conclusion to his speech when introducing the first Home Rule Bill. 'Think, I beseech you, think well, think wisely, think not for a moment, but for the years that are to come, before you reject the Bill.' These phrases cast into pallor the machinations, the political calculations, the deviousness, the long period of disinterest that also characterise Gladstone's connection with Ireland. Gladstone gave Irish nationalism and its demands a liberal and democratic character and a parliamentary tradition, that transcend the immediate context of his policies. He gave the Irish Question the kind of moral dimension that he, and he alone of British politicians, could give it.

Source 6: From E.J. Feuchtwanger, *Gladstone*, published in 1975.

Instead he took the fateful decision not only to continue to lead the Liberals through the next election, but after the election to attempt the Home Rule solution for Ireland, which must seriously divide his followers. In many ways it was a heroic effort, justified in the light of history because it was one of the few real opportunities to cut through the unhappy tangle of Anglo-Irish relations. But it was largely due to Gladstone's personality and his handling of the Home Rule crisis that so deep, damaging and lasting a split occurred in the Liberal ranks. In this lay the obverse of his greatness and his genius. The question arises how great a blight not only the split but the further continuation of Gladstone's leadership for another eight years cast upon Liberal prospects. In many ways the party was not ready to produce the new progressive policies which the conditions of the age and the electors increasingly demanded and even if Gladstone had retired in 1885 it would have required time to find new leaders and new ideas and adapt the structure of the party to changing needs.

Source 7: From Eugenio F. Biagini, *Gladstone*, published in 2000.

By way of conclusion, it is appropriate to consider the impact of the Home Rule split on the performance of the Liberal party during the next thirty years. Some historians have seen 1886 as the 'crisis' of Liberalism, and have ascribed it to Gladstone's 'obsession' with Ireland, which was, in their view, a mere sideshow, a pawn in the game between the two parties. The extent to which this interpretation ignores the political and constitutional reality of the United Kingdom at this time is quite astonishing. It is important to note that most of Gladstone's contemporaries took a different line: indeed, the Irish issue generated an enormous amount of interest and passion in Britain, and there is evidence to suggest that popular support for Home Rule was culturally deeper, and politically much more significant, than has hitherto been conceded.

The traditional view is that British working-class voters were uninterested in Home Rule. Poll results seem to bear out this conclusion. Yet, electoral evidence cuts both ways: after all, the Liberal party retained most of its popular support both in 1886 and in 1892. Furthermore, after Gladstone's retirement in 1894, his successors remained loyal to Home Rule, which became one of the Liberal party's trademarks.

In terms of popular support it is also significant that from as early as 1874 most working-class parliamentary candidates and Lib-Lab MPs endorsed the Irish demand for a Parliament in Dublin. Behind such support, the weight, and significance of which would deserve a longer discussion, there was an unbroken tradition of concern and sympathy for what was described as 'the sister island', while Chartists had consistently upheld the Irish demand for the repeal of the Act of Union, and as late as the 1850s their last meetings had been enlivened by toasts 'to the Irish patriots'. . . . Proposals for radical land reform and even nationalization were commonplace in the radical press. In 1881 Gladstone's Land Act was welcomed as a major step in the right direction, but his renewal of coercion was taken as conclusive evidence that the Home Rulers were right to demand constitutional reform and even independence. . . . Thus in 1885 . . . the unity and viability of the Liberals as the workers' main party was threatened not by class struggle, but by 'external' questions such as Ireland, the Empire and foreign policy. By opting for Home Rule, Gladstone pre-empted a crisis on the left at the cost of another one on the right.

Source 8: From Jonathan Parry, *The Rise and Fall of Liberal Government in Victorian Britain*, published in 1993.

It was the determination of Gladstone to stay in charge and to redefine Liberalism around Home Rule that caused so many crippling defections from the Liberal party. Neither Hartington and his followers, nor Chamberlain and his, wished to leave. Few of them were enamoured of the Conservatives' apparently irrational, prejudiced, unintelligent governing style. The departure of each group was at first provisional; they stayed in the wings throughout 1886 and 1887, hoping that Gladstone would retire or that the party would turn its attention elsewhere. After all, most of those Liberals who remained loyal to Gladstone probably did not care much for Home Rule. They took their stand on personal admiration for their leader, confidence in his popular rapport, cowardice in the face of the rank-and-file, or a hope that the new policy would be only a temporary aberration.

The division of 1886 was an accident, not a long-expected socio-economic combustion. But it was also more than a personality quarrel. At root, it was, unsurprisingly, about Ireland. But, to a lot of Unionists, it was also about the moral dimensions of political leadership in a proto-democracy. Gladstone's commitment to Home Rule was the most convincing demonstration imaginable that his priorities were at odds with those of the mainstream nineteenth-century Liberal tradition. . . . In 1886, Gladstone *did* spectacularly misinterpret and idealise the will of the political nation. Unionists were able to ignore his call for Home Rule not only because their judgment pointed in that direction, but also because a mass popular movement for it never materialised. Indeed, two of the most high-profile Liberal tribunes, Chamberlain and Bright, were on the Unionist side. Gladstone's relentless crusader politics alienated the bulk of those who believed in an administrative, rational, didactic, consensual and parliamentary conception of Liberalism – who believed in it both for its policy results, and as the best way to keep a loose but invincibly large coalition of propertied and popular sentiment together under cultured leadership. Gladstone's impulsive, sentimental, evangelising, over-active political temper was a much greater threat to that conception than Chamberlain's 'socialism', because it could strike many more chords with provincial Dissenters and Liberal working-men. Crude class interpretations have no place in explaining the division of 1886. When Liberal Unionists merged with Conservatives, they did so in defence of manly, progressive, considered imperial administration by 'the property, the wealth, the intelligence, and the industry of the country' – the very forces that the whig reformers had sought to represent in parliament fifty-five years before.

Questions

1. Compare the arguments in Sources 7 and 8 on how Gladstone's policy on Home Rule reflected public opinion. (15)

2. 'The debate among historians is not so much whether Gladstone failed over Home Rule – but whether he really deserved to succeed.' Do you agree with this view? (30)

Total (45)

8

GLADSTONE, DISRAELI AND THEIR POLITICAL PARTIES

BACKGROUND

The issue of political parties has been left until this final chapter since so much that is relevant to it has already been covered. A parliamentary system presupposes the existence of organised political action and much of the careers of Gladstone and Disraeli was devoted to this. The common unit of organisation was, in all cases, the political party. Everything, therefore, comes within its scope.

In summary, Chapter 1 dealt with two politicians who entered Parliament as Tories but who went on to play a key role in different parties – Disraeli reviving the Conservatives and Gladstone eventually leading a new Whig–Peelite–Radical combination renamed as the Liberals. The ideas and influences behind this political transformation were the theme of Chapter 2, with a particular focus on the extent to which there was ever a party ideology. As the Liberals and Conservatives won power they introduced reforms with a particular party stamp. These were considered in the form of economic, social and institutional reforms (Chapter 3) and parliamentary reform (Chapter 4). Similarly, the political parties revolved around distinctive positions over foreign policy (Chapter 5) and imperial policies (Chapter 6). The Irish Question refocused party loyalties, consolidating the Conservatives, but splitting the Liberals; the reasons for and results of this were considered in Chapter 7. What remains is an overall assessment of the contributions made by Gladstone and Disraeli to their parties, rather than to the nation *through* them. A broader background perspective of the development of the British party system might be useful, as a context in which to place some of the comments about Gladstone and Disraeli after their own era.

The evolution of the political parties in Britain 1783–2001

Britain has traditionally been under a two-party system. The original seventeenth-century rivalry was between the Tories (inclined to be pro-court) and the Whigs, the 'country' party taking their stand more on the privilege of Parliament. Both had an aristocratic base and were heavily lubricated by patronage. From 1714 the Whigs were the dominant party, particularly during the premiership of Walpole (1721–42). The Tories revived, although in somewhat different form, under William Pitt the Younger (1783–1801 and 1804–6). From 1806 until 1830 the Tories dominated British politics, especially under Lord Liverpool (1812–27).

Between 1830 and 1841 the initiative passed to the Whigs, who introduced a series of reforms, starting with the extension of the franchise in 1832. This was the decade in which both Gladstone and Disraeli started their careers, the former joining Peel's cabinet after the Tories (now renamed Conservatives) returned to power in 1841. Peel's decision to repeal the Corn Laws in 1846 split the Conservative party. Gladstone joined Peel in political exile and the Peelites gradually moved towards a new alignment with the Whigs and Radicals in 1859 to form the Liberal party – first under Palmerston, then Russell and finally under Gladstone. Meanwhile, Derby and Disraeli kept together what was left of the Conservative party which was, nevertheless, in a much weaker position after 1846.

A more genuine period of two-party politics resumed after the 1867 Reform Act, with government alternating between the Liberals (1868–74), the Conservatives (1874–80) and the Liberals again (1880–5). The next twenty years, however, saw the Liberal party split by the Irish issue just as damagingly as the Conservatives had been split by the repeal of the Corn Laws. The result was two decades of Conservative domination, mainly under Lord Salisbury, interspersed with brief periods of Liberal rule under Gladstone (1886 and 1892–4) and Rosebery (1894–5).

This predominance ended with the swing of the pendulum of controversy back to the Conservatives. The party was divided by Joseph Chamberlain (who had defected to the Conservatives as a Liberal Unionist) over the issue of tariff reform and lost by a landslide in the 1906 general election. A new Liberal government, under Campbell Bannerman and, from 1908, Asquith, introduced a series of social reforms which were more sweeping than anything Gladstone had envisaged. Their majority was, however, removed in two general elections held in 1910 brought about by a conflict with the House of Lords. They remained in power with the support of the Irish Nationalists, whose price was the introduction of a third Home Rule Bill. This was already in trouble when it was suspended by the government in 1914 as Asquith focused his attention on the war with Germany.

Meanwhile, the Liberals were also coming under pressure from the emergence of a new party on their left. The Labour Representation Committee was established in 1900 and soon renamed the Labour party. After an electoral pact which helped both parties in the 1906 election, Labour became the junior partner of the reforming Liberal government, although it was as yet unable to break through in its own right.

The First World War proved a catalyst for a major political change. Asquith was challenged for the leadership by his former Chancellor of the Exchequer and surrendered the premiership to him in 1916. Lloyd George remained in power as Coalition Prime Minister until 1922, in the process collaborating with the Conservatives. The internal split proved fatal for the Liberal party, which never challenged for government again. The Representation of the People Act (1918) expanded the electoral base of the Labour party, which now gradually replaced the Liberals as the main alternative to the Conservatives.

The period between the two world wars (1918–39) was strangely paradoxical. The Conservatives, largely under Baldwin, had huge electoral support, while Labour, under Ramsay MacDonald, had not yet fully risen because the Liberals had not yet fully collapsed. Yet the Conservatives formed only two governments (1922–3 and 1924–9), while Labour had two spells in power, with Liberal support (1924 and 1929–31). The economic crisis from 1929 had a dramatic impact on British politics. Ramsay MacDonald formed a National government in 1931 and was expelled from the Labour party for his action. The rest of the 1930s saw a series of National governments, which acquired an increasingly Conservative appearance after 1935 – under Baldwin and then Neville Chamberlain. Labour, meanwhile, were defeated in two Conservative landslides (1931 and 1935). After the outbreak of war in 1939 the National government was transformed into a Coalition as Churchill assumed the premiership in 1940.

The First World War demolished the Liberal party; the Second World War consolidated the rise of Labour. In the first general election for ten years, Labour under Attlee won a landslide in 1945 and proceeded to introduce a welfare state and a limited programme of nationalisation. The impetus had slowed by 1951 and there followed a 'Conservative decade' until 1964 – under Churchill, Eden, Macmillan and Douglas-Home. Labour returned in 1964 with a commitment from Wilson to modernise the welfare state. The rest of the 1960s and the 1970s were beset with economic problems and industrial unrest which affected Wilson, Heath (the latter during an interlude of Conservative rule between 1970 and 1974) and Callaghan.

The year 1979 saw one of the key general election results of the twentieth century as the Conservatives swept back to power with a radical agenda for reform under Margaret Thatcher. Committed to privatisation and reducing trade union influence, she moved Britain to the right. Labour, in response, lurched to the left, losing its own right wing, which broke away as the Social Democrats and eventually joined the Liberals to form the Liberal Democratic party. The Conservatives won the next three general elections (1983, 1987 and 1992), forcing Labour into a prolonged process of internal examination and reform. The eventual result was the emergence of 'New Labour' which contested the central ground in British politics and won successive landslides in 1997 and 2001. The Conservatives, in their turn, experienced internal divisions and, by 2004, were still trying to rediscover their former stability and electoral support. The Liberal Democrats, meanwhile, had gradually consolidated their own support without, however, managing to break out of their position as a third party.

Patterns and trends

From this outline several trends can be deduced. The first is the periodic realignment of British political parties. This occurred after

1846 with the division of the Conservatives and the subsequent emergence of the Liberals as the merger between the Whigs, Peelites and Radicals. The Liberals, in turn, split over Irish Home Rule, a substantial number of Liberal Unionists moving over to the Conservatives after 1886. The third major example of political mergers involving splinter groups was the secession of the Social Democrats from Labour and their union with the Liberals in the 1980s.

A second trend is the dominance of two political parties. The British electoral system has proved unable to accommodate more than two large parties for any length of time. Throughout the nineteenth century power was contested between the Whigs and Tories and then the Liberals and Conservatives. After the First World War the place of the Liberals was gradually assumed by Labour. But two-party politics has not necessarily meant alternating governments. The trend has more commonly been the dominance exerted by one of the parties over a substantial period, with a brief intrusion of alternate party rule. Hence the Tories dominated the first third of the nineteenth century, the Whigs the second third and the Conservatives the last quarter. During the twentieth century the Conservatives controlled the periods 1951–64 and 1979–97, while Labour were in control between 1945 and 1951, for all but four years of the period 1964–1979, and from 1997 onwards.

A third feature has been the repackaging of political parties at certain stages as an attempt to modernise their appeal. This occurred with the Conservatives under Peel and Disraeli, and again under Lord Randolph Churchill and Salisbury. Baldwin further changed the image of the Conservatives in the 1920s, as did Macmillan in the 1950s and Thatcher in the 1970s. Significantly, the connection with Disraeli was frequently emphasised by most of his successors – with the notable exception of Thatcher. Gladstone reconstructed the political image of the political left in the 1860s and 1870s, before splitting it over Ireland in the 1880s and 1890s. The 'New Liberals' were a further renovation after 1900, with a focus on social reform. There is a strong parallel between the 'New Liberal' revival at the beginning of the twentieth century, after a damaging internal crisis, and the emergence of 'New Labour' towards the end of the century after a similar upheaval. Gladstone's name is mentioned less often than Disraeli's – but parallels will be suggested in Analysis 2.

ANALYSIS 1: COMPARE THE CONTRIBUTIONS MADE TO THEIR POLITICAL PARTIES BY GLADSTONE AND DISRAELI.

Since both Gladstone and Disraeli started their careers as Conservatives, their roles are directly comparable during the first two decades of their careers. Gladstone contributed more directly to the Conservative party in government – as President of the Board of Trade (1843–5). He also supported Peel's attempts to re-educate the party in the principles of free trade. Disraeli's attitude in the same period was more critical: sometimes this was constructive, but usually it was motivated by the absence of his own political advancement. The prime responsibility for the damage inflicted by the confrontation over the repeal of the Corn Laws is debatable. It was Disraeli who mobilised the protectionist interest within the Conservative party in defiance of Peel. It was Peel who defied the opposition within his own ranks and sought Whig support to see the measure through. Gladstone's role was subordinate to Peel's and therefore less directly responsible than Disraeli's for the subsequent party split.

During the period 1846–68, therefore, their careers diverged. Gladstone played an important part in the realignment of the various political groups – at the expense of the Conservatives – while it was Disraeli who held the Conservative rump together during this critical period. Gladstone led the Peelites into union with the Whigs and Radicals at the Willis's Room meeting in 1861 and subsequently adjusted the Liberals to a new world without Palmerston, who died in 1865. He assumed the leadership of the Liberals, after a brief interlude under Russell, in 1868. Disraeli was responsible for the Conservatives in the House of Commons under the overall control of the Earl of Derby; Disraeli, too, assumed the leadership in 1868. Gladstone therefore played a key role in mobilising a new party, while Disraeli revived and reactivated an old one. At the same time, each had to deal with party leaders who were members of the aristocratic elite. Disraeli's relations with Derby were certainly more constructive than Gladstone's with Palmerston. There was therefore a smoother transition to the eventual emergence of Disraeli than to that of Gladstone.

Both of these roles involved the re-education of the respective parties. Disraeli's contributions were varied. He had persuaded his party by 1852 to abandon the lost cause of protectionism and to come to terms with free trade. This may have antagonised some of the landed interest, but it opened the way for the manufacturing and mercantile interests to come to terms with the Conservatives during the 1860s and 1870s. Second, he broadened the electoral base, assuming that the Conservative party would benefit from an extension of the franchise to the upper levels of the working class. This may not have paid off in the 1868 general election, but it did enable the Conservatives to win in 1874 their first outright majority since 1841. He also provided the Conservatives with something resembling a programme: his speeches in 1872 at the Free Trade Hall in Manchester and at Crystal Palace managed to combine the traditional bases of Conservative policy – the aristocracy, the Church and the monarchy – with a new emphasis on social reform. From this time onwards Conservatives would aim to maintain the institutions of the country, maintain the Empire and 'elevate the condition of the people'. Whether or not his statements on social reform carried any real depth of intention, Disraeli did, nevertheless, give the Conservative party an appeal which penetrated all classes and which survived for the rest of the century.

The Liberal appeal established by Gladstone is harder to define. The Liberals appealed less to Empire and imperialism and more to cost-effective government, less to an active and unilateralist foreign policy and more to concert diplomacy based on a sense of morality. Neither of these was likely to be of instinctive appeal to the electorate other than in exceptional circumstances. These, however, Gladstone did manage to create, especially in the Midlothian campaign of 1879–80. Like Disraeli, he was also aware of the importance of exerting a party appeal to the working class. It was he who introduced the first measure for parlia-mentary reform in 1866 and, although Disraeli saw it through to the statute book in 1867, it was the Liberals who benefited in the 1868 general election. Gladstone was less successful in maintaining the support which the middle classes had traditionally shown for the Whigs; much of this went over to the Conservatives in the form of 'villa Toryism'. Even the increased working-class base, which the Liberals might have expected from the 1884 Reform Act, failed to materialise, as the twenty years which followed were dominated by Conservative governments.

Both leaders benefited from improvements in party organisation. The National Union of Conservative Associations was formed in 1867, with Gorst as the Principal Agent from 1870, while the Liberal party's equivalent was the National Liberal Federation set up from Birmingham in 1877. These were, however, in their early stages and neither Gladstone nor Disraeli had much to do with them directly. The constituency organ-isations in the Liberal party developed a considerable degree of autonomy, which sometimes pulled apart from the control which Gladstone tried to exercise over the highest level of the party during the 1880s. Conservative organisation was less loose in the constituencies and there was less tension with the centre because of Disraeli's more relaxed authority over his colleagues. Ultimately the Liberal model fostered regional strengths, especially in Wales and Scotland, while the Conservative network was more effective in England. This pattern overlapped with the new shape of constituencies which emerged as a result of the 1885 Redistribution Act. Gladstone's Liberal party received its strongest support in the Celtic fringe, whereas the Conservatives became strongest in England. The latter trend was, however, largely post-Disraelian.

Gladstone and Disraeli contested three general elections against each other, of which Gladstone won two. His electioneering campaigns on behalf of the Liberals were especially effective in 1868 and 1880. In 1868 he promised the disestablishment of the Irish Church (particularly popular in Ireland and with the Irish vote in Lancashire), educational reform in Britain and reduced taxation through more efficient government. Through this he managed to persuade much of the newly enfranchised working class to abandon the Conservatives who had expected to gain their support in response to the 1867 Reform Act; the result was a Liberal victory by 387 seats to 271. In 1880 Gladstone conducted the more spectacular Midlothian campaign in which he made maximum use of his talent for public speaking and gained widespread press coverage. He also delivered a scathing attack on all aspects of Disraeli's record between 1874 and 1880, including his policy towards the Balkans, his failure in Zululand and Afghanistan and his apparent inability to deal with the onset of depression in 1879. The electorate were sufficiently convinced by Gladstone's rhetoric on 'Beaconsfieldism' to return 353 Liberals to 238 Conservatives. Disraeli, however, also proved adept at campaigning and lambasting the government. His election campaign in 1874 was particularly effective: he accused Gladstone of 'blundering and plundering', stressing that he had 'harassed every trade, worried every profession, and assailed or menaced every class, institution, and species of property in the country'. This time the Conservatives won the general election by 342 to 251. This was a period when the two parties were more evenly matched, so that the image of their leaders and the effectiveness of their campaigns did make a substantial difference to the result.

A key factor in party leadership is the degree of cohesion and unity maintained. After his iconoclastic behaviour in the 1830s and 1840s, Disraeli settled down to become the main reconciling influence within the Conservative party. Gladstone, by contrast, appeared to become more divisive, particularly during the 1880s. This difference is partly the result of different priorities. Disraeli tended to match his policies and priorities to his career and to the needs of the Conservative party (which generally overlapped). Hence he was adaptable and was always careful to focus on issues which would win votes. In some cases this was straightforward: the Conservatives were bound to identify with monarchy, the Church and empire. But Disraeli also persuaded them to accept free trade in 1852, a wider franchise in 1867 and social reform in the 1870s. It probably helped that his leadership of the cabinet while in office was relatively low-key and that, in domestic affairs at least, he provided the climate within which others were able to provide the detailed changes. Gladstone could also be persuasive, especially over his economic policies and his plans to reform institutions like the civil service and the army. But sometimes he chose not to be, preferring to involve the Liberals in a crusade rather than a more diverse set of policies. This was particularly the case with Irish Home Rule after 1885. Gladstone failed to convince either of the wings of the party – the Whigs or the Radicals – and, in the process, alienated colleagues like Chamberlain and Hartington, who eventually took their talents with them into the Conservative party. It may well be that Gladstone was right in the more contentious policies that he pursued. But being right can, as Disraeli realised, be both unsettling and divisive.

This brings us, finally, to the state of their two parties at the end of their careers. On the death of Disraeli in 1881, the Conservatives had been defeated by the Liberals and Gladstone seemed set for a pro-longed spell in power. But they had one major advantage. They were still relatively cohesive as a party and, even if they appeared uninspired at this stage, they had the capacity for a swift recovery should the Liberals stumble in the future. Disraeli therefore left them undistinguished but not in disarray. Gladstone's impact was altogether different. In 1886 and again between 1892 and 1894 he gave the Liberals a major cause and an impassioned belief which inspired some of the greatest speeches of the nineteenth century. The result, however, was a damaging rift which enabled Salisbury to take Disraeli's Conservative party into a period of unprecedented domination at the expense of the Gladstonian Liberals.

ANALYSIS 2: HOW HAVE HISTORIANS INTERPRETED THE CONTRIBUTIONS OF GLADSTONE AND DISRAELI TO THEIR PARTIES?

This analysis pulls together the themes relating to the political parties covered elsewhere in Chapters 1 to 7, while adding material to fill any remaining gaps.

The development of the political parties before the mid-1860s was referred to in Chapter 1. The debate focused primarily on whether the contributions made by Gladstone and Disraeli to the development of the Conservatives and Liberals were either significant or positive. For example, did Gladstone help bring about the reorientation of British politics after 1846 and the development of a progressive political force in the form of a new Liberal party? Or did he merely distort the 'liberal' direction already being taken by the Whigs and, through his own disruptive influence, implant the seeds of division in the Liberal party? Did Disraeli rescue the Conservative party from a spiralling decline after 1846 and consolidate it in anticipation of better times to come? Or did he make no essential difference between 1846 and 1866, merely taking advantage of the changed fortunes of the Conservatives after 1866? There is plenty of controversy here – but with one theme in common. The parties are seen as separate entities, with identifiable differences, while Gladstone and Disraeli are seen, as individuals, to have had a direct influence on them – whether positive or negative.

In fundamental contrast to this is a more deterministic argument that political parties were shaped not so much by individuals as by the economic infrastructures. This case was put by Hobsbawm, who provided very few direct references to Gladstone and Disraeli in describing the political development of Britain. Instead of competing parties shaped by individual leaders, he saw shifting classes below the surface giving rise to variations in political organisation and expression on the surface. Any changes in party politics in the nineteenth century can be attributed to the growing wealth and influence of the mercantile middle class and its aspiration to merge with the aristocracy. 'Nothing was more natural than that other types of businessmen – like Robert Peel Se., the cotton-master – should climb the same slope of wealth and public honour, at the peak of which there beckoned government, or even (as for Peel's son and the son of Gladstone, the Liverpool merchant) the post of Prime Minister.' There was to Hobsbawm an inevitability about the emergence of representatives of the business classes to lead their country. Any changes in the parties themselves can also be explained in terms of the shifting economic base: this applies especially to the crucial period of realignment between 1846 and 1866. According to Hobsbawm, 'the so-called "Peelite" group in Parliament in the second third of the nineteenth century represented very much this group of business families assimilated into a landed oligarchy, though at odds with it when the economic interests of land and business clashed'.[1] There are no references to clashes between Peel and Disraeli in 1846, or to Gladstone's political exile, or to his reluctant accommodation with Palmerston and the Whigs, or to Disraeli's influence in holding the Conservatives together after 1846. Britain was moved not by political machination but by the shifting tectonic plates of social classes.

Whether Gladstone and Disraeli provided the Liberal and Conservative parties with a distinctive theory based, perhaps, on their own development and ideas, was considered in Chapter 2. What were the components of 'Gladstonian Liberalism' and did they provide the Liberal party with any 'ideological cohesion'? Was there any such thing as 'Tory Democracy' or was this merely read back into the Disraelian Conservative party by later leaders? Chapter 3 considered whether there was anything distinctive about the economic policies of the two leaders – and whether there was any practical application for Gladstonian Liberalism and Tory Democracy in Liberal or Conservative party policy during the ministries of 1868–74, 1874–80, 1880–5, 1886 and 1892–4. A similar focus was provided in Chapter 4, but on the theme of parliamentary reform and its impact on the parties. Party policy was explored in Chapter 5 concerning foreign affairs and Chapter 6 on the Empire – and the extent to which this was shaped by Gladstone and Disraeli while they were in power and in opposition. The Irish situation (Chapter 8) had a particular bearing on the parties. Did Disraeli use it merely as a means of uniting the Conservatives against Liberal vulnerability? Or did he provide the basis of a longer-term policy on Ireland which eventually led the Conservatives to change their name to Unionists? Did Gladstone sacrifice the unity of the Liberal party to the principle of Home Rule, thus condemning it to twenty years largely in opposition? Or did he exploit the principle of Home Rule to try to force the Liberal party to unite behind a crusade as an alternative to its previous divisions over piecemeal reform? Ireland certainly had a direct impact on British party politics: but precisely how?

The issue which now requires further examination is the style of leadership imposed by Gladstone and Disraeli and the direction in which this moved the Liberal and Conservative parties in the future.

Gladstone as Liberal leader

The traditional view of Gladstone is that economic principles moved him out of the Conservative party and into the formation of a new party – which he then divided on the Irish issue. This is in contrast with Disraeli, whose principles were aimed at holding the Conservatives together. The view of Magnus is typical here. He argued that 'Gladstone regarded Party as an alliance of enlightened individuals formed to serve a series of high moral causes, such as his mission to pacify Ireland'. Gladstone conceived it his duty as leader 'to devise such missions, and he was convinced that the electors could be taught to respond to the voice of God appealing directly to their consciences'.[2] The party, in other words, was a channel for progressive and enlightened policy, as interpreted and formulated by Gladstone himself. This overlaps with the earlier view of Hammond that, 'Once a Liberal, Gladstone differed from all other Liberal leaders both in the tone of his politics and in the source of his principles. Yet his moral ascendancy over the party that he led was almost unrivalled.'[3]

Whether Gladstone's leadership was entirely *principled* is, of course, open to debate. A second possibility is that, during the 1880s, he felt that the Liberal party was in danger of being taken over by the radicalism of Joseph Chamberlain as a means of reviving its reforming impetus. Ramm summarised the dilemma Gladstone faced during his second ministry from 1880: although 'he cast a backward look to 1874', he found it impossible 'to pick up the legislative or policy threads of the first administration'.[4] He was also increasingly preoccupied by the 'sects which nestle within this party' and the 'divisive courses of sectional opinion' which threatened the party's 'aggregate energy'.[5] What could he do? According to historians like Ramm, Vincent and Hamer, Gladstone adopted the single-issue approach as a way of maintaining the party's 'aggregate energy' – but under his authority. This amounted to the same overall result as the one expressed by Magnus and Hammond, but it comes at this result from a different direction. It also allows for a greater degree of calculation and opportunism on Gladstone's part. It should be remembered that Gladstone's self-confidence had been greatly increased by his sudden and dramatic return to the Liberal leadership in 1876 over the Bulgarian issue, the huge success of his Midlothian campaign (1879–80) and victory in the 1880 general election. Matthew emphasised how adept Gladstone was in his 'extra-parliamentary speech-making' and that his Midlothian campaign 'represented the flowering of a new style of politics, long in germination'.[6] Hence he could well have been influenced as much by power as by principle. He was confident that he had the answers for big issues like Ireland and felt that he *could* apply them; this was just as important to him as the feeling that he *should*.

How effective did all this make him as a party leader? The main approaches here seem to divide between the view that his leadership was positive – but ultimately flawed – and a more negative conclusion that Gladstone's leadership was more consistently damaging.

Hamer, for example, emphasised Gladstone's firm management: the very purpose of his crusading politics, especially over Ireland, was to transcend the party structure, remain detached from the details of party management and assume the role of national statesman[7] – a style which had already been established in the Midlothian campaign. Feuchtwanger, too, stressed Gladstone's personality and leadership as 'two of the key factors in the formation of the Liberal party and in the history of the party for the next quarter of a century'.[8] He was, indeed, 'a leader detached from those he led and that is how he saw his position'.[9] The problem, of course, was that he selected an issue – Home Rule – over which he eventually failed. The strength of his leadership therefore had a damaging impact on the party.

More severe criticism was expressed by a number of other historians – on the grounds that Gladstone not only failed to provide party unity but also failed the individual components of the Liberals. One example is his misunderstanding and misuse of the Whigs, especially men like Hartington and Granville. The argument is that leading Whigs eventually broke with the Liberals not just because of their opposition to Home Rule, but because of Gladstone himself. This point was particularly strongly made by Parry. We have already looked at his view that Gladstone did not provide the liberal impetus before 1866 (see Chapter 1) and that more important in this respect was the work of the Whigs – the genuine influence for progress. What Gladstone did was to impose a less tolerant form, along with an authoritarian style, of leadership. The damage was, however, intensified after he became Prime Minister as his style became increasingly divisive. Parry maintained that the man with the real ability for sustaining unity was Hartington, who was 'like Palmerston in his astuteness about how to keep the Liberal coalition together'.[10] He related far more effectively than Gladstone to the different elements of support, whereas 'Gladstone despised the new plutocracy'. Although he 'did not intend to be a divisive politician', he was anything but 'a coalition-builder by temperament'.[11] Most tellingly of all, Parry claimed that 'The Liberal party did not fall apart because of "sectionalism" or whig "inflexibility" but because of Gladstone's distance from the Liberal tradition.'[12] This takes us back to Parry's central argument – that the real origins of Liberalism were the Whig reforming impetus, which was actually distorted by Gladstone.

There has also been criticism of the way in which Gladstone alienated the other wing of the Liberal party – the Radicals. This has been approached on the basis of Gladstone's inherent caution on social reform, which made him wary of the pressures of Chamberlain and Bright (leaders respectively of the 'new' and 'old' Radicals). Here Gladstone saw a conflict between those who wanted to expand the involvement of the state and his own preference for minimising what he saw as state interference. Hobsbawm provided a more sweeping condemnation, claiming that the Liberal party failed to gain the lasting support of the workers because of 'the reluctance of older politicians like Gladstone and of certain groups of business men in the party to pay the necessary price in "government interference"'.[13] This approach probably under-emphasises the importance of Gladstone's public appeal, but it does have the advantage of recognising his anachronistic attitudes when compared with the rise of Labour.

Gladstone's legacy to the Liberal party can be drawn from these views on his leadership. As we saw in Chapter 7, much of this is related to the split experienced by the Liberals during the 1880s and 1890s which is, in turn, connected in some way to the controversy over Home Rule.

There are two main approaches to Gladstone's impact on the Liberals during the 1880s and 1890s. The first is that Gladstone wrecked a Liberal party which had won a second term in office in 1880, with a chance to continue the earlier reforming impetus of 1868–74. Instead, Gladstone chose to limit the programme of social reform and, in 1885 and 1886, severely damaged the Liberals by launching a crusade over Home Rule. Whether this was done through high principles or through mistaken political opportunism, the result was disaster. Feuchtwanger maintained that 'it was largely due to Gladstone's personality and his handling of the Home Rule crisis that so deep, damaging and lasting a split occurred in the Liberal ranks. In this lay the obverse of his genius.' Indeed, 'The split of 1886 was a major blow that stacked the cards against the Liberals for many years to come.'[14] What made matters worse was that Gladstone was an impossible act to follow for the Liberal party. 'The continuing presence of Gladstone's towering figure until 1894 made the emergence of new leaders and new ideas much more difficult.'[15] We might deduce from this a legacy of almost reckless momentum – as a result of which the Liberal party crashed.

An alternative approach is that the Liberal party was already in serious difficulties and that Gladstone's emphasis on Home Rule finished off an already weakening consensus. According to Shannon, 'The Liberal split over Home Rule registered the end of the old political era. Home Rule itself, however, was the occasion rather than the cause of this.'[16] The only alternative to Liberal unity through the Irish cause was an agenda set by radicalism and Chamberlain. Gladstone had already discharged his post-1880 obligations through the 1884 Reform Act. Home Rule was now the only way to justify Gladstone's 'deciding for continuation in office and in a fully committed political life'.[17] Unless, of course, Gladstone should decide to intensify the Liberal programme of reform. That, however, would play into the hands of the radicals. The implication is that Gladstone was deliberately choosing a policy which would prevent the Liberal party from moving *forward*: 'the fundamental point that emerges in 1886 is his insistence on committing Liberalism to a future within, and not beyond, the limits prescribed in the assumptions inherited from the formative years of the 1860s'.[18] Because of Gladstone's leadership, Radicalism was ruined, with the Liberal party being 'diverted from its logical path of becoming a party under predominantly Radical inspiration and control'.[19] Gladstone's legacy, it could be argued, was to bring the Liberal party to an abrupt halt.

Gladstone had the historical disadvantage of leading a party which claimed to be on the progressive wing of British politics but which was shortly to be displaced by another. This is bound to reflect on his image as a party leader. Although his reputation as an individual statesman and campaigner with a remarkable intellect and high moral character continued to thrive, the party after him preferred to see him in isolation from the party – preferably on a pedestal. The Liberal party, faced with growing competition from a new Labour, had to renovate itself after 1900. 'New Liberalism' – by definition – involved cutting some of the connections with Gladstonian Liberalism. This issue is explored at greater length in the final section.

Disraeli as Conservative leader

Disraeli is usually given more credit than Gladstone for relating to his party and developing a more cohesive strategy for it. Whether there were any principles behind this is another matter.

Not surprisingly, this is claimed by Disraeli's most favourable biographers, Monypenny and Buckle, who maintained that Disraeli also showed 'exceptional greatness, only just short of supreme mastery'. He was 'a grand and magnificent figure, standing solitary, towering above his contemporaries'. He showed a 'vision wide and deep, amid a nation of narrow practical minds'. Furthermore, Disraeli had maintained the high ideals of Conservatism from the past.[20]

Although somewhat less eulogistic about Disraeli's leadership, Jenkins points to a positive impact on the party. The main difference from Monypenny and Buckle, however, is that political ability is allied with opportunism rather than high principles. Disraeli was particularly effective in his 1872 speeches at the Free Trade Hall in Manchester and at Crystal Palace. 'In tactical terms . . . Disraeli was seizing the opportunity to exploit the growing unpopularity of Gladstone's ministry in order to reinforce the "Tory" strategy which he had been pursuing for over a decade.'[21] He was also receptive to new ideas and approaches. His appreciation of 'the merits of "social" reform was the one aspect of the "Tory" platform that was comparatively new'.[22] He may not even have been fully committed to it. He remained 'politely aloof from what came to be known as the "new social alliance", but it at least pointed to the political potential in Conservative action on social reform, which offered a means of appeasing the newly-enfranchised working classes'.[23] Blake adopted a more restricted approach, with less emphasis on content but more on display. 'Where Disraeli excelled was in the art of presentation. He was an impresario and an actor manager. He was a superb parliamentarian, one of the half dozen greatest in our history.'[24]

Against all this are dissenting views – that Disraeli's leadership was without either principle or ability and accomplished very little for the Conservatives. Smith argued that his leadership was entirely unexceptional. The period of his power was not earned on his own merits. 'The Conservative party did not so much mount to victory as find itself suddenly exposed by the ebbing of the Liberal tide which had submerged it for nearly thirty years.'[25] Smith maintained that 'almost any' leader could have won the 1874 general election. Disraeli's reforms were 'uncontroversial' and 'bi-partisan', while his desire to leave a mark in 'assertive foreign policy' resulted only in the destruction of 'the newly won Conservative majority'.[26] Besides, there were few 'Disraelian policies, legislative or administrative, by which national unity could be promoted or national purpose effectively implemented'.[27]

The legacy of Disraeli to the Conservative party might be categorised as 'intended', 'created' or 'unintended'.

There is no shortage of historians to put the case for Disraeli having a broadly positive influence on the Conservatives, although after the most unpromising of starts. Machin's view is not untypical: 'Disraeli is a great and central figure in the history of the Conservative party. He revived its fortunes, even if he had first destroyed them.'[28] McWilliam emphasised the way in which Disraeli broadened the party's base and widened its appeal, thus enabling it to compete on more equal terms with the Whigs and Liberals. 'Disraeli's legacy to the Conservatives was that he took a party of the landed elite and turned it into a force that did not look out of place in a more democratic age.' He did this by extending the vote to the working classes and because he 'annexed the issues of nation, monarchy, Empire and the Church of England'.[29] Blake emphasised another contribution – the importance of imperialism. 'Under Derby the party had not been empire-minded or in favour of gunboat diplomacy.' Indeed, 'the early prophets of imperialism were largely Liberals'. Disraeli reversed this. 'His attitude decisively orientated the Conservative party for many years to come, and the tradition which he started was probably a bigger electoral asset in winning working-class support during the last quarter of the nineteenth century than anything else, though he himself did not live to see its fruits.'[30]

This line has not, however, attracted other historians, who tend to see Disraeli's legacy as one which was created later and attributed back to him. At the time of his death the Conservative party was in a parlous condition, having been defeated in the 1880 general election by a reinvigorated Gladstone. The Liberals looked set for a decade or more in power, especially as Home Rule had not yet emerged as an issue to divide them. Indeed, Disraeli was reduced in his election campaign to accusing Gladstone, without evidence, of being about to adopt Home Rule. Disraeli was therefore reduced to inventing Liberal divisions, being at this stage unaware that they would produce their own. His desperation was, however, later put down to foresight, as indeed were many of his other ideas. Feuchtwanger put forward a strong argument for this. 'The weak situation in which he left his party made it all the more tempting for those who sought his succession to pick over the entrails of his legacy and to extract what suited their agenda.'[31] This applied to a wide range of issues. 'Tory Democracy', for example, became increasingly associated with Disraeli's leadership, even though it was 'a term Disraeli never used'. The reality was that Disraeli left his party in a state of turmoil. The aristocracy were still the most influential sector, but were being badly affected by the depression, while the middle classes, who were turning to it, 'had not yet been allotted a major place in the party'.[32] Disraeli was therefore far from being the unifying figure he was later purported to have been.

A third possibility is that the legacy of Disraeli was real enough – but unintended. Shannon took issue with the 'received Disraeli myth' that he educated his party 'to become the mass popular party of the 1870s and 1880s' on the basis of the 'doctrinal foundations of the Young England movement'. Nor is there any evidence that Disraeli 'anticipated that the future of Conservatism would be based upon a "national" working-class electorate'. Far from it; instead, his hopes 'for a revived Conservatism' really rested on 'the party's gaining a sufficient majority on a traditional basis'.[33] The key to Disraeli's contribution to Conservative success was not so much the creation of a mass party but rather the provision of a 'refuge for the bourgeoisie anxious about that very same popular element in politics'. But was this planned? According to Shannon, 'In the long run this can certainly be accepted as Disraeli's legacy to his party; but it was a legacy Disraeli was not intending to pass on.'[34]

Other arguments have made Disraeli's legacy to the Conservative party even more indirect. According to Jenkins, it 'appeared to be ambiguous' at the time of his death in 1881.[35] Although the Conservatives had won their first election majority in a generation in 1874, the 1880 election was 'a catastrophe for the Conservatives' and there was no discernible prospect for renewed growth. What actually happened was a revival in 1885 through winning a majority of seats in the English boroughs. Disraeli has received some of the credit for this in terms of broadening the party's base. But should he? The real factor in this revival was the Redistribution Act of 1885 which transferred seats from small to larger boroughs and introduced single-member constituencies, both of which worked in the Conservatives' favour. The credit for this should go to Lord Salisbury, who made 'effective use of the political leverage supplied by the Conservatives' majority in the House of Lords' to block Gladstone's franchise reform until the latter agreed to the seat redistribution on which Salisbury insisted. It was also the case that the Conservative ascendancy of the late Victorian period depended on 'the Liberal schism of 1886, provoked by Gladstone's attempt to grant Home Rule to Ireland'.[36] This 'served to accelerate the middle class drift towards Conservatism' and forged an alliance with the Liberal Unionists.

The real Disraeli is therefore as difficult for historians to agree on as is the real Gladstone. Politicians, characteristically, seem to have found it all rather easier.

Conservative and Liberal perceptions of Disraeli and Gladstone *after* Disraeli and Gladstone

The later Conservative party had much occasion to quote Disraeli and to invoke his memory. This applied particularly to imperialism and One-Nation Conservatism.

Imperialism remained an important issue to the Conservatives well into the twentieth century. Disraeli was seen as a powerful initial influence – partly because of the rousing speeches he made on the subject and partly because of bold strokes like the purchase of the Suez Canal shares in 1875. It is true that Lord Salisbury presided in the late 1880s and the 1890s over a much larger territorial addition to the British Empire (and, indeed, Disraeli never had a new city named after him). Yet Salisbury was always a 'reluctant imperialist', conscious as much of the cost and administrative inconvenience of Empire as of the theoretical advantages. Joseph Chamberlain was much more enthusiastic about the whole imperial ethos. But Chamberlain was an ex-Liberal (or worse, still a Radical). It was therefore safer and more convenient to associate the imperial temper of the Conservative party with its most eloquent historical spokesman. Disraeli was still much invoked after 1900. The Conservatives tried to keep alive popular enthusiasm for the Empire at a time when the Liberals were focusing their attentions on welfare reforms. Since, however, the Boer War (1899–1902) had left a nasty after-taste, it seemed safer to foster the Disraelian tradition on imperialism and to bypass more recent events.

The association between Disraeli and Empire faded with the Empire itself. After the Second World War, especially, Empire became as much an embarrassment to the Conservatives as an asset. Instead, Macmillan's 'winds of change' speech switched the emphasis to decolonisation and Commonwealth. Yet there was one link between Conservative policy and Disraeli. Ironically it was a Thatcherite one – the swift response to the Argentine occupation of the Falklands in 1982. Since, however, Mrs Thatcher was no admirer of Disraeli, the connection remained unacknowledged. Mrs Thatcher always saw herself as fulfilling a Churchillian role. In foreign policy, however, she was more strikingly Disraelian – although she lacked any of his vision in her domestic policy.

One-Nation Conservatism has had a much longer influence on the Conservative party. It has always been associated directly with Disraeli and has made periodic revivals in the 120-or-so years since his death. It was systematically exploited with the formation of the Primrose League as early as 1883, aimed at achieving a mass working-class membership of the Conservative party, although with a definite aristocratic patronage and direction. April 19 became Primrose Day, the anniversary of Disraeli's death. Disraelianism exerted a double influence in the inter-war period. Baldwin and the mainstream of the Conservative party quoted Disraeli to keep the Conservatives steering in the direction of moderation and 'a further period of ordered progress in the tradition of that greatest of our leaders, Lord Beaconsfield'.[37] At the same time, Macmillan and the younger section of the party used Disraeli's ideas to suggest more radical approaches to social reform in the 1920s.

Conservative ascendancy was ended by the 1945 Labour landslide and the introduction of the welfare state between 1945 and 1951. The Conservative response was to set up the One Nation Group, with the intention to 'reconcile an industrial democracy with economic and social inequalities'.[38] During the 1950s, Winston Churchill emphasised that Conservative reforms had a historical precedent in 'the Tory Democracy of Lord Beaconsfield and after him, Lord Randolph Churchill'.[39] Disraeli's influence faded a little in the 1960s and 1970s, while, during the 1980s, Thatcherite Conservatism largely disregarded him. This was partly because Conservatism itself had changed, now emphasising monetarism as an economic policy, the contraction of the state's role in welfare provision and individual opportunity rather than social unity. In response, the

Conservative party developed a 'wet' tendency, which expressed concern about the return to the Two Nations. Disraeli was also invoked by those Conservatives who wanted to justify the acceptance of the European social charter. Heath, for example, argued in 1989 that 'Social policy is not socialism. . . . We Conservatives have possessed a social policy ever since Disraeli, more than a century ago.'[40]

There were also ways in which Gladstone was seen to be relevant to the twentieth century. This applied especially to the period after the First World War, with the establishment of the League of Nations and the focus on national self-determination in the creation of a series of new states in Europe. Gladstone received more than a cursory acknowledgement here for his foreign policy in the 1870s. He was also remembered with some gratitude in Ireland following the establishment of the Irish Free State in 1922. But there is rather less of a Gladstonian legacy for the Liberal party. Indeed, the latter has made far fewer connections with Gladstone than have the Conservatives with Disraeli. There is no enduring Gladstonian myth in modern Liberalism.

There are several possible reasons for this. One is that Gladstone was less obviously a party man than Disraeli. He did, after all, contribute towards the splitting of two parties during his career, which means that his particular contributions tend to be seen in the context of his individuality and statesmanship. He is more of a national – and international – than a Liberal figure. Second, over the broader timescale his was not seen as the most progressive form of Liberalism. The 'New Liberalism' of Campbell-Bannerman, Asquith and Lloyd George after 1905 placed much more of a focus on social reform and, in the process, had to reverse many of the 'self-help' assumptions of Gladstonian Liberalism. Lloyd George therefore has as much a place in Liberal mythology as Gladstone. And third, the Liberal party declined in the twentieth century, whereas the Conservatives remained – consistently – one of the two major parties. Party icons are normally associated with a continuous line rather than with a broken one. The modern Liberal party, which, it should be remembered, won only six seats in the 1950 general election, has had to base its revival on a vision of the future rather than the inspiration of the past. With the British electoral system stacked against them, Liberals and Liberal Democrats have had to focus on a radicalism which has sometimes seemed to be overtaking Labour on its left. Liberalism, unlike Conservatism, has no need for icons. Thus the political memory of Gladstone has been diluted by the subsequent political decline of his party. Conversely, the political reputation of Disraeli has been preserved by the continuity of Conservatism. Historians have debated the contributions of each in their lifetime but ultimately it is the politician who claims – or declines – the heritage.

This might have something to do with a general impression that I have gained in researching and writing this book. Disraeli's reputation was to be systematically dissected by historians – but embalmed by politicians. Gladstone's career, on the other hand, was given a post-mortem and decent funeral by most historians – and a respectful silence by politicians.

Questions

1. Radicals   Gladstonian Liberals   Whigs
   a. How did Gladstone relate to each of these sectors of the party?
   b. Which was the dominant influence?
   c. Was his connection with them positive or negative?
2. Landowners   Professional middle classes and commercial interests   Skilled workers
   a. Who was seen by future politicians to have adapted his party more to the needs of these sectors – Gladstone or Disraeli?
   b. Who did more to adapt his party more to the needs of these sectors: Gladstone or Disraeli?
3. Who was more relevant to *twentieth*-century Britain: Gladstone or Disraeli?

SOURCES

1. THE ELECTORAL PERFORMANCE OF THE LIBERALS AND CONSERVATIVES 1865–95

Source 1: General election results 1865–95.

	Lib	Con	IN	Lib U	Total
1865	370	288	–	–	658
1868	387	271	–	–	658
1874	251	342	59	–	652
1880	353	238	61	–	652
1885	335	249	86	–	670
1886	191	317	85	77	670
1892	272	268	80	46	670 (including 4 'others')
1895	177	340	82	71	670

Lib: Liberals
Con: Conservatives
IN: Irish Nationalists
Lib U: Liberal Unionists

Source 2: Lines from *Iolanthe*, a satirical comic opera by Gilbert and Sullivan, first performed in 1882.

I often think it comical
That nature doth contrive
That every boy and every gal
That's born into the world alive
Is either a little Liberal
Or else a little Conservative.

Source 3: A cartoon from *Punch*, August 1878.

A BAD EXAMPLE
Dr Punch: 'What's all this? You, the two head boys of the school, throwing mud! You ought to be ashamed of yourselves!'

Source 4: From a speech by Disraeli, April 1872.

As time advanced it was not difficult to perceive that extravagance was being substituted for energy by the Government. The unnatural stimulus was subsiding. Their paroxysms ended in prostration. Some took refuge in melancholy, and their eminent chief alternated between a menace and a sigh. As I sat opposite the Treasury Bench the Ministers reminded me of one of those marine landscapes not very uncommon on the coasts of South America. You behold a range of exhausted volcanoes. Not a flame flickers on a single pallid crest. But the situation is still dangerous. There are occasional earthquakes, and ever and anon the dark rumbling of the sea.

Source 5: From J. Morley, *Life of Gladstone*, published in 1903. Morley, who wrote the first major biography of Gladstone, had also served under Gladstone as a minister. The following description is based on Morley's own witnessing of the Midlothian election campaign of 1879.

People came from the Hebrides to hear Mr Gladstone speak. Where there were six thousand seats the applicants were forty or fifty thousand. The weather was bitter and the hills were covered with snow, but this made no difference in cavalcades, processions and the rest of the outdoor demonstrations. . . . An aristocratic minister, speaking in Edinburgh soon after, estimated the number of words in Mr Gladstone's Midlothian speeches in 1879 at 85,840 and declared that his verbosity had become 'a positive danger to the commonwealth'. Tory critics solemnly declared that such performances were an innovation on the constitution, and aggravated the evil tendencies of democracy. Talk of this kind did not really impose for an instant on any man or woman of common sense. . . .

It was an orator of concrete detail, of inductive instances, of energetic and immediate object; the orator confidently and by sure touch startling into watchfulness the whole spirit of civil duty in a man. . . . In a word, it was a man impressing himself upon the kindled throngs by the breadth of his survey of great affairs of life and nations, by the depth of his vision, by the power of his stroke. . . .

All this was Mr Gladstone in Midlothian.

Questions

1. Explain the significance of the cartoon and caption in Source 3. (3)
2. Use your own knowledge to explain why Disraeli was attacking the Liberals in 1872 (Source 4) and Gladstone the Conservatives in 1879 (Source 5). (5)
3. How far does the information in Source 1 confirm the view expressed in Source 2? (5)

4. Compare the value of Sources 4 and 5 in the study of the campaigning methods of Disraeli and Gladstone. (5)
5. 'The Liberal and Conservative parties fought each other on petty issues between 1868 and 1886.' How far do Sources 1 to 5, and your knowledge, confirm this view? (12)

Total (30)

2. GLADSTONE, DISRAELI AND 'MASS' APPEAL

Source 6: From a chapter in a book entitled *The Life of William Ewart Gladstone*, published in 1899. This extract is on Disraeli.

Only a man whose political conscience was a blank could have tried; only a man whose political courage was an unlimited quantity could have succeeded. Divested of the one and invested with the other, Disraeli usurped Radicalism, dished Whiggism, and educated Toryism. From that time the Conservative party, having, in Lord Cranborne's words, 'borrowed the ethics of the political adventurer,' and having learned at the appropriate moment to sink its prejudices, ceased to be 'stupid'.

Source 7: From John Vincent, *Disraeli*, published in 1990.

Still, endings do matter; and the ending of the 1870s owed much to Disraeli's ideas of the 1830s. And what was an ending for Disraeli, was for English Conservatism the beginning of a largely successful century managed on broadly Disraelian lines. An adversarial party system probably has room for only one party of national identity at a time – meaning English national identity, and leaving Scotland, Ireland, and perhaps Wales out of it, as aspects of the un-Englishness of the opposition. This began as an anti-O'Connell tactic in the 1830s; generalized, it became a stable component of political culture. It was a close-run thing for the Tories. They did not necessarily have to end up as the party uniting – or appearing to unite – social cohesion and national identity. Palmerston nearly appropriated the latter, while Gladstone made a good try at making social cohesion the Liberal trade mark. Many Conservative parties elsewhere failed to make the crucial move from elite parties to mass parties, partly because they did not have a brand image, or not one that could be put across in popular terms. It is to Disraeli's mental footwork as much as anything that the Conservatives owe their survival.

Source 8: From Eugenio Biagini, *Gladstone*, published in 2000.

Gladstone's political activities and convictions can best be understood in the context of the changing relationship between rulers and ruled in nineteenth-century Western Europe and North America. The formation of mass party organisations, the role of the press and the evolution of forms of charismatic leadership will be discussed. Gladstone's understanding of finance and taxation, as well as of international relations and the future of the United Kingdom and British Empire were influenced both by his classical education – then typical of most of the European aristocratic ruling elite – and by his ecumenical Christianity, particularly in his sense of a 'Christian Europe' within which Britain had developed and flourished. These also informed his sensitiveness to the strength of nationalism both abroad and at home, when confronted with the claims of Wales, Scotland and Ireland.

Source 9: From Jonathan Parry, *The Rise and Fall of Liberal Government in Victorian Britain*, published in 1993.

Gladstone's behaviour in 1886 turned the Liberal party from a great party of government into a gaggle of outsiders. From then on, its attachment to the principle of popular control became increasingly monotonous – hence Gladstone's motto, 'trust the people', at the 1892 election. Its critics satirised the canting sanctimonious uplift generated by Liberal platform orators who talked of 'God's people'. In order to win Welsh and Scottish sympathy for Irish self-government, Gladstone chose to pander to those Celtic Liberals who were most conscious of the cultural distinctness of their countries. At Swansea in 1887, he announced that 'Welsh nationality is as great a reality as English nationality', and in 1891 he finally committed himself to Welsh church disestablishment. Though he was not foolish enough to call for Home Rule for Wales and Scotland as well, such declarations generated more distrust of him in England, especially among those most anxious for Great Britain to play a forceful international role. His approach to cultivating Welsh and Scottish sentiment was certainly very different from the anti-clericalism and periodic anti-Popery associated with Russell and Palmerston, which had allowed Celtic Dissenters to expend their political energies in a self-consciously *British* cause. More generally, whereas Palmerston and Russell had used Protestantism and constitutional and fiscal liberty to construct a notion of Britishness which large numbers of men in all classes found sympathetic, and which bound them to Liberalism, Gladstone became less and less successful, as time went on, in his attempt to redefine that Britishness. Concepts such as devolution, church–state separation, local democracy, passionate moral crusades and non-assertion abroad were inspiring to many diverse groups, but they lacked the breadth of appeal necessary to hold the centre-ground of politics. Too many people saw the aged Gladstone's religious, Irish and foreign policy attitudes as unmanly, a betrayal of the attractive national identity constructed by his Liberal predecessors.

Questions

1. Compare the views expressed in Sources 7 and 8 on the attempts of Gladstone and Disraeli to give their parties a British appeal. (15)

2. 'Disraeli was more successful than Gladstone in giving his party a mass appeal.' How far is this view backed by Sources 6 to 9 and by your own knowledge of the historiographical debate on Gladstone and Disraeli? (30)

Total (45)

NOTES

1. GLADSTONE AND DISRAELI BEFORE 1868

Analysis 2

1 J.L. Hammond and M.R.D. Foot: *Gladstone and Liberalism* (London 1952), p. 1.
2 See D.A. Hamer: *Liberal Policies in the Age of Gladstone and Rosebery* (Oxford 1972).
3 See W.F. Monypenny and G.E. Buckle: *The Life of Benjamin Disraeli* (London 1910–20).
4 See P. Smith: *Disraeli: A Brief Life* (Cambridge 1996).
5 R. Blake: *Disraeli* (London 1966), p. 496.
6 Blake, p. 242
7 Ibid.
8 Blake, p. 243.
9 Ibid.
10 See J. Vincent: *Disraeli* (Oxford 1990).
11 Smith, p. 211.
12 Smith, p. 212.
13 J. Parry: The *Rise and Fall of Liberal Government in Victorian Britain* (New Haven and London 1993), p. 24.
14 Parry, p. 25.
15 Parry, ch. 8.
16 Hammond and Foot, p. vi.
Source 1: Mansell Collection.
Source 2: B. Disraeli: *Sybil; or the Two Nations* (London, 1845).
Source 3: *The Times*, 1860.

Source 4: P. Adelman: *Gladstone, Disraeli and Later Victorian Politics* (London, 1970).

Source 5: W. Gladstone: *Protectionism* (1860).

Source 6: N. Gash: 'The Peelites after Peel', *Modern History Review*.

Source 7: M. Winstanley, *Gladstone and the Liberal Party* (1990).

Source 8: J. Morley: *The Life of William Ewart Gladstone* (London 1908), vol. i, p. 199.

Source 9: J. Parry: *The Rise and Fall of Liberal Government in Victorian Britain* (New Haven 1993), p. 20.

2. THE IDEAS OF GLADSTONE AND DISRAELI

Analysis 1

1 Quoted in J.R. Vincent (ed.): *Disraeli, Derby and the Conservative Party* (Hassocks 1978), ch. 2.
2 B. Disraeli: *Whigs and Whiggism* (London 1913), p. 340.
3 B. Disraeli: *Sybil* (London, 1845).
4 B. Disraeli: *Vindication of the English Constitution in a Letter to a Noble and Learned Lord* (1835), pp. 182–3.
5 Quoted in N. Brasher: *Arguments in History* (London 1968), ch. 5.
6 Quoted in M. Chamberlain: *Pax Britannica? British Foreign Policy 1879–1914* (London 1988), ch. 8.
7 Quoted in P. Knaplund: *Gladstone and Britain's Imperial Policy* (London 1966), ch. 4.
8 Quoted in Chamberlain, ch. 8.

Analysis 2

1 Quoted in J. Morley: *The Life of William Ewart Gladstone* (London 1908), vol. i, p. 198.
2 Morley, i, p. 453.
3 Morley, i, p. 190.
4 See J.L. Hammond and M.R.D. Foot: *Gladstone and Liberalism* (London 1952).
5 Quotations from Hammond and Foot.
6 Sir Wemyss Reid: 'Mr Gladstone's character and career: a general appreciation', in Reid (ed.): *The Life Of William Ewart Gladstone* (London 1899), p. 44.
7 F.W. Hirst: 'Mr Gladstone as a Peelite', in Reid, pp. 386 and 398.
8 A. Ramm: *William Ewart Gladstone* (Cardiff 1989), p. 23.
9 P. Magnus: *Gladstone. A Biography* (London 1954), p. 165.
10 See J. Parry: *The Rise and Fall of Liberal Government in Victorian Britain* (New Haven and London 1993).
11 Hirst, p. 493.

12 R. Blake: *Disraeli* (Oxford 1990), p. 764.
13 E. Feuchtwanger: *Disraeli* (London 2000), pp. 212–13.
14 J. Vincent: *Disraeli* (Oxford 1990), p. 18.
15 Vincent, p. 19.
16 Vincent, p. 23.
17 Vincent, p. 49.
18 Vincent, p. 50.
19 C.J. Lewis: 'Theory versus expediency in the policy of Disraeli', *Victorian Studies*, 4, pp. 237–58.
20 Morley, vol. i, p. 200.
21 Magnus, pp. 440–1.
22 P. Butler: *Gladstone. Church, State and Tractarianism* (Oxford 1982), p. 233.
23 Parry, ch. 9.
24 Quoted in T. Endelman and T. Kushner: *Disraeli's Jewishness* (London 2002), p. 8.
25 P. Smith: *Disraeli: A Brief Life* (Cambridge 1996), p. 105.
26 Vincent, p. 27.
27 P.R. Ghosh: 'Disraelian Conservatism: a financial approach', in *English Historical Review*, 98 (1984), p. 286.
28 Quoted in G.M. Young: *Mr Gladstone* (1944), p. 4.
Source 1: Mansell Collection.
Source 2: A.J.P. Taylor: 'Dizzy', in *Essays in English History* (Harmondsworth 1976).
Source 3: T.E. Kebel (ed.): *Selected Speeches of the Earl of Beaconsfield*, vol. ii (1882), quoted in P. Adelman: *Gladstone, Disraeli and Later Victorian Politics* (London 1970), p. 89.
Source 4: T.L. Jarman: *Democracy and World Conflict 1868–1970* (Blandford 1963), pp. 9–14.
Source 5: P. Magnus: *Gladstone: A Biography* (London 1978), pp. 440–1.
Source 6: R. Shannon: *Gladstone: Heroic Minister 1865–1898* (Harmondsworth 1999), p. xii.
Source 7: J. Parry: *The Rise and Fall of Liberal Government in Victorian Britain* (New Haven and London 1993), pp. 247–8.
Source 8: T.A. Jenkins: *Gladstone, Whiggery and the Liberal Party 1874–1886* (Oxford 1988), pp. 19–20.

3. SOCIAL, ECONOMIC AND INSTITUTIONAL REFORMS

Analysis 1

1 W. Gladstone: *Protectionism 1840–60* (London 1894).
2 Quoted in P. Stansky: *Gladstone: A Progress in Politics* (Boston and Toronto 1979), epilogue.

3 Quoted in P. Adelman: 'Gladstone and Liberalism: changes in political outlook', *Modern History Review*, February (1991), p. 25.
4 Quoted in P. Smith: *Disraeli: A Brief Life* (Cambridge 1996), p. 122.
5 T.A. Jenkins: *Disraeli and Victorian Conservatism* (Basingstoke 1996), p. 114.

Analysis 2

1 E.J. Hobsbawm: *The Age of Empire 1875–1914* (London 1987), ch. 2.
2 Ibid.
3 P.R. Ghosh: 'Disraelian Conservatism: a financial approach', *English Historical Review*, 98 (1984), p. 281.
4 Jenkins, *Disraeli*, p. 42.
5 P. Smith: *Disraelian Conservatism and Social Reform* (London 1967), p. 122.
6 E.F. Biagini: *Gladstone* (Basingstoke 2000), p. 32.
7 Biagini, *Gladstone*, p. 33.
8 Biagini, *Gladstone*, p. 33.
9 Biagini, *Gladstone*, p. 55.
10 T.A. Jenkins: *The Liberal Ascendancy* (Basingstoke 1994), p. 112.
11 E.F. Biagini: *Liberty, Retrenchment and Reform: Popular Liberalism in the Age of Gladstone 1860–1880* (Cambridge 1992), p. 4.
12 E.J. Feuchtwanger: *Democracy and Empire: Britain 1865–1914* (London 1985) p. 68.
13 P. Adelman: 'Gladstone and Liberalism', in P. Catterall (ed.): *Britain 1867–1918* (Oxford 1994), p. 15.
14 T.E. Kebel (ed.): *Selected Speeches of Benjamin Disraeli, Earl of Beaconsfield* (London 1882), vol. 2, p. 511.
15 W.J. Wilkinson: *Tory Democracy* (New York 1925), p. 35.
16 D. Cooper: 'Disraeli, Salisbury and the Conservative Party', in M. Scott-Baumann (ed.): *Years of Expansion: Britain 1815–1914* (London 1995), pp. 348 and 351 ff.
17 Cooper, p. 356.
18 Ibid.
19 Adelman, p. 29.
20 I. Machin: *Disraeli* (Harlow 1995), p. 135.
21 Smith: *Disraelian Conservatism and Social Reform*, introduction.
22 Feuchtwanger, *Democracy and Empire*, p. 85.
23 R. Blake: *Disraeli* (Oxford 1990), p. 759.
24 T.A. Jenkins: *Disraeli and Victorian Conservatism* (Basingstoke 1996), p. 110.
25 Jenkins, *Disraeli*, p. 111.
26 Jenkins, *Disraeli*, pp. 110–12.
27 Jenkins, *Disraeli*, pp. 115–16.

28 Feuchtwanger, *Democracy and Empire*, p. 60.
29 Feuchtwanger, *Democracy and Empire*, p. 84.
30 Biagini, *Gladstone*, p. 50.
31 Jenkins, *The Liberal Ascendancy*, p. 131.
32 Jenkins, *The Liberal Ascendancy*, p. 132.
33 J. Parry: *The Rise and Fall of Liberal Government in Victorian Britain* (New Haven and London 1993), ch. 11.
34 Parry, p. 254.
35 Extract from R.A. Cross: *A Political History* (1903), p. 135.
36 D. Watts: *Tories, Conservatives and Unionists 1815–1914* (London 1994), p. 97.
37 Watts, p. 100.
38 Jenkins, *Disraeli*, p. 115.
39 Ibid.
Source 1: *Punch*, 6 March 1875.
Source 2: Quoted in M. Lynch: *Gladstone and Disraeli* (London, 1991), p. 45.
Source 3: *Hansard*, 8 February 1875, vol. 222, p. 100.
Source 4: R. Cross: *A Political History* (1903).
Source 5: *Hansard*, 24 June 1875, 3rd series, vol. 225.
Source 6: T.A. Jenkins: *Disraeli and Victorian Conservatism* (Basingstoke 1996), pp. 111–12.
Source 7: L.C.B. Seaman: *Victorian England* (London 1973), pp. 168–9.
Source 8: E.F. Biagini: *Gladstone* (Basingstoke 2000), pp. 47–8 and 50.

4. CONSTITUTIONAL REFORM

Analysis 1

1 Quoted in R. Quainault: 'Gladstone and Parliamentary reform', in D. Bebbington and R. Swift (eds): *Gladstone Centenary Essays* (Liverpool 2000), p. 81.
2 Quoted in Quainault, p. 80.
3 Quoted in D. Morgan: *Suffragists and Liberals* (Oxford 1975), p. 12.
4 Quoted in Quainault, p. 89.
5 Quoted in E.J. Feuchtwanger: *Disraeli* (Oxford 2000), p. 73.

Analysis 2

1 W.F. Monypenny and G.E. Buckle: *The Life of Benjamin Disraeli* (London 1910–20).
2 G. Himmelfarb: 'The politics of democracy: the English Reform Act of 1867', *Journal of British Studies*, 6 (1) (1966).

3 R. Blake: *Disraeli* (London 1966), ch. 21.
4 Ibid.
5 J. Morley: *The Life of William Ewart Gladstone* (London 1908), vol. 1, pp. 643–50.
6 See G.M. Trevelyan: *British History in the Nineteenth Century and After, 1782–1919* (London 1937), pp. 335–8.
7 R. Harrison: *Before the Socialists* (London 1965), ch. 3.
8 M. Cowling: *1867: Disraeli, Gladstone and Revolution* (Cambridge 1967), ch. 1.
9 E.J. Feuchtwanger: *Democracy and Empire: Britain 1865–1914* (London 1985), ch. 1.
10 J.K. Walton: *The Second Reform Act* (London 1987), ch. 3.
11 Blake, ch. 21.
12 Cowling, ch. 1.
13 Feuchtwanger, *Democracy and Empire*, pp. 45–6.
14 I. Machin: *Disraeli* (Harlow 1995), p. 105.
15 Machin, p. 110.
16 Machin, p. 111.
17 N. Gash: 'Parliament and democracy in Britain: the three nineteenth-century Reform Acts', in *Pillars of Government and other Essays on State and Society c. 1770–c. 1880* (London 1986).
18 E.F. Biagini: *Gladstone* (Basingstoke 2000), p. 95.
19 Ibid.
20 T.A. Jenkins: *The Liberal Ascendancy* (Basingstoke 1994), p. 201.
21 B.H. Abbott: *Gladstone and Disraeli* (London 1972), p. 75.
22 W.A. Hayes: *The Background and Passage of the Third Reform Act* (New York and London 1982), ch. 11.
Source 1: Mary Evans Picture Library.
Source 2: *Hansard*, 28 February 1884, vol. 285, p. 109.
Source 3: C.W. Boyd (ed.): *Mr Chamberlain's Speeches* (vol. I) (London 1914), p. 131.
Source 4: J. McCarthy: *A History of Our Own Times from 1880 to the Diamond Jubilee* (1897), pp. 165–7.
Source 5: Quoted in M. Lynch: *Gladstone and Disraeli* (London 1991), p. 25.
Source 6: Quoted in Lynch, p. 26.
Source 7: R. Blake: *Disraeli* (London 1966).
Source 8: P. Smith: *Disraeli: A Brief Life* (Cambridge 1996), p. 144.
Source 9: Paul Adelman: *Gladstone, Disraeli and Later Victorian Politics* (Harlow 1970), pp. 12–13.

5. FOREIGN POLICY

Analysis 1

1 Quoted in R. Ensor: *England 1870–1914* (Oxford 1936), ch. 2.
2 Quoted in N. Brasher: *Arguments in History* (London 1968), ch. 5.
3 Quoted in W.F. Monypenny and G.E. Buckle: *The Life of Benjamin Disraeli* (London 1910–20), vol. ii, p. 473.

Analysis 2

1 H. Paul: *A History of England*, vol. IV (London 1905).
2 J.L. Hammond and M.R.D. Foot: *Gladstone and Liberalism* (London 1952), p. 19.
3 E.F. Biagini: *Gladstone* (Basingstoke 2000), p. 82.
4 P. Smith: *Disraeli: A Brief Life* (Cambridge 1996), p. 190.
5 Hammond and Foot, p. 19.
6 Smith, p. 189.
7 Quoted in Smith, p. 189.
8 Chamberlain, p. 139.
9 Seaman, p. 97.
10 R.W. Davis: *Disraeli* (London 1976), p. 197.
11 E. Feuchtwanger: *Disraeli* (London 2000), p. 188.
12 Smith, p. 193.
13 Lloyd in B.L. Kinzer (ed.): *The Gladstonian Turn of Mind* (1985), pp. 260–1.
14 *The Times*, 16 July 1878.
15 R. Blake: *Disraeli* (London 1966), ch. 5.
16 Davis, p. 205.
17 Ibid.
18 Davis, p. 206.
19 R. Shannon: *The Crisis of Imperialism* (London 1976), p. 134.
20 Paul, vol. V, p. 58.
21 M.C. Morgan: *Foreign Affairs 1886–1914* (London 1973), pp. 13–21.
22 R. Ensor: *England 1870–1914* (Oxford 1936), p. 52.
23 L.S. Stavrianos: *The Balkans Since 1453* (New York 1958), p. 412.
24 Davis, p. 207.
25 Quoted in Smith, p. 190.
26 Quoted in Smith, p. 191.
Source 1: Mary Evans Picture Library.
Source 2: W.E. Gladstone: *The Bulgarian Horrors and the Question of the East* (1876), pp. 11–12.
Source 3: *Hansard*, 11 August 1876, vol. 231, p. 1145.
Source 4: B.H. Abbott: *Gladstone and Disraeli* (London 1972), p. 96.

Source 5: *The Times*, 17 July 1878.
Source 6: R. Blake: *Disraeli* (London 1966), ch. 5.
Source 7: R.W. Davis: *Disraeli* (London 1976), p. 205.
Source 8: R. Shannon: *The Crisis of Imperialism* (London 1976), pp. 19–20.

6. IMPERIALISM AND EMPIRE

Analysis 1

1 Quoted in J.K. Walton: *Disraeli* (London 1990), ch. 4.
2 Quoted in M.E. Chamberlain: *'Pax Britannica'? British Foreign Policy 1789–1914* (Harlow 1988), p. 126.
3 P. Knaplund: *Gladstone and Britain's Imperial Policy* (London 1966), ch. 4.
4 Knaplund, ch. 5.
5 Quoted in P. Magnus: *Gladstone. A Biography* (London 1954), ch. 12.
6 Quoted in Chamberlain, ch. 8.
7 Quoted in L.C.B. Seaman: *Victorian England* (London 1973), ch. 11.
8 Quoted in N. Brasher: *Arguments in History* (London 1968), ch. 6.
9 Quoted in Brasher, p. 126.
10 Quoted in R.W. Davis: *Disraeli* (London 1976), p. 192.
11 Quoted in Davis, p. 211.
12 Quoted in Brasher, p. 126.
13 W.D. Rubinstein: *Britain's Century* (London 1998), p. 178.

Analysis 2

1 P. Smith: *Disraeli* (Cambridge 1996), p. 164.
2 R. Blake: *Disraeli* (London 1966), ch. 4.
3 L.H. Gann and P. Duignan: *The Rulers of British Africa* (London 1978), ch. 1.
4 Quoted in Davis, p. 186.
5 I. Machin: *Disraeli* (Harlow 1995), p. 5.
6 Smith, pp. 198–9.
7 R. Shannon: 'Midlothian: 100 years after', in P.J. Jagger (ed.): *Gladstone, Politics and Religion* (London 1983).
8 E.F. Biagini: *Gladstone* (Basingstoke 2000), p. 85.
9 E.F. Biagini: 'Exporting "Western & Beneficent Institutions": Gladstone and Empire, 1880–1885', in D. Bebbington and R. Swift (eds): *Gladstone Centenary Essays* (Liverpool 2000), p. 205.

10 D.K. Fieldhouse: 'Imperialism; an historiographical revision', *Economic History Review*, 14 (1961), pp. 187–209.
11 D. Thomson: *Europe Since Napoleon* (London 1957), ch. 20.
12 J.A. Hobson: *Imperialism: A Study* (London 1902).
13 E.J. Hobsbawm: *Industry and Empire* (Harmondsworth 1981), p. 130.
14 Hobsbawm, p. 131.
15 R. Robinson and J. Gallagher: *Africa and the Victorians* (London 1961), p. 465.
Source 1: Mary Evans Picture Library.
Source 2: E. Feuchtwanger: *Disraeli* (London 2000), p. 199.
Source 3: W.F. Monypenny and G.E. Buckle: *The Life of Benjamin Disraeli* (London 1910–20), vol. vi, p. 382.
Source 4: Speech made by Disraeli (now Earl of Beaconsfield) in the House of Lords, 10 December 1878.
Source 5: R. Salter; *Peel, Gladstone and Disraeli* (Basingstoke 1991), p. 92.
Source 6: *Hansard*, 25 July 1882, vol. 272, pp. 1705–7.
Source 7: Quoted in M. Willis: *Gladstone and Disraeli: Principles and Policies* (Cambridge 1989), pp. 94–5.
Source 8: Quoted in M. Lynch: *Gladstone and Disraeli* (London 1991), pp. 63–4.
Source 9: D. Judd: *Empire: The British Imperial Experience, from 1765 to the Present* (London 1996), pp. 95 and 96.
Source 10: R. Robinson and J. Gallagher: *Africa and the Victorians* (London 1961).

7. IRELAND

Analysis 1

1 Quoted in R. Blake: *Disraeli* (London 1966), p. 179.
2 T.A. Jenkins: *Disraeli and Victorian Conservatism* (Basingstoke 1996), p. 81.
3 Quoted in Jenkins, p. 93.
4 Quoted in Jenkins, p. 131.
5 R. Shannon: *The Age of Disraeli, 1868–71: The Rise of Tory Democracy* (Harlow 1992), p. 341.
6 Quoted in Shannon, p. 341.

Analysis 2

1 J.L. Hammond: *Gladstone and the Irish Nation* (London 1938). All quotations from ch. 35.
2 P.S. O'Hegarty: *A History of Ireland Under the Union* (London 1952), p. 458.

3 N. Mansergh: *Ireland in the Age of Reform and Revolution 1840–1921* (London 1940), p. 100.
4 O. MacDonagh: *Ireland: The Union and its Aftermath* (London 1977), p. 48.
5 MacDonagh, pp. 63–4.
6 R.F. Foster: *Modern Ireland, 1600–1972* (London 1989), p. 423.
7 J. Vincent: 'Gladstone and Ireland', *Proceedings of the British Academy*, 63 (1977).
8 D.A. Hamer: *Liberal Policies in the Age of Gladstone and Rosebery* (Oxford 1972), ch. 5.
9 J. Loughlin: *Gladstone, Home Rule and the Ulster Question 1882–93* (Dublin 1986), conclusion.
10 D.G. Boyce: 'Gladstone and the Unionists of Ireland, 1868–1893', in D. Bebbington and R. Swift (eds): *Gladstone Centenary Essays* (Liverpool 2000), p. 197.
11 E.F. Biagini: *Gladstone* (Basingstoke 2000), p. 104.
12 E.J. Feuchtwanger: *Gladstone* (London 1975), p. 237.
13 Quoted in Boyce, p. 185.
14 Boyce, p. 187.
15 Boyce, p. 188.
16 Feuchtwanger, p. 281.
17 J. Parry: *The Rise and Fall of Liberal Government in Victorian Britain* (New Haven and London 1993), ch. 11.
18 Quoted in T.A. Jenkins: *Gladstone, Whiggery and the Liberal Party 1874–1886* (Oxford 1988), p. 285.
19 N. Brasher: *Arguments in History* (London 1968), ch. 5.
20 Biagini, p. 110.
21 Biagini, p. 111.
22 Biagini, p. 112.
23 Lord Eversley: *Gladstone and Ireland* (1912).
24 Quoted in Boyce, p. 106.
25 Boyce, p. 122.
Source 1: Mansell Collection.
Source 2: Quoted in N. Lowe: *Making Modern British History* (London 1989), p. 309.
Source 3: Quoted in E. Curtis and R.B. McDowell (eds): *Irish Historical Documents* (1943), pp. 285–6.
Source 4: Quoted in M. Willis: *Gladstone and Disraeli: Principles and Policies* (Cambridge 1989), pp. 74–5.
Source 5: D.G. Boyce: 'Gladstone and Ireland', in P.J. Jagger (ed.): *Gladstone* (London 1998), p. 122.
Source 6: E.J. Feuchtwanger: *Gladstone* (London 1975), p. 281.
Source 7: E.F. Biagini: *Gladstone* (Basingstoke 2000), pp. 109–11.
Source 8: J. Parry: *The Rise and Fall of Liberal Government in Victorian Britain* (London and New Haven 1993), pp. 302–3.

8. GLADSTONE, DISRAELI AND THEIR POLITICAL PARTIES

Analysis 2

1 E.J. Hobsbawm: *Industry and Empire* (Harmondsworth 1981), p. 83.
2 P. Magnus: *Gladstone. A Biography* (London 1954), p. 441.
3 J.L. Hammond and M.R.D. Foot: *Gladstone and Liberalism* (London 1952), p. 2.
4 A. Ramm: *William Ewart Gladstone* (Cardiff 1989), ch. 4.
5 Quoted in D.A. Hamer: *Liberal Policies in the Age of Gladstone and Rosebery* (Oxford 1972), ch. 3.
6 H.C.G. Matthew (ed.): *Gladstone Diaries*, vol. IX (London 1986), introduction.
7 Hamer, ch. 3.
8 E.J. Feuchtwanger: *Gladstone* (London 1975), p. 278.
9 Feuchtwanger, p. 279.
10 J. Parry: *The Rise and Fall of Liberal Government in Victorian Britain* (New Haven and London), ch. 11. See also T.A. Jenkins: *Gladstone, Whiggery and the Liberal Party, 1874–1886* (Oxford 1988).
11 Parry, ch. 10.
12 Parry, ch. 9.
13 E.J. Hobsbawm: 'Trends in the British Labour movement since 1850', in *Labouring Men: Studies in the History of Labour* (London 1964), p. 338.
14 Feuchtwanger, p. 281.
15 Ibid.
16 R. Shannon: *The Crisis of Imperialism 1865–1915* (St Albans 1976), p. 192.
17 Ibid.
18 Shannon, p. 194.
19 R.T. Shannon: *Gladstone and the Bulgarian Agitation 1876* (London 1975), p. 273.
20 W.F. Monypenny and G.E. Buckle: *The Life of Benjamin Disraeli* (London 1910–20), vol. II, pp. 1517–19.
21 T.A. Jenkins: *Disraeli and Victorian Conservatism* (Basingstoke 1996), p. 88.
22 Jenkins, p. 92.
23 Ibid.
24 R. Blake: *Disraeli* (London 1966), p. 764.
25 P. Smith: *Disraeli: A Brief Life* (Cambridge 1996), p. 223.
26 Ibid.
27 Smith, p. 217.
28 I. Machin: *Disraeli* (Harlow 1995), p. 169.
29 R. McWilliam: 'Popular Conservatism in Britain, 1867–1914', in

New Perspective (2000). See also R. McWilliam: *Popular Politics in Nineteenth Century England* (London 1998).

30 Blake, p. 760.
31 E.J. Feuchtwanger: *Disraeli* (London 2000), p. 210.
32 Feuchtwanger, p. 212.
33 R. Shannon: *The Crisis of Imperialism 1865–1915* (St Albans 1976), p. 67.
34 Shannon, p. 69.
35 Jenkins, p. 135.
36 Jenkins, p. 137.
37 D. Watts: *Tories, Conservatives and Unionists 1815–1914* (London 1994), p. 108.
38 Quoted in J.K. Walton: *Disraeli* (London 1990), p. 65.
39 Watts, p. 108.
40 Quoted in Walton, p. 66.
Source 3: Mansell Collection.
Source 4: Quoted in M. Lynch: *Gladstone and Disraeli: History at Source* (London 1991), p. 36.
Source 5: J. Morley: *Life of Gladstone* (1903).
Source 6: F.W. Hirst: 'Mr Gladstone as a Peelite', in W. Reid (ed.): *The Life of William Ewart Gladstone* (London 1899), p. 493.
Source 7: J. Vincent: *Disraeli* (Oxford 1990), p. 116.
Source 8: E. Biagini: *Gladstone* (Basingstoke 2000), p. 3.
Source 9: J. Parry: *The Rise and Fall of Liberal Government in Victorian Britain* (New Haven and London 1993), p. 306.

SELECT BIBLIOGRAPHY

This makes no claim to be a complete bibliography – but rather a brief list of the works I have found most useful in writing this book. Most have been referred to in Analysis 2 in each chapter and many have provided extracts for use as sources.

PRIMARY SOURCES

Three concise but valuable selections of documents on Gladstone and Disraeli are: M. Lynch: *Gladstone and Disraeli* (London 1991); M. Willis: *Gladstone and Disraeli: Principles and Policies* (Cambridge 1989); and R. Salter: *Peel, Gladstone and Disraeli* (Basingstoke 1991).

More detailed selections are contained in H.C.G. Matthew (ed.): *Gladstone Diaries*; T.E. Kebel (ed.): *Selected Speeches of the Earl of Beaconsfield* (1882); and J. Matthews and M.G. Wiebe (eds): *Benjamin Disraeli Letters* in five volumes (Toronto 1982–93). It is also worth looking at W.E. Gladstone: *The Bulgarian Horrors and the Question of the East* (1876); W.E. Gladstone: *Protectionism 1840–60* (London 1894); H.M. Swartz and M. Swartz (eds): *Disraeli's Reminiscences* (London 1975); and W. Hutcheon (ed.): *Whigs and Whiggism: Political Writings of Benjamin Disraeli* (London 1913). Three of Disraeli's novels which are worth looking at are: *Coningsby or the New Generation* (1844); *Sybil; or the Two Nations* (1845); and *Tancred or the New Crusade* (1847).

SECONDARY SOURCES

Both Gladstone and Disraeli

Gladstone and Disraeli are covered in a huge range of general works. The following are worth particular mention: R. Ensor: *England 1870-1914* (Oxford 1936); R. Shannon: *The Crisis of Imperialism* (London 1976); P. Adelman: *Gladstone, Disraeli and Later Victorian Politics* (Harlow 1970); L.C.B. Seaman: *Victorian England* (London 1973); and E.J. Feuchtwanger: *Democracy and Empire: Britain 1865-1914* (London 1985).

Foreign policy and the Empire are covered in M. Chamberlain: *Pax Britannica? British Foreign Policy 1879-1914* (London 1988); and R. Robinson and J. Gallagher: *Africa and the Victorians* (London 1961). Marxist views can be found in E.J. Hobsbawm: *The Age of Empire 1875-1914* (London 1987); and E.J. Hobsbawm: *Industry and Empire* (Harmondsworth 1981).

More detailed coverage of specific issues concerning both Gladstone and Disraeli can be found in: M. Cowling: *1867: Disraeli, Gladstone and Revolution* (Cambridge 1967); N. Gash: 'Parliament and democracy in Britain: the three nineteenth-century Reform Acts', in *Pillars of Government and Other Essays on State and Society c. 1770-c. 1880* (London 1986); and W.A. Hayes: *The Background and Passage of the Third Reform Act* (New York and London 1982).

Gladstone

Three collections of essays have provided a varied insight into Gladstone's thinking and policies: P.J. Jagger (ed.): *Gladstone, Politics and Religion* (London 1983); and D. Bebbington and R. Swift (eds): *Gladstone Centenary Essays* (Liverpool 2000).

The main biographies of Gladstone are: J. Morley: *The Life of William Ewart Gladstone* (London 1908); P. Magnus: *Gladstone. A Biography* (London 1954); P. Stansky: *Gladstone: A Progress in Politics* (Boston and Toronto 1979); R. Shannon: *Gladstone: Heroic Minister 1865-1898*, in two volumes (London 1982 and 1999); R. Jenkins: *Gladstone* (London 1995); and H.C.G. Matthew: *Gladstone 1875-1898*, in two volumes (Oxford 1986 and 1995). Shorter biographies are: J.L. Hammond and M.R.D. Foot: *Gladstone and Liberalism* (London 1952); A. Ramm: *William Ewart Gladstone* (Cardiff 1989); E.J.

Feuchtwanger: *Gladstone* (London 1975); and E.F. Biagini: *Gladstone* (Basingstoke 2000). The last of these is particularly readable and original.

The following are essential for references on politics, the economy, the Liberal party and public opinion: J. Vincent: *The Formation of the British Liberal Party 1857–68* (London 1966); T.A. Jenkins: *The Liberal Ascendancy* (Basingstoke 1994); T.A. Jenkins: *Gladstone, Whiggery and the Liberal Party 1874–1886* (Oxford 1988); M. Cowling: *1867: Disraeli, Gladstone and Revolution* (Cambridge 1967); D.A. Hamer: *Liberal Policies in the Age of Gladstone and Rosebery* (Oxford 1972); E.F. Biagini: *Liberty, Retrenchment and Reform. Popular Liberalism in the Age of Gladstone 1860–1880* (Cambridge 1992); and J. Parry: *Democracy and Religion. Gladstone and the Liberal Party 1867–1875* (New Haven and London 1986). An important revisionist view of Gladstone is J. Parry: *The Rise and Fall of Liberal Government in Victorian Britain* (New Haven and London 1993).

Religion is covered in: P. Butler: *Gladstone. Church, State and Tractarianism* (Oxford 1982); P.J. Jagger: *Gladstone: The Making of a Christian Politician* (London 1991); and D.W. Bebbington: *William Ewart Gladstone. Faith and Politics in Victorian Britain* (Liverpool 1993). The Irish issue is dealt with in a wide range of books. Two of particular interest are: J.L. Hammond: *Gladstone and the Irish Nation* (London 1938); and J. Loughlin: *Gladstone, Home Rule and the Ulster Question 1882–93* (Dublin 1986). Foreign and imperial affairs are given detailed treatment in: P. Knaplund: *Gladstone and Britain's Imperial Policy* (London 1966); and R.T. Shannon: *Gladstone and the Bulgarian Agitation 1876* (London 1975).

Disraeli

The main biographies of Disraeli are: W.F. Monypenny and G.E. Buckle: *The Life of Benjamin Disraeli*, in six volumes (London 1910–20); R. Blake: *Disraeli* (London 1966); and, most recently, R. Shannon: *Disraeli*, in two volumes (London 1982). There are many shorter biographies, including: R.W. Davis: *Disraeli* (London 1976); J.K. Walton: *Disraeli* (London 1990); J. Vincent: *Disraeli* (Oxford 1990); E. Feuchtwanger: *Disraeli* (London 2000); P. Smith: *Disraeli: A Brief Life* (Cambridge 1996); and T.A. Jenkins: *Disraeli and Victorian Conservatism* (Basingstoke 1996). Some of these authors have also written on Gladstone (see above).

Politics, the Conservative party and reform are covered in a considerable number of books, of which the following are the most important: R. Stewart: *The Foundation of the Conservative Party 1830–1867* (London 1978); R. Blake: *The Conservative Party from Peel to Thatcher* (London 1978); W.J. Wilkinson: *Tory Democracy* (New York 1925); P. Smith: *Disraelian Conservatism and Social Reform* (London 1967); R. Shannon: *The Age of Disraeli, 1868–71: The Rise of Tory Democracy* (Harlow 1992); J.R. Vincent (ed.): *Disraeli, Derby and the Conservative Party* (Hassocks 1978); F.B. Smith: *The Making of the Second Reform Act* (Cambridge 1966); M. Cowling: *1867: Disraeli, Gladstone and Revolution* (Cambridge 1967); J.K. Walton: *The Second Reform Act* (London 1987); E.J. Feuchtwanger: *Disraeli, Democracy and the Tory Party* (Oxford 1968); and H.J. Hanham: *Elections and Party Management: Politics in the Time of Disraeli and Gladstone* (Hassocks 1978).

Rather less is available on foreign and imperial policies but the following are widely used: R.W. Seton-Watson: *Disraeli, Gladstone and the Eastern Question* (London 1935); R. Millman: *Britain and the Eastern Question, 1875–1878* (Oxford 1979); and M. Swartz: *The Politics of British Foreign Policy in the Era of Disraeli and Gladstone* (London 1985).

Finally, there has been recent interest in Disraeli's Jewish background. This is explored in all the biographies of the past three decades and is dealt with in detail in T. Endelman and T. Kushner: *Disraeli's Jewishness* (London 2002).

INDEX